The Symbolism of Subordination

THE SYMBOLISM OF SUBORDINATION

Indian Identity in a Guatemalan Town

By Kay B. Warren

with a new Introduction

University of Texas Press, Austin

Requests for permission to reproduce material from
this work should be sent to Permissions, University
of Texas Press, Box 7819, Austin, Texas 78713-7819.

Library of Congress Cataloging in Publication Data

Warren, Kay B   , 1947–
   The symbolism of subordination.

   Bibliography: p.
   Includes index.
   1. Cakchikel Indians—Ethnic identity. 2. Indians
of Central America—Guatemala—Ethnic identity.
3. Cakchikel Indians—Religion and mythology.
4. Indians of Central America—Guatemala—Religion and
mythology. 5. San Andrés Semetabaj, Guatemala—Social
life and customs. 6. Catholic action—Guatemala.
I. Title.
F1465.2.C3W37   301.45'19'707281   78-9763
ISBN 0-292-77621-7

To my family

Contents

Plates

Preface

Ethnic subordination has been a constant in the lives of Guatemalan Indians since the Spanish conquest in the sixteenth century. Yet the historical circumstances of ethnic subordination—that is, the kinds of contact Indians have had with non-Indians and the mechanisms crafted to perpetuate political and economic inequities—have changed dramatically over time. This study examines Indian responses to the constant and historically changing aspects of subordination in a bi-ethnic society where daily life is circumscribed, if not defined, by another ethnic group. In the present, Indian society is dominated by the cultural descendents of the Spanish colonists, by Ladinos as they call themselves. After 450 years of contact, both Ladinos and Indians are *mestizos* in the sense of sharing the same gene pool. Differences between these ethnic groups are more accurately phrased in terms of their distinctive cultural systems and contrasting patterns of access to society's crucial resources.

To develop an anthropological understanding of how Indians deal with the continuing problems of powerlessness and racism I have pursued an interpretive analysis of their world views, of the systems of knowledge through which Indians narrate their changing understandings of self and other, of moral action, and of political order. What I have found in the community of San Andrés Semetabaj in the western highlands of Guatemala are striking attempts by Indians to reformulate their ethnic identity and the symbolism of subordination.

For Mayan Indians time flows in spiraling cycles; events turn back on themselves not for a simple reenactment so much as for clarification. It is in this spirit that I have written a new preface and introduction to the paperback edition of this ethnographic study of the town of San Andrés. The body of the analysis remains the same in this edition, though I have had to resist the temptation after ten years have passed to change some terminology. For instance, Mayan healers who diagnose physical and moral illness, but who may also be paid to curse and bring disease, are most often called "diviners" rather than "sorcerers" in current anthropological studies. "Peasants" are referred to as "agriculturalists" now. "Symbolic anthropology" sounds out of date as the subfield has become "interpretive anthropology." The discipline of anthropology is continually transforming its own descriptive languages, not in search of perfect, neutral terms but rather as a result of self-examination about how language colors our representations of "the other." In this edition readers will encounter subtle contrasts in terminology between the introductory sections, which suggest how the work should now be read, and the body of the ethnography. These shifts mark this edition as a historical product of both the seventies and the eighties, something that needs to be underscored in a work that argues that cultures and nations (and academic disciplines as well) are in continual transformation.

In revising the introduction it has become clear to me how this work bridges the anthropological concerns of both decades. In the seventies the issue in Latin American studies was to challenge the view that Indian communities were cultural isolates and impediments to national development. Spurred by dependency theory, anthropologists documented the ways in which Indian communities were parts of larger economic systems which historically perpetuated the marginality of rural populations. For anthropologists the challenge was to show how hierarchies of class and control were perpetuated and whose interests they served. The rural Indian was the victim. In the eighties there has been a growing desire in anthropology and some branches of political science to reanimate people in our ethnographic narratives of inequality, to give a voice to those who were muted by the earlier focus on economic systems and political histories. In giving voice to muted constructions of reality, analysts are finding acts and understandings which critique domination and exploitation and coalesce into cultures of resistance.[1] This study poses important questions for those who see strategic assimilation and the subversion of dominant culture as a way for subordinate populations to resist domination. Unlike other cases where critiques of domination may be veiled or implicit, in the community of San Andrés the critique of racism is explicit and integral to Indian culture. The limits of existing critiques are what has preoccupied two recent generations of young-adult Indians.

The ethnographic present in this study is the early seventies. This should not be seen as a time of peaceful innocence before violence and the militarization of civilian life swept Guatemala in the late seventies and eighties. The late sixties and early seventies prefigured later conflicts—curfews and states of siege involving the suspension of civil rights were called by the Méndez Montenegro and Arana Osorio regimes. Military authorities routinely stopped buses, searching passengers at gun point, to show their strength and to intimidate. Bodies of young soldiers killed in skirmishes with guerrillas in the Petén jungles were brought home to the highlands for burial. The capital city was surrounded at one point by the military, who sought to search entire neighborhoods for subversives. Anthropologists had nightmares of being wrongly caught and harmed in military investigations of rural populations. And there were unspoken rules about what could be comfortably discussed in rural communities.

In this tense atmosphere, religion flourished, as it had in the past, serving as a focal point of social activity in towns like San Andrés. I wondered about the diversity of religious groups in one small town, the local issues reflected in their practices, and the connections these groups had with national organizations. I was to find that conflict, both within and outside the Indian community, was a central religious concern. So I was turned back to the issue of cultural distrust so endemic to Guatemala, even as we avoided current volatile issues in interviews, in discussions, and certainly in field notes.

This account stops before the late seventies when violence escalated in Guatemala, communities were subject to direct military intervention, hundreds of thousands of Guatemalans became refugees, and local civil defense committees were organized by the military. I hope to begin field work soon for a twenty-year restudy of the community, which will allow me to fill in the gaps and pursue other dimensions of change in Guatemala. For the moment, however, readers should turn to other sources for an understanding of recent events. Carmack's *Harvest of Violence* (1988), Manz's *Refugees of a Hidden War* (1988), Montejo's *Testimony: Death of a Guatemalan Village* (1987), and Burgos-Debray's *I . . . Rigoberta Menchú* (1984) are excellent places to start.

I am indebted to the institutional sponsors of this research: Princeton University's Department of Anthropology and Program in Latin American Studies, the Fulbright-Hays Commission, and Mount Holyoke College. Their generous financial support allowed me to visit Guatemala in 1969 and to spend a total of fourteen months, between September 1970 and January 1972, in the community of San Andrés and the surrounding highlands. I returned to San Andrés for a brief visit in 1974 and pursued archival work on Catholic Action and the counterrevolution at the University of Texas at Austin in 1976.

The most important contributors to this study have been Guatemalans, both Indians and Ladinos. They showed great openness and patience when faced with the queries of a novice fieldworker in the early seventies. In the bilingual town of San Andrés I conducted interviews and the business of everyday life in Spanish, with a smattering of Cakchiquel. I began work with the help of a group of young-adult Indian field assistants. They provided help with Cakchiquel and translations when necessary, as well as facilitating interviews and the taping of public events. These assistants proved to be invaluable for doing research in an agrarian town where the population was either dispersed in the outlying fields during workdays or congregated in large simultaneous celebrations during religious festivals lasting several days and nights at a time. In addition, during my field work I participated as an informal member in the major religious organizations in town, including the traditionalist brotherhood (*cofradía*) of María, Catholic Action, and the protestant Central American Mission. These groups have my appreciation for their acceptance of my unconventional, multiple religious involvements and for their detailed explanations of the significance of religious acts and knowledge. I spent long, thought-provoking hours talking with members of each group and gained exposure to a variety of moral philosophies as living systems.

After much thought I have decided not to acknowledge individual Guatemalans by name in order to protect their privacy and to emphasize the reality that I alone assume responsibility for the analysis and findings of this research. Nevertheless, the friendships which grew out of sharing experiences and uncertainties with individual Guatemalans were central aspects of field work for me. To these friends and to the town of San Andrés as a whole I give grateful thanks for their generosity and rugged acceptance.

Administrators of the Instituto Indigenista Nacional, faculty and students at the Universidad del Valle, members of the Tikal Association, and the Guatemalan family I stayed with when visiting the capital shared time and their views of Guatemalan society. I spent many rewarding hours outside my field research working with members of the Proyecto Lingüístico Francisco Marroquín. The Proyecto is committed to the value of studying Mayan languages, training Mayan linguists and administrators, and producing materials designed and written by Mayas. The group's dedication to cooperation among Mayas, Ladinos, and North Americans is exemplary for its consciousness of the difficulties that must be continually dealt with in cross-cultural collaboration. At the Proyecto, in addition to my Guatemalan teachers and friends, Bob Gersony, Jo Froman, Nora England, Tony Jackson, and Will Norman were important sources of friendship and support during my field work.

I completed the first stage of this analysis at Princeton and Mount Holyoke as I finished my dissertation and began teaching; the paperback edition was produced after my return to Princeton eight years later. It is a great pleasure to acknowledge the help I received over the years from my Princeton colleagues, both faculty and students: Martin G. Silverman and Fred D'Agostino, as well as Sherry Ortner, Tom Kirsch, Alfonso Ortiz, Mark Leone, Janet Dolgin, Barbara Frankel, Gwen Lewis, JoAnn Magdoff, Rick Parmentier, and Steve Barnett were sources of anthropological stimulation in the old days. Richard N. Adams, June Nash, Frank Reynolds, and Nancy Munn offered important feedback as the project evolved into publication. Susan C. Bourque was a wonderful source of friendship and intellectual challenge throughout the process. Our subsequent collaborative work in Peru allowed me to pursue unfinished questions from Guatemala and will doubtlessly continue to enrich and complicate my restudy of San Andrés.[2] Marjorie Childers, Jean Grossholtz, Penny Gill, Romeo Grenier, Martha Ackelsberg, Donna Divine, Tom Divine, and Sylvia Forman were other vital colleagues at Mount Holyoke, Smith, and the University of Massachusetts. Most recently, Natalie Davis, as well as Joan Scott, Rena Lederman, Davida Wood, Begoña Aretxaga, Mike Hanchard, Carla Hesse, Hildred Geertz, Gananath Obeyesekere, Larry Rosen, and Henry Bienen among many others in Princeton's anthropology, women's studies, and Woodrow Wilson School networks have brought fresh challenges. Mary Moran, Vanessa Schwartz, Elissa Adair, Loy Ann Carrington, and Luis Arriola have my thanks for their great energy and endurance as research assistants, as does Carol Tobin for her resourcefulness at the Firestone Library.

Working with the editorial staff at the University of Texas Press on both editions has been thoroughly pleasurable. For the countless hours of work that went into typing and copy editing the first versions of this study, I owe heartfelt precomputer debts to Mary W. Shaughnessy, Jane Pierce, and Pat Kuc.

Throughout my years of study and research, I have gained strength and support from my family. Marjorie and Bernie Jensen first kindled my interest in anthropology many years ago in northern Nigeria. Bob and the late Barbara Ebersole graciously opened their home to me as an urban way station in the field. Bruce Warren, Elva Ristau Warren, Wendy Warren, and the memory of Kim Warren have provided love and encouragement that have helped me to follow through in my concerns with anthropology, university teaching, and field research. They have my thanks and great affection.

The Symbolism of Subordination

Introduction

This study of contemporary Mayan Indian identity and ethnic subordination is set in the highland Guatemalan community of San Andrés Semetabaj. In the last three decades, anthropologists have examined the social and economic processes that subordinate Indian populations to non-Indian national society in countries like Mexico and Guatemala. Yet few analysts have focused their energies on the ways in which Indians' resistence to subordination and powerlessness colors their self-conceptions and their cultural understandings of society and morality. Relatively little attention has been paid to the ways in which subordination is portrayed in Indian systems of knowledge, such as religion and oral history.[3] Nor has enough research been done on Indians' consciousness of their own social position or on ethnic identity as a collage of meanings that Indians continually redefine in action. In focusing on these issues, this study employs an interpretive approach to analyze changes in belief and action that have resulted in transformations of the experience and the significance of being Indian in contemporary Guatemala.

In the following introductory pages, I critically examine assumptions that are often made about "traditional" or "indigenous" culture and the unfortunate impact these conceptions have had on understandings of change and Indianness in Mexico and Guatemala. Then I demonstrate how conventional analyses of ethnic stratification, which examine international and national political and economic forces as the determining factors, would benefit from interpretive approaches which explore Indian world views and systems of knowledge.

Questioning the Sources of "Tradition"

For many the following description of change in a rural Guatemalan community, which is drawn from my 1971 field notes, would be taken as another example of time and the forces of modernization suddenly catching up with a traditional Mayan Indian population that had remained at the margins of a national society:

All agree that the highland Guatemalan town of San Andrés Semetabaj has gone through a period of rapid social change in the last twenty-five years. Some Indians fear these changes as a sign of growing disorder, of the impending judgment and destruction of the world by God. Others point to the same changes as progress which has brought a better material life for Indians and more respect from non-Indians. In the seventies, Indian youth dress in non-Indian, commercially produced clothing, carry on conversations in Spanish instead of Cakchiquel, and make plans to continue studies outside town or to migrate to urban centers in search of non-agricultural employment. Agriculturalists wait in line at the cooperative building for credits in the form of seed and fertilizers. While elders gather on the steps of the municipal building complaining of difficulties in recruiting new members for traditional Indian religious brotherhoods, voices can be heard reciting passages from the catechism in the old colonial church. A glimpse of the town twenty-five years ago would have shown *none* of these activities.

In assessing such changes, one might, with sympathetic cultural relativism, mourn the passing of ethnic distinctiveness and an indigenous Mayan heritage as expressed in hand-woven dress, traditional religion, the authority of Indian elders, and a native American language. The problem is that labels like "traditional" and "indigenous" for Indian culture mislead because they create an image of a timeless past from which change is measured.[4] This construction may blind us to the immensity of cultural change that has taken place historically. In questioning the origin of "traditional" forms in Guatemala, it is vital to examine Indian communities and ethnic identity as they have been shaped by the Spanish conquest and over 450 years of subsequent contact between prehispanic Mesoamerican populations, the Spaniards, and both groups' descendents. Indians have not retained a separate culture. Instead, ethnicity has been very much the product of the interplay of Indian and non-Indian responses to colonially created cultural identities as they are embedded in national systems of ideology, economics, and politics (cf. Carmack 1981; Hawkins 1984; Hobsbawm and Ranger 1983). Some anthropologists see so much change during the colonial period that they doubt the appropriateness of studying Indians as an ethnic group at all. Instead they suggest that we should focus on the same populations as the rural poor whose life chances are determined by their marginal class positions.

Judith Friedlander's study of Hueyapán in Morelos, Mexico, has contributed an important correction to misreadings of ethnic distinctiveness. Friedlander critiques the anthropological use of such terms as traditional and indigenous for characterizing languages, dress, and rituals that are said to mark Indians off from the larger non-Indian population. Her analysis concludes that present-day Indian language, spinning and weaving, clothing, domestic technology, food, healing, and religion are largely Spanish or hispanic-Mexican, derived from cultural transformations that took place during the colonial and republican periods. Throughout the colonial period, many aspects of Indian culture were redefined through a process whereby practices were intentionally stripped of their original religious significance and reworked to fit into colonial Christian ideology. Thus it would be a mistake to see these practices—which in the case of local religion were used to facilitate conversion by dramatizing European Catholic themes and values—as evidence of an ongoing indigenous tradition (1975:83–100, 103).

Friedlander concludes that Indian culture in central Mexico does not involve value systems or world views that are in any sense separate from those of urban society. Indianness is better understood as an emblem of low status in a class-stratified society than as evidence of continuing cultural pluralism. In the context of a class-stratified society, "Indian" has become an adjective used to talk in a depreciating way about lack of sophistication, lack of education, and poverty in comparison to the valued sophistication, education, and relative wealth of the non-Indian Mexican society. Significantly, while the content of Indians' identity has changed, their social position in a class-stratified society, or their structural subordination, has been held largely constant over time (Friedlander, 1975:xv, 71–74).

San Andrés, the subject of this study, contrasts sharply with Hueyapán in several significant ways.[5] First, in the Guatemalan community of San Andrés, ethnic identity has legitimized world views and social arrangements that contrast with those of non-Indian society. Second, ethnicity in the eyes of Indians does not operate as an exclusively negative definition of what Indians lack with respect to the broader society. Nor is the concept "Indian" used as a relative adjective to characterize some behaviors or individuals as being "*more* Indian" than others. Non-Indians (or Ladinos, as they are called), however, do define Indians negatively and use ethnic labels as relative adjectives in Guatemala.[6] A third significant contrast between the two communities is that in San Andrés the Indians have a clearly formulated consciousness of their subordinate position. They have come to fresh understandings of the strength and persistence of structural inequalities through local experiments in religious and social reform, as will be detailed in the body of this study.

Despite these contrasts, Friedlander's study contains several important lessons that are directly applicable to the present analysis of Guatemalan ethnicity. Indian identity is not a set of beliefs, social forms, and economic specializations that were created from scratch in the prehispanic past. Rather, Indian identity is a response of diverse Mayan groups to the colonial society that introduced Catholicism, resettled and reorganized Indian communities, and used Indians as a source of labor for plantation agriculture. As a result, this analysis is not likely to shed a great deal of light on prehispanic Mayan society, although it examines the postconquest descendents of a Mayan group. Instead, I will stress the interactive aspect of Indian identity by concentrating on the ways in which Indians have created a social philosophy to make sense of their subordination to non-Indians.

A second problem with anthropological discussions of "traditions" and "indigenous culture" is that change is almost inevitably portrayed as the loss or impoverishment of culture. This representation creates a passive rather than an active role for Indian populations. The challenge for studies of Indian communities is to do justice to a history of colonial and contemporary domination during which Indians were victimized and, at the same time, to understand the part that Indians played in transforming their own culture in the process.

The final lesson from Friedlander is that the content of an ethnic identity may change without the structural position, or the subordination, of the group being transformed. In other words, Indians may assimilate a great deal of non-Indian culture without gaining equivalent status, as a group, to that of non-Indians. The following chapters will suggest that Guatemala shares in this situation of continuing subordination despite changes in the content of Indian identity. In addition, this analysis will discuss specific *cultural* issues (along with economic realities) that make structural change a very frustrating goal.

Toward a Historical Understanding of Ethnic Identity

Analyses of colonial and contemporary history present useful overviews of the impact that changing economic and political policies have had on Indian identity and on relations between Indians and non-Indians. The basic structure of Indian-Ladino relations was defined during the colonial period and further refined in the late nineteenth century by policies that controlled land, labor, and trade as well as by Indian reactions to these policies. As Handy concludes: ". . . the general perception of Indians during the colonial period as a reluctant but necessary source of labor that needed to be compelled to work by a number of legal and illegal coercive measures has continued to shape the treatment of labor in Guatemala" (1984:15). The following account of Guatemalan labor policy and political-economy is drawn from detailed studies by Chester Lloyd Jones (1940), Eric Wolf (1959), Marvin Harris (1964), Richard N. Adams (1970), Manning Nash (1970), Rodolfo Stavenhagen (1970), Thomas Melville and Marjorie Melville (1971), Mary Helms (1975), Robert Carmack (1981), William Sherman (1979), Robert Wasserstrom (1983), and Jim Handy (1984).

The abusive exploitation of *los indios* came at the heels of Pedro de Alvarado's conquest of Guatemala in 1524. Two kinds of slaves were branded by the Spaniards: *esclavos de guerra*, meaning those taken in Spanish wars of conquest, and *esclavos de rescate*, those who were already slaves among their own people (see Carmack 1981 and Sherman 1979). In addition, trusteeships, called *encomiendas*, gave powerful Spaniards free access to Indian labor within a defined region with the often-ignored charge that they had the duty to protect and convert their tributaries (*tributarios*). *Encomenderos*, often using Indian elites as intermediaries, drafted labor and collected tribute from indigenous communities within their grants; Spaniards were not, however, given the land itself. Indian towns were forced to provide workers for the building of colonial towns, for mining and gold washing, as well as for agriculture and domestic service. Tribute was exacted in specified amounts of spun and woven cotton, fowls, cacao, corn, and other foodstuffs. Those drafted for labor service were often sent to work on colonial landholdings far outside the *encomiendas*. *Encomenderos* most often administered their grants and landholdings from Spanish towns rather than living in the rural hinterlands.

Forced labor exhausted Indian communities, which were faced with insurmountable demands for tribute and labor and were left with insufficient time during the agricultural cycle to cultivate for their own subsistence. Most dreaded was the work of the long-distance burden carriers (*tamemes*), who hauled colonial commerce on their backs with straps across their foreheads. The Crown, responding to criticisms from determined priests like Bartolomé de las Casas, brought forth the New Laws in 1542 to regulate abusive treatment of Indian populations, limit unreasonable demands for tribute, and halt further distribution and inheritance of *encomiendas*. The colonists strongly objected to these regulations, which, like much protective legislation, were rarely enforced (Sherman 1979).

In Mesoamerica, some Mayan Indian elites were rewarded with *encomiendas* and the right to continue to hold slaves and collect tribute. They were further assimilated into Spanish society through intermarriage. More often those who satisfactorily established descent from Mayan aristocracy—and, as a result, were called *caciques* (chiefs) and *principales* (members of the upper class) by the Spaniards—were used for conquerors' ends to collect tribute, organize work parties, and judge local disputes. In exchange they were freed from tribute and forced labor demands. More commonly, Indian elites either perished in the brutality and rebellions of the conquest or lost their wealth and were absorbed into peasant communities. Both processes weakened the regional powers of preconquest states and confederacies as well as the economic and political stratification of colonial Indian society. Those who tried to hold on to local power were caught in the struggles between *encomenderos*, priests, Crown officials, elected Indian authorities, and the local populace. Spaniards organized local governments into a hierarchy of positions, including Indian mayors (*alcaldes ordinarios*) to oversee local justice, municipal councilmen (*regidores*), and their assistants (*alguaciles*) to keep order and run errands. Over time elite powers were eroded and replaced by the collective authority of Indian elders (the new transformation of *principales*) who jointly assigned local offices in a system of rotating authority linked to a hierarchy of tasks and prestige (Carmack 1981:305–324; Sherman 1979).

Slavery was abolished by 1550; the *encomienda* became less important after the sixteenth century as the Crown sought to centralize control over colonists. In response to a precipitous decline in Indian population—due to epidemics of smallpox, influenza, and bubonic plague as well as dislocation and mistreatment—the Crown turned to state-directed forced-labor policies (called the *mandamiento* and *repartimiento*). Indian communities had to provide a labor pool from which the Crown drafted manual laborers to work on Spanish plantations and on the construction of roads, municipal offices, and churches. Under the *mandamiento*, all Indians were obligated to work a set number of weeks each year. For instance, late in the seventeenth century Indians in Guatemala were required to work sixteen weeks a year in one-week shifts. The only Indians exempted from forced labor were those holding office as governors or mayors of rural communities (Jones 1940:139). Alternatively, under the forced-labor policy called the *repar-*

timiento, colonial landowners petitioned government officials for specific numbers of laborers from the Indian communities of a particular region. Governmental authorities saw to it that communities furnished the required labor force, at times allocating several hundred laborers to a single plantation.

The conversion of Indians and the administration of labor policies were facilitated by the Dominican priests who worked to resettle populations, which had been dispersed by disease or the desire to avoid labor drafts, into communities called *reducciones.* These towns were given limited inalienable communal lands to be worked by Indians for their own subsistence. *Reducciones,* which numbered seven hundred settlements by 1600, served as focal points for the introduction of Indians to Catholicism and to Spanish local government (Handy 1984:23). Religious brotherhoods *(cofradías)* were organized by the Spaniards to structure Indian religious devotion and to provide priests with incomes in exchange for their services. With the economic decline of the seventeenth and eighteenth centuries and the continuing concentration of the Spanish population in the capital city, Spanish priests were the only consistent European contacts for many rural Indian communities.

Debt slavery, through which Indians were tied to particular plantations by advances of wages and accumulated indebtedness, became common later in the seventeenth century. Most commonly, Indians were advanced money for expenses incurred during community fiestas. By accepting such advances, individual Indians were obligated to migrate to plantations in order to work off debts at very low wages. Together, debt slavery and the *mandamiento* (which was not always clearly distinguished from the *repartimiento* by colonists) were the primary mechanisms for the regulation of Indian labor for some three hundred years.

The history of Guatemalan production for the international market was rocky at best before the late nineteenth century. Shortly after the conquest it was clear that Guatemala would not become a mining center. The late sixteenth and seventeenth centuries brought a period of economic depression during which the colony was virtually ignored by Spain because it had few resources that were attractive for international commerce. Only limited numbers of Spaniards had settled in the colony, *mestizos* (mixed Spaniards and Indians) were still a very small proportion of the population, and Indian populations had grown increasingly isolated from the colony's administrative center. Apparently, many Indians were successful in avoiding tribute payments. Some impoverished *encomenderos* moved out into the countryside to set up isolated, feudal *haciendas* for subsistence. Later Guatemala was to make a foray into international trade by exporting natural dyes, the blues of indigo and the red tones of cochineal. Unfortunately, the European production of aniline dyes at a lower cost permanently displaced Guatemalan producers (Handy 1984).

Guatemala's involvement in the production and export of coffee eclipsed earlier efforts at international trade. In 1872, acting president Justino Rufino Barrios began to promote the planting of coffee trees in western Guatemala and other regions with favorable climates. Land was also made available to Ladino businessmen for the development of plantations for rubber, sarsaparilla, and cacao and for cattle ranches. During this period the north coast banana industry and quinine and cotton production were also supported. Barrios committed the country to a program of economic development based on the attraction of foreign capital and entrepreneurs and on the use of Indians as a source of labor for the production of export crops on commercial plantations. In rural areas, provincial governors (*jefes políticos*) were enjoined to assist farmers in arranging a steady stream of laborers. Success in coffee cultivation was thought to depend on a generous supply of cheap labor secured through seasonal migration to plantations located primarily in the southern piedmont. Most assumed that adequate labor supplies could not be maintained without some form of compulsion. Debt bondage was the most common way of compelling Indian agriculturalists to work on plantations, although forced-labor laws were also issued by Barrios. Barrios advocated the nineteenth-century credo that the position of the Indian population would only improve with increasing contact with Ladinos, who he felt would accustom Indians to productive labor and expose them to new needs (Skinner-Klée 1954:34–43). To further this integration, he abolished communal lands in Indian communities and encouraged the settlement of Ladinos in the Indian countryside (Adams 1967:480). During the late nineteenth century, Ladinos were given direct access to lands around Indian communities which they purchased or acquired extralegally. Indians, thus deprived of their subsistence base, were compelled to work as seasonal migrants or permanent laborers on newly created plantations.

Wolf (1959), M. Nash (1970:173–176), Helms (1975:197–200), Wasserstrom (1983), and Handy (1984) argue that the nineteenth century was a definitive period for Indian communities. Indian reactions to government policy and to the economic impact of plantation agriculture gave rise at that time to forms of community organization and Indian identity that have persisted to the present. While the administrative structure of Indian communities was a product of the Spanish period, it was the increasing contact between Indians and non-Indians during the nineteenth century that caused a "passive, defensive resistance" on the part of Indians who adopted a hostile attitude toward outsiders.[7] Indian communities restricted membership through endogamy and control over the allocation of agricultural lands within their jurisdictions. They created social institutions that acted to distribute or destroy surplus wealth.[8] Finally, communities erected barriers to the entry of material goods and values from the larger society (Wolf 1957:6). Indians minimized contact with others by creating separate social and religious institutions (referred to as the "civil-religious hierarchy" in anthropological literature), excluding non-Indians from participation. Indians transformed religious brotherhoods (or *cofradías*, which were initially introduced by the Spaniards to promote devotion to the saints) so that they provided a sense of common identity and a source of prestige in return for community service. Through these "closed corporate communities" Indians maintained values, beliefs, and social practices that were distinct from those of non-Indian society and minimized the significance of economic stratification among Indians.

Harris (1964:26–34) and Wolf (1957) stress another aspect of the crystallization of the closed corporate Indian community: it was a social form shaped by the requirements of national and international plantation economics. This economic system required a source of manual labor during active periods of the cash-crop cycle yet showed little interest in the maintenance of laborers or concern with their subsistence throughout the continuous subsistence agricultural cycle. Harris notes that the closed corporate reaction to plantation economics fragmented the Indian population by restricting political and religious authority to the confines of a given community. Although adjoining communities recognized that they had similar civil and religious organizations, they did not develop secular or religious authorities with regional powers. Moreover, religious brotherhoods had the ironic effect of forcing Indians to spend unusual amounts of cash on commodities like liquor, clothing, candles, and fireworks for communal religious observances. These expenditures were often financed through loans from non-Indians and purchased from non-Indian businessmen. Thus, the price of community-centered and collectivist Indian identities has been continual dependency on the external non-Indian economy that drains off economic surplus from Indian agriculturalists.

Both the structure of the closed corporate community and the authority of Indian elders to oversee civil and religious organizations have

been challenged since the 1930s by increasing central-government intervention in community affairs. When Jorge Ubico became president in
1931, Guatemala was in serious economic difficulties because the world
depression had severely constricted the international coffee market.
Moving to centralize the control over labor, Ubico abolished debt
peonage and created a vagrancy law that required peasants with minor
landholdings, or without any land at all, to show that they had worked
for 100 to 150 days a year (cf. Skinner-Klée 1954:110–114, 118–119).
The new labor laws meant that Indians had an obligation to work at
very low wages whether or not they were in debt (Jones 1940:162).
Through vagrancy legislation, the government assured a readily available labor force for plantation agriculture. In addition, Ubico em-
barked on a program to centralize political power which had been
previously exercized by local and regional elites. He eliminated local
elections and appointed local mayors who were brought from other
parts of the country. Thus, the loyalty of mayors was to the national
government, not the patronage of local elites. Adams concludes that
the shift from individualized debt peonage to government vagrancy
control had a centralizing effect that paralleled the change from local
mayors to nationally appointed civil authorities (1970:176–177).

   The fall of Ubico in 1944 and the subsequent elections of, first, Juan
José Arévalo and, then, Jacobo Arbenz marked the beginning of a ten-
year "revolutionary" period in Guatemalan history. During this period,
reforms eroded the control that landowning elites and Indian elders
had exercised over rural communities. Urban and rural workers were
mobilized through unions, peasant leagues, and, later, agrarian reform
committees which had direct access to national agencies. Labor courts
heard cases from workers' points of view; agrarian reform committees,
organized to expropriate idle lands, did not include local landholding
elites. Laws of forced rental compelled local landowners to rent unused
lands to peasants for minor fees or to fear expropriation. In rural
areas, the franchise was extended to illiterate males, and political parties were encouraged to organize and promote competing slates of local
candidates. Local positions that had been nationally appointed under
Ubico became locally contested. Wider involvement of Indians during
the revolutionary period politicized a younger generation who became
local leaders although they had not proven themselves through years
of loyalty to elders in the closed corporate community. In short, the
social-structural basis of Indian identity had been transformed with the
addition of new and competing alternatives to earlier patterns of community authority, cooperation, and participation (Adams 1957b).

In 1954 Carlos Castillo Armas overthrew Arbenz in a U.S.-sponsored invasion and counterrevolution, motivated by growing fears of communism and potential expropriation of North American business investments. Castillo Armas returned expropriated lands to their owners, dissolved labor organizations, and disenfranchised the illiterate vote. Yet, the incomplete experiments of the revolutionary period could not be totally ignored, especially when they had involved the rural populace whose potential radicalism worried subsequent administrations. Politics after the counterrevolution showed a concern with social welfare through the establishment of agricultural cooperatives, new land colonization programs in the south coast and Petén regions, and the increasing involvement of the Catholic Church and the U.S. Peace Corps in development projects. Some programs hoped to increase productivity so that subsistence farming in the highlands would be an alternative to seasonal migration to commercial plantations. Others promoted Indian "integration" into national life through education and participation in grass-roots organizations with national ties. (The irony here, of course, is that Indians were always integrated into national life through administrative, labor, and religious policies.) Still other programs, such as land colonization efforts, underscored the magnitude of the land distribution problem that Guatemala had not faced squarely (cf. Melville and Melville 1971).

In sum, throughout Guatemalan history Spaniards and, later, Ladinos conceived of Indians as semi-subsistence farm workers who produced surpluses for regional consumption and were available for draft as low-cost laborers for *haciendas* and the export economy. Labor policy has taken various forms: the *encomienda*, the *mandamiento*, the *repartimiento*, debt bondage, vagrancy laws, and, more recently, a relatively free market. Generally, the goals of these policies have been to provide local and larger coastal plantations with steady labor supplies, given historical variations in the international market, the number of Indian workers available, and national development ideologies. Adams argues that until 1940 peasants would have benefited from a free labor market instead of forced-labor policies (1970:425–426). Forced labor correlated with high demands for the production of export crops, whereas the free market in migratory labor did not develop until the rural population exceeded plantations' needs for laborers. Adams concludes that present-day rural workers are in poor positions to bargain for more adequate housing, better treatment on their jobs, or higher wages because plantation owners assume that, with an excess labor force available, they will not have to negotiate demands seriously.

Nevertheless, migration to the south coast or major cities continues to be one of the few options open to land-poor workers who are unable to support their families locally.

Rodolfo Stavenhagen offers a useful language for grasping key dimensions of the historical process through which Indians have been defined as subordinates. He distinguishes "colonial relations" and "class relations," both of which have shaped Ladino-Indian ethnic relations. In broad terms, colonial relations defined Indians as an ethnic unit, despite individual differences in socioeconomic positions. Interethnic relations were characterized by "ethnic discrimination, political dependence, social inferiority, residential segregation, economic subjection and juridical incapacity," which originated under the Spaniards (1970:269). Indians created the closed corporate community, which defined alternative sources of individual prestige and value, as a defensive reaction to the long-term effects of social discrimination.

Stavenhagen argues that colonial relations were shaped by an economic system that required cheap labor for agriculture when other alternatives, such as industrialization, were not regionally or nationally feasible (1970:277). In this situation the categorical difference of Ladinos and Indians was emphasized and Indian acculturation of Ladino values minimized. Ladinos maintained superiority and power through specialized knowledge and manipulation of the economic and legal systems (not to speak of the advantage of their fluency and literacy in the national language). Colonial relations reinforced a class structure defined by labor and property relations that closely paralleled the ethnic division.

Stavenhagen notes that Ladino-Indian relations have incorporated a class dimension in that "the former produce exclusively for the market, while the latter produce primarily for their own consumption; Ladinos accumulate capital, Indians sell their farming products only in order to buy goods for consumption; Ladinos are employers and Indians laborers" (1970:244–245). Further, he notes that the pervasiveness of ethnic stratification means that, even when Indians and Ladinos share similar economic levels, cultural values and ethnic attitudes will intervene to make these relations hierarchical. Economic parity does not transform expectations of paternalistic behavior on the part of Ladinos and the requirement for acquiescence and submission from Indians (1970:262–266).

Significantly, Stavenhagen emphasizes that class relations are not always parallel to ethnic, or colonial, relations. In fact, he argues that the two diverge with increasing national "development." Ultimately, class relations push for the assimilation of Indians into Ladino society (1970:269–270). As Indians are increasingly required for nonagricultural labor and cast in the role of consumers of manufactured goods, class relations are stressed at the expense of colonial relations.[9] Indians who are pulled away from corporate communities enter the Ladino class-stratified society, leaving behind colonial relations and their invidious ethnic identity. "Passing" from one ethnic group to another is possible, but unidirectional, because ethnicity in Guatemala is based not on mutually exclusive phenotypic or racial differences but rather on cultural differences. Indians may find class relations outside their home communities an attractive option because the larger economy offers a wider range of economic opportunities than those found in agrarian communities (1970:281).

Stavenhagen situates the study of ethnicity within an examination of Guatemalan economics and suggests that ethnic identity reflects the subordination of Indians in terms of colonial and class relations. Because these sets of relations are influenced by changes in the national economy (changes caused by the expansion of capitalism and accompanied by industrialization, regional economic integration, and a consumer-oriented market), ethnicity is not static but subject to redefinition by national society and by local populations in response.

Anthropologists have been intrigued by the sometimes rigid, sometimes flexible nature of ethnic boundaries which often discourage the assimilation of Ladino culture in the corporate Indian community, yet allow Indians to pass as Ladinos outside their home communities (Colby and van den Berghe 1969). In urban or coastal plantation settings, Indian migrants no longer have access to the social institutions that reinforce the ethic of the corporate community and delimit the boundary between Indians and Ladinos. As a result, they rapidly adopt the lifestyles and emblems of Ladino identity, such as western dress and Spanish language. A similar identity change may occur when Indians migrate to other corporate communities, particularly if they are viewed as strangers and are not given access to the community-centered institutions that define Indianness. Members of the corporate Indian community are ambivalent toward other Indians because ethnicity is anchored to each particular town which practices its own *costumbre* (tradition) inherited from its own ancestors. However, as we will see, in the case of San Andrés, ambivalence toward strangers and rigid ethnic boundaries forced one ambitious family of new residents to experiment with and ultimately transform local definitions of Indianness.

Despite the passing of individuals, ethnic labels are still used to classify all individuals in rural communities, and Indians continue to be subordinated as a group to Ladinos. Ladino and Indian participation in the same institution is structured hierarchically, in the form of patron-client relations. In bi-ethnic towns, Ladinos are most often employers, labor recruiters, and bureaucrats. Only in exceptional, and very specific, circumstances do Ladinos work for Indians. In ritual kinship, Ladinos are asked to be godparents for Indian children, never the other way around. These social institutions are said to integrate Indians and Ladinos in bi-ethnic communities. At the same time they may also lead to ethnic conflict because of their hierarchical structuring of roles and the resulting skewed distribution of power and social rewards. Large areas of social life stand outside the arena of ethnic contact: marriage, kinship, religious, and civic celebrations are separately organized by each group. These observations have led some analysts of Guatemalan society to conclude that rural communities have experienced little real change in the social structure that defines ethnicity. They believe that urban settlements and commercial plantations are the significant sources of ethnic redefinition. In contrast, this study finds local communities to be important sources of cultural creativity and experimentation.

Colby and van den Berghe (1969), who have studied ethnic identity on a regional basis, argue that when Indians assimilate Ladino characteristics, such as town residence, literacy in Spanish, and nonagricultural employment, they do not locally challenge the hierarchical patterning of social roles or the rigidity of ethnic boundaries. Rather, attributes of ladinoized identity come to represent classlike differences within Indian society itself (Smith 1977). Education, new technical skills, and new occupations in the commercial sector suggest that Indian identity is changing in rural communities, although the colonial nature of ethnic relations persists. Apparently, a great deal of movement toward Ladino values has occurred without weakening the ethnic boundary.[10]

Adams takes a different point of view from that of the boundary theorists and stresses change in the content of Indian identity. He sees the process of "ladinoization" (also called "ladinization" in the literature) as composed of individual mobility through ethnic passing outside one's home community and of collective transculturation whereby Indian communities lose "indigenous" traits while assimilating ladinoized characteristics (1959). On the one hand, the introduction of coffee as a major export commodity at the end of the nineteenth century, coupled with growing scarcities of fertile lands in Indian control, has promoted Indian migration to commercial plantations on the south coast. On the other hand, political and religious change has influenced the organization of Indian communities for those who have avoided permanent migration. Central-government intervention in local Indian government has created organizations that compete with councils of Indian elders and their civil appointees. The advent of political parties in rural areas during the revolutionary period of the 1940s and 1950s has undermined the civil-religious hierarchy and created new activist roles for Indian youths. In addition, the close corporateness of Indian communities has been challenged by religious movements, such as Catholic Action, which sought to revitalize Catholic orthodoxy. As the council of Indian elders must now adjust to political factions created by new ideologies, so the Indian religious brotherhoods must adapt to the presence of competing religious organizations. In short, the civil-religious hierarchy no longer enjoys a monopoly in the organization of Indian affairs or the perpetuation of key emblems of ethnic identity.

The foregoing analyses—which examine the patterning of social institutions, ethnic boundaries, and ladinoization—go a long way toward explaining how passing occurs on a national level while ethnic categories persist on a local, rural level. In Stavenhagen's terminology, colonial relations still continue within bi-ethnic rural communities; yet class relations predominate in urban areas and on coastal plantations. More than Indian and local Ladino resistance to change, however, has perpetuated ethnic boundaries and colonial relations in the present. Another important factor has been the willingness of those who have introduced businesses and other organizations to adapt to hierarchical Indian-Ladino social roles. For example, a textile factory that was introduced into the community of Cantel operated much like a rural agricultural plantation, with hierarchical yet personalistic relations between the owner and laborers, an ethnic division of labor between the clerical staff and workers, loans of land to Indian workers, and time off for Indians so that they could fulfill their obligations to the civil-religious hierarchy (Nash 1958).

Approaching the Study of Ethnic Identity and Local Culture

It is not the goal of the present study to extend the economic and political arguments of writers like Harris and Stavenhagen. Rather, I am concerned with a closer view of Indian-Ladino communities, with the internal dynamics of local culture. If subordination is so funda-

mental and pervasive, then it is important to ask how Indian constructions of "self" and "other" influence and respond to changing colonial
and class relations. Nor will I pursue the work of Colby and van den
Berghe, which focuses on the social boundaries between ethnic groups,
defined through patterns of participation in joint versus separate institutions. Instead, I will ask if assimilation of Ladino culture by Indians
is accompanied by changes in the meaning of subordination or by a
changing awareness of the processes that re-create hierarchy in ethnic
difference.

Anthropologists working on Guatemala have often approached the
issue of self-perception by weighing the implications of what they term
"separate value systems." Colby and van den Berghe find that Ixil communities in the western Guatemalan highlands "value their way of life
and reject the ladino definition of their culture as 'pagan,' 'backward,'
and 'inferior.'" They "resent the overbearing and superior attitude of
many Ladinos" (1969:146, 155). Julian Pitt-Rivers wonders why Indians
in Chiapas, Mexico, fail to challenge the subordinate position that
Ladinos have established for them. He concludes that Indians do not
accept Ladino values, including their assessment of Indian inferiority
(1967:76). Similarly, John Gillin (1947) and Melvin Tumin (1945) present evidence from the Guatemalan town of San Luis Jilotepeque that
suggests that separate Indian and Ladino definitions of prestige, work,
and religion block Indians from full knowledge of their subordinate
position.

Tumin's analysis (1949) of interethnic relations shows that Ladinos
justify separatism in terms of Indian inferiority, while Indians speak
of separatism as motivated by a desire to "keep with one's own kind."
His ethnographic material suggests that, in cases of joint participation
in godparenthood, the hierarchical structuring of the relations between
Ladino godparents and Indian parents has different meanings for Ladinos and Indians. Indians may ask Ladinos to be the godparents of their
children because this relation brings economic advantages, such as access to land, a protector in the event of difficulties with Ladino authorities, and the softening of overtly degrading behavior. For their part,
Ladinos gain prestige in their own group by having dependent clients
and serving the poor (Tumin 1949:20–21). Tumin's analysis implies
that the combination of separatism and joint participation mutes Indian perceptions of their structural subordination.

In short, analysts who stress distinctive value systems argue that
Indians may be aware of but nevertheless reject racist stereotypes of
their inferiority. They also argue that Indians have a limited con-

sciousness of subordination and are oblivious, because of their separate values, to the range of situations in which they must accept an inferior social position.

I am not sure, however, that it is appropriate to generalize these conclusions without examining Indian world views in action over time. The issue is not a light-switch judgment about whether Indians are aware or not of subordination. Rather, the issue is how social ideologies are used and transformed by Mayan populations to understand the larger social world in which their everyday lives are embedded. The challenge here is that nothing is static: world views, social life, and the wider political-economy are in constant flux. Interpretive strategies need to tackle this flux with queries about the ways individuals re-create and transform their own analyses in action (cf. Sexton 1985 and Burgos-Debray 1984). Do Indian populations see their own analyses as problematic, under pressure, and changing (cf. Warren 1986)? When does the significance of subordination become disputed or contested in a community? In what terms and with what consequences? Are there contrasts between what the analyst and the individuals in the community see as "resistance" to Ladino domination?

One way to study Indian's self-conception is to ask Indians directly about such issues as differences between ethnic groups, the value placed on manual labor, the desirability of interethnic ritual kinship, and the possibilities of ethnic passing. Tumin's study of San Luis Jilotepeque in Guatemala (1945) has done precisely this, documenting the attitudes that govern interethnic relations. Colby, in his study of Zinacantan in Chiapas, Mexico (1966), has analyzed variations in ethnic attitudes and modes of behavior, classifying them as paternalistic, egalitarian, or competitive. Another way to study self-perception is to look at interethnic stereotypes conveyed through proverbs and folk tales, as Colby (1966) has done for Chiapas. Alternatively, one can adopt a symbolic approach that looks specifically at the ways Indians organize their knowledge and assessments of the social universe in which they live. Although not aimed at the study of ethnicity, Robert Hinshaw's follow-up study of Panajachel (1975) has taken one symbolic approach to analyzing beliefs by looking for the set of premises that stand behind a broad range of discrete beliefs. Other interpretive approaches take a more interactive view, asking how systems of knowledge inform action and how knowledge emerges as the product of history and social interaction.[11]

Contemporary anthropology has edged away from thinking of culturally distinctive world views and systems of knowledge as stable systems of cultural categories, as neatly ordered systems of logic evolved to impose order on the world, or as systems of rules that people conform to or flaunt. Increasingly, the field is concerned with meanings in action, with the forging and manipulation of value and significance in the practice of everyday life, with the ongoing experience of reasoning for individuals and groups (cf. Wallace 1972; Tedlock 1982; Bourdieu 1977; Geertz 1973, 1983; Turner and Bruner 1986). As a result, interpretive anthropologists have focused their examinations on the contested meanings and the ambiguities of images, metaphors, and cultural narratives. We are centrally concerned with understanding how people use narratives to inform and justify social arrangements and action and how social arrangements and actions shape cultural meanings. The ways that ideologies mandate or subvert the authority of particular individuals and groups, the capacity of power structures to mute or give voice to distinctive groups, and the tug of war between those who would impose their constructions of reality and others who subvert and transform from below are political dimensions of this inquiry. This approach is a far cry from earlier studies that listed interethnic attitudes gathered from survey research. It involves a very different theory of meaning and culture.

There is good evidence that Indian religion deals expressly with Indian-Ladino relations at the same time it portrays a distinct system of values. In analyzing the ritual re-enactment of the Passion in Holy Week ceremonies, June Nash finds that these dramas serve as vehicles for the expression of "pre-Columbian" themes and for a presentation of contemporary ethnic relations.[12] Through these dramas, Indians "reveal a sense of their oppression, a definition of the dominant group as oppressors and an imagined victory over their masters" (J. Nash 1967/68:318). That Christ and Mary are of secondary importance in these dramas shows the extent to which Indians have rephrased the Passion story so that it might express their cultural preoccupations at the same time it deals with Indian images of Ladinos. These rituals focus on various manifestations of Judas, who is clearly identified as a Ladino. That Judas is both castrated and propitiated and that he may symbolize a commercial trickster, a guardian of sexual fertility, and a hated enemy in different towns hints at the complexity of the image of the Ladino. Nash suggests that this diversity can be explained in terms of the cultural emphasis and patterns of social relations in each community. I would add that such symbols gain significance as they are related to other aspects of local social ideologies and historical events in each community.

Ricardo Falla (1971) has found that Indians express images of their exploitation through the character of Juan Noj, who is the subject of mythology common to communities throughout Guatemala and highland Chiapas. In these myths Juan Noj is presented as a supernatural being who offers to make pacts with Indians, who in turn become rich in this life in exchange for their labors after death on the guardian's plantation located within a volcano. Juan Noj may be paternalistic, rewarding the poor without necessarily requiring repayment. Or, arbitrarily, he may demand repayment after death. On the other hand, he inevitably punishes the ambitious for their greed. Juan Noj is portrayed by Indians as a Ladino landowner. Falla, in a detailed analysis, argues that these myths express Indian conceptions of an economic exploitation that reinforces dependence on Ladino landowners. Ladinos are associated in these myths with limits placed on the accumulation of wealth in Indian communities. The resulting leveling of economic differences is fundamental to the Indians' conception of community. The portrayal of exploitation as both necessary and inescapable leads Falla to conclude that this belief system gives Indians insight into the structure that limits them economically but blocks a political consciousness of subordination. Falla's analysis is another excellent example of an interpretive approach used to examine how Indian systems of knowledge deal explicitly with bi-ethnic relations and subordination.

The complexity of the image of the Ladino is also conveyed in Victoria Bricker's study (1973) of ritual humor in highland Chiapas. She finds that Indians express social criticism of ladinoized behavior by ritually associating Ladinos with specific kinds of wild animals. Through celebrations in which they impersonate animals and dress as Ladinos, Indians mock Ladino wealth, conspicuous consumption, dietary differences, and promiscuous sexuality. Furthermore, Indians represent Ladino superiority and their own inferiority by associating each ethnic group with animals that are felt to exemplify contrasting characteristics (in this case, the iguana and the squirrel). The construction is a subtle one: powerful Ladinos are portrayed as moral inferiors because, as animals, they are guided by "impulse" while Indians are guided by "reason." The message of these rituals in terms of ethnicity is that, while Ladinos may be politically and economically superior, morally they are not quite human (1973:160–166).

Like Nash, Falla, and Bricker, I will look at the ways in which Indians construct and represent their experience in a bi-ethnic society. This analysis examines meaning systems—whether they be ritual, myth, history, political ideology, or national policy—as ways of structuring knowledge and social experience. As has just been shown, Judas, Juan Noj, and the iguana are central symbols in mythic and ritual narratives in various Indian communities. As symbols, they are vehicles for conceptions, in this case, for Indians' conceptions of Ladinos. These symbols and their accompanying narratives incorporate complex, paradoxical meanings. Judas represents a commercial trickster, a guardian of sexual fertility, and an enemy. Juan Noj becomes a capricious supernatural who sometimes rewards the poor and often punishes the ambitious. The iguana can claim superiority to the squirrel in terms of power; yet, like all animals, it is in the end a moral inferior because impulse rather than reason guides its actions. Judas, Juan Noj, and the iguana are identified by Indians as representations of Ladinos. By studying such representations in particular bodies of ritual and myth, one can begin to understand the interplay of "self" and "other" that is central to Indian identity.

Just as important, however, is the closely related study of the contexts in which an array of narratives are evoked, argued, or questioned. As will be described in detail in the following chapters, the Indians of San Andrés have not one but several origin myths, not one but several available conceptions of the individual as a moral actor, not one but two radically different narratives for Indians who assimilate Ladino culture. One goal of this analysis is to detect patterns in this diversity (cf. Warren 1985a). On the one hand, the apparent lack of consensus and diversity of narratives in San Andrés reflects individual variations in belief, which are both observed and expected by Indians and thus subject to cultural explanation. On the other hand, this variation is a historical product of competing local groups whose definitions of reality have influenced each other even as one gained adherents and the other felt endangered.[13]

This study uses interpretive strategies for understanding how the Indians of San Andrés phrase their own cultural identity or ethnicity.[14] With few exceptions, which are carefully noted, the ethnographic data for this study is drawn from Indians' points of view. To demonstrate their views and present evidence for the analysis, I have translated passages from interviews, public meetings, and ceremonies that were taped during my field work. These passages—from Indian elders, civil-religious hierarchy officials, diviners, catechists, and other townspeople —appear throughout the following chapters, in verbatum in indented quotes or paraphrased in the text. They include narrations of myths, ritual prayers, oral histories, and commentaries on local politics and race relations. In reviewing my field notes I am struck by how directly my commentary and analysis flow from the original interviews. However, the overall model of how world views and ideologies fit together, in a community rife with conflict, is mine. When I returned to Guatemala after completing the analysis, I translated the entire work orally to the field assistant who had been most involved with the study. Though he agreed with the specifics, he found it difficult to fathom the interplay of the religious ideologies of different groups. To him it was clear that one group was correct and the other a liability to the coming generations. I hope that this analysis successfully gives voice to a variety of partisan views in San Andrés. With this in mind, I have tried to clarify the affiliations of those quoted in the text without identifying individuals specifically by name. Whenever possible, I have presented materials on variations in Indians' knowledge and interpretations of belief.

By studying the way Indians represent their social world in a variety of meaning systems, we are able to examine the ways in which this world view addresses the issue of subordination. In addition, we will be able to ask about the cultural forms through which Indians express their political consciousness of the processes that historically and currently contribute to their subordination. Finally, we will be able to evaluate whether changes in Indian world view reflect Stavenhagen's model. His analysis suggests that class relations will increasingly undermine definitions of Indian ethnicity based on colonial relations. Stavenhagen predicts that Indians' assimilation into a class-stratified national society will undermine Indian culture and the social organization of the corporate Indian community.

The Setting for a Re-examination of Indian Identity

This work is a study of the dynamics of Indian cultural identity in the bi-ethnic highland Guatemalan town of San Andrés Semetabaj. Located in the heavily dissected western highlands, the community of San Andrés rests on a narrow east-west shelf a thousand feet above the northern shores of Lake Atitlán. Although rugged topography restricts the growth of the town on three sides and limits the availability of flat land for agriculture, the climate and geographical situation of San Andrés have contributed to its commercial success as a producer of such staples as maize, beans, and wheat.

The climate of San Andrés is largely determined by elevation and proximity to Lake Atitlán. At 6,300 feet, the town lies in the *tierra fría* (cold country) with daytime temperatures of approximately 70°F and nighttime temperatures of 50–55°F. The relative stability of temperatures during the year contrasts with seasonality in rainfall. Rainfall patterns define cycles of planting and harvesting in a community whose economy is centered on the production of grains. The dry season (*el verano*) lasting from November to early April alternates with the wet season (*el invierno*) from mid-April to October. Several varieties of corn and beans are planted with the first rains in mid-April and harvested as they mature at various times throughout the first months of the dry season. Wheat, which is the community's most important cash crop, is planted twice a year in late May and mid-September and harvested in September and February. The double harvests of wheat, the result of an unusually favorable climate, find a ready market on the national level.

By selecting varieties of subsistence crops that produce staggered harvests, peasant agriculturalists exert a measure of control over the temporal distribution of labor-intensive tasks involving the use of a wide-bladed hoe, digging stick, and machete. The demanding work required for harvesting, transportation of crops from outlying fields, and storage is spread over the months of September to February. In addition, serial planting limits the consequence of the failure of a particular crop and ensures a continual inflow of agricultural produce that may be consumed, stored for future use, or sold.

The combination of subsistence and cash crops along with access to a network of local and national markets has made San Andrés an important commercial center during several periods in this century. In the first decades of the century, the town's location at the midway point of a two-day journey between the urban centers of Quezaltenango and Guatemala City made it a common rest stop for commerce and communications flowing between the western highlands and the capital city. Subsequently, when the south coast was developed for plantation agriculture, San Andrés furnished corn for new settlements and laborers for commercial agriculture. In the sixties, the town was bypassed by the completion of the Inter-American Highway, which connects population centers north of the lake region. Despite a less-than-central position in the country's transportation network, San Andrés gained recognition as a regional administrative center for a national association of agricultural cooperatives and as an important producer of wheat.

On the local level, San Andrés maintains commercial ties through a weekly round of market days with neighboring towns north of the lake, including Panajachel, Patzún, Tecpán, Chichicastenango, and the departmental capital of Sololá (cf. de Dios Rosales 1968). Commerce is dominated by women who sell surpluses of staples as well as small amounts of locally produced squash, lima beans, oranges, avocados, and handwoven textiles in the town's plaza on Tuesdays or visit nearby markets on other days of the week. In exchange, women buy fruit, vegetables, condiments, soap, coffee, brown sugar, pottery, textiles, and other staple goods not produced in the town.

San Andrés is the administrative center for the *municipio* (township) of the same name, which serves some 3,500 inhabitants of the town, surrounding hamlets, and nearby plantations.[15] The town itself has approximately one thousand inhabitants, subdivided into 180 families. While the nuclear family predominates as an economic unit, Indian adult sons ideally build homes within paternal compounds so that the extended family is maintained as a residential unit. Within the low mud walls of each compound, nuclear families eat and sleep separately.

At the center of the settlement is a spacial plaza where the local market is held once a week, children play while the school is not in session, and adults congregate while waiting to transact business or to attend town meetings. The plaza is ringed by municipal offices, a newly constructed health center, the colonial plaza church, and the headquarters of the agricultural cooperative. A second church building, the *calvario* chapel, overlooks the plaza from a nearby hill.

The residential area immediately surrounding the plaza is inhabited exclusively by one segment of the bi-ethnic community, the Ladinos. Ladinos, who consider themselves the descendents of the Spanish conquerors of Guatemala, make up about 26 percent of the town's population, a figure unusually high for rural communities in this area of the highlands. They run small shops attached to their homes, work in the offices adjoining the plaza, and manage or own nearby plantations. The Mayan segment of the bi-ethnic community, the Trixanos, as they call themselves, lives around the Ladino core of the town. Trixanos consider themselves to be the local descendents of the Cakchiquel Indians, who form the second largest Mayan linguistic group in Guatemala and now inhabit towns in the departments of Guatemala, Chimaltenango, Sacatepéquez, and Escuintla. Trixanos are peasant agriculturalists who independently farm small plots of land or work as day laborers on local plantations. Men supplement the incomes of nuclear families through a variety of occupations, including tilemaking and brickmaking, house construction, bread baking, small-scale businesses, and more lucrative work on highway repair crews. Women, in addition to domestic duties and assistance in some agricultural tasks, weave textiles on backstrap looms, market agricultural surpluses, or work as domestic servants.

Transformations of Indian Identity in San Andrés Semetabaj

From a distance one could argue that the Guatemalan case is an archetypal transition from traditional to modern, involving the rejection of a communal social order for individualism (Migdal 1974). In fact, this study of San Andrés Semetabaj reveals a much more complex pattern of moral debate, institutional transformation, and a growing questioning of the accepted terms of ethnic difference. As in other highland communities, the 1940s to 1970s was a period when a singular Indian world view, the fundamental source of authority for Indian elders and the civil-religious hierarchy, was challenged by a younger generation, who embraced individualized religious doctrines, cultural assimilation, and work opportunities outside the conventional ethnic division of labor (cf. Carmack 1981:360–367; Brintnall 1979; Falla 1978; Smith 1977). The political experiments of the 1945–1954 revolutionary period weakened the powers of Mayan elders. Youths experienced the turmoil of Indian elders and Ladino landowners when the revolutionary government recruited young literate Indians to new local leadership roles in a largely unsuccessful attempt to institute agrarian reform. These youths were also the focus of the Catholic Church and, later, the counterrevolutionary government of 1954, which encouraged groups like Catholic Action to missionize rural communities in order to depoliticize the poor, who it was feared might be responsive to leftist politicization.

From an interpretive point of view, it is clear that, although national politics and economics may shape the raw material for change, they do not mechanically create its terms. Thus, to understand the significance of the disruption of Indian power structures, the following chapters examine the world views of Indian elders and traditionalists, the emergence of alternative visions of reality as the younger generation became active in Catholic Action, and the consequences of new religious pluralism for Indians' formulation of their own identity. What this study uncovers, for both traditionalists (who I also refer to as Trixanos or old Catholics) and Catholic Action converts (who I also call orthodox Catholics and catechists), is a continual process of cultural reformulation through which Indians have created their own understandings of change, tested them, and found grounds for challenging the status quo of ethnic relations. At the heart of the world views of both traditionalists and converts is a concern with ethics, specifically with the relation of the individual to community in a world of injustice.

Part One of this book describes the way Trixano traditionalists sought and found symbolic separation, in religion, from those who structurally subordinated them. "Traditionalist" in this case is *their* construction, for these Indians root the moral legitimacy of their structure of authority and religious world view in *costumbre* (tradition) inherited from the first *antepasados* (ancestors). In blending their own version of Mayan and colonial Spanish beliefs, Indian populations transformed colonial religious language in order to present their own understandings of culture contact. In the Trixano case reworking occurred in several ways. First, traditionalists narrate a series of interlocking origin myths through which they offer explanations of the creation of a bi-ethnic town by the Spaniards as well as the perpetuation of an Indian community distinct from the aftermath of the conquest. Origin myths and traditionalist constructions of colonial history are merged in these meaning systems. The analysis of origin mythology demonstrates how Indians contrast the acceptance of an imposed system with resistance to it through distinctive constructions of community and the past. Second, Indians appropriated and recombined the religious imagery of sixteenth-century Catholicism (cf. Christian 1981), infusing it with new meanings. Satan and Judas appear as non-Indian Ladinos in Trixano myth, folklore, and ritual; the Mayan Lord of the Volcano and Lord of the Wilds (cf. Carmack 1981) are also thought of as the ethnic other. Third, Trixanos redirected the religious brotherhoods (*cofradías*), initially founded by Spanish missionaries, to serve as the mainspring of a separatist Indian culture with its own ritual language and valued images of behavior. In the ceremonies of the brotherhoods, ritual guides (*camol beij*) represent the apex of a Trixano hierarchy, which all adult men ascend during the course of their lives to become *principales* (elders). As the following chapters will show, the guides represent the valued transcendence of the communal order over the natural diversity of individual motives and concerns, rather than the mediation of religious experience by elites. The guides and elders enforce an egalitarian ethic within the Indian sector, arguing for the identification of individual Indians with all others in their community, stressing the interdependence of the generations, and requiring those with greater financial resources to contribute to community rituals and festivals.

Mythology, ethnic symbolism, brotherhood organization, and rituals are products of the conquest; they are also "radical imaginings" of a self-defined identity, social order, and ethical system. An implicit cultural critique is made explicit as Indians identify the egalitarian model for social relations as "the law of Christ" in contrast to the exploitative "law of the Devil" governing the bi-ethnic community.[16] Trixanos believe that moral action (that is, expressions of the individual's *voluntad*, or will) is not possible by definition in those situations where "the law of the Devil" robs individuals of choice. Moral refuge is found in the separatist Indian community and the *cofradias*, where the "law of Christ" prevails.

This critique is further refined in traditionalist belief by pacts with the devil. An analysis of these pacts—in which individuals trade wealth in this world for eternal suffering in the next—will show how they can be read as critiques of the assimilation of Ladino culture. Pacts express the fear that Indians who defy the moral necessity of suffering in this world will use their wealth to exploit other Indians. As will be shown in detail in Part One, the twist that traditionalist world view gives to these pacts is that they are not entered into voluntarily.[17] Consequently, change is portrayed as outside the control of the individual and the Indian community.

Part Two of this study opens with the entrance of Catholic Action (Acción Católica) into the town of San Andrés in 1952 and the subsequent reformulation of the Trixano world view by local Indian catechists who sought to stress a universalistic, trans-ethnic religious identity over the traditionalist understanding of Indianness as town-specific. Initially a handful of Indian converts began to explore an alternative social world view through their new orthodox group, while the rest of the Indian population continued involvement, one way or another, in the community-wide celebrations of the older civil-religious hierarchy. Although converts to the orthodox movement attempted to work alongside the brotherhoods to revitalize Catholicism, they soon discovered that their universalistic beliefs were incompatible with the world view and social ideology of the civil-religious hierarchy. Today members of Catholic Action form the strongest religious group in San Andrés. The civil-religious hierarchy currently faces the prospect of consolidating religious brotherhoods or closing down the less important ones and perhaps even returning images of the saints to the bi-ethnic chapel.

The task of relating Catholic Action religious ideology to social life fell almost exclusively to Indians in the town, rather than to missionaries or to the formal hierarchy of the Catholic Church, due to the decentralization of Catholic Action in the highlands and a national scarcity of parish priests. Decentralization may have contributed to a more rapid acceptance of the new religious belief system because it allowed local catechists to appropriate religious language for a social critique that demanded change in this world. Modern Catholic orthodoxy has given Indians a set of contrasting categories (such as material/ spiritual and body/soul), which converts have used to reinterpret the existing social order, to analyze their position within it, and to envision an alternative. As this analysis will show, new Catholics have linked their religious critique to a historical analysis of the impact of national policies—including forced labor and educational reforms—on local affairs in order to talk about the social and political processes that created present-day ethnic hierarchies.

The central metaphor in Catholic Action belief is a contrast between allegiance to God and to the World, between the "spiritual" and "material" aspects of life. For these converts, allegiance to the spiritual is marked by belief in the equivalence of all souls, unlike the material world, in which distinctions are based upon the dominant group's judgment of the social worth of each person. Most significantly, Indian converts associate the racism of Ladinos *and* the belief system of the Trixano civil-religious hierarchy with the material world. What they have done is to make an important connection between the Ladino subordination of Indians in daily life and the separatism of the civil-religious hierarchy, which they believe contributes to subordination.

Indian converts to Catholic orthodoxy reintroduce the possibility of moral action by calling on all individuals to choose between the spiritual and material orderings of society. In religious terms, such a choice demonstrates commitment to the sacraments of the Church, which work to rebalance the spiritual and material aspects of the individual's behavior so that the soul will remain in a state of grace. In social terms, moral action means choosing to emphasize religious over ethnic identity. Believing that the spiritual should predominate over the material in the secular world as well, Catholic Action members have become involved in bi-ethnic affairs in San Andrés. This activism centers on the goal of achieving equality through the end of discrimination in the bi-ethnic, material world that would parallel the universalism of the Catholic Church in spiritual matters. Following these precepts, members of Catholic Action have been active in secular institutions, like the regional agricultural cooperative that is tied into a national association of agricultural cooperatives. Through this organization, orthodox Catholic Indians hope to work toward greater economic parity between the two ethnic groups.

As this analysis will document, catechists have evolved their understandings through action. They have found contemporary political history to be increasingly relevant to their formulations, because it can be used to explain why equity in the present fails to narrow gaps between the rich and the poor, between Ladinos and Indians. Their understandings of history and contemporary society have led converts to feel ambivalent about the success they might have in practicing their social vision in a bi-ethnic community. They have come to wonder about the ultimate wisdom of promoting an egalitarianism that rests on a de-emphasis of ethnicity and seeing "progress" for Indians as selective ladinoization.

Finally, at the close of this study, I will return to the issue of Indians' political consciousness and their changing explanations of subordination. Specifically, I will be concerned with analyzing the overall impact of changes in the representation of "self" and "other," redefinitions of community and individual moral action, and transformations of the sources of authority for the Indian community. What this study finds is that resistance to and subversion of cultural impositions is not a single act but rather a patterned social and historical process of responses to power, and therefore its successes and failures must be seen in the wider context of possibilities and constraints. In closing, I will outline varying anthropological interpretations of what may be a radical reformulation of Indian identity in San Andrés Semetabaj.

PART ONE

Indian Costumbre *and the*
Image of the Devil

1. Creation of the Indian World in Myth

No single myth describes how the Trixano world was created. Rather, an oral tradition of mythology, short commentaries, and interpretations tells of a series of creations and destructions during which the world was formed and ordered and humanity's relation to the Eternal Father (Padre Eterno) was elaborated with the addition of his Son, Jesus Christ (Jesucristo), and the saints as sacred intermediaries. The chronology of creation is divided by the Trixanos into three periods (*épocas*): (*a*) the epoch of the Eternal Father, (*b*) the life and subsequent crucifixion of Jesus Christ, and (*c*) the division of the earth's population into towns governed by the saints. Each period marks the addition of a new level of intermediaries (*intermediarios*) to the sacred hierarchy and the division of the world into more specific domains.

The Trixanos involved in the civil-religious hierarchy describe the dynamics of creation and the division of the world into more specific domains in terms of an agricultural metaphor. Each set of sacred intermediaries has its "cultivated fields," which become increasingly specific as new levels are added and time passes in the chronology of creation. God created the highest level of cultivated fields, the universe, and sent his Son to give order to a more restricted domain, the world. Jesus Christ divided his cultivated fields by distributing the towns of the world to the Apostles, so that each would have his own fields to watch over. San Andrés received the town that is named after him as a product of this division.

The cycles that formed the sacred hierarchy are conceptualized by the Trixanos in the terms of the agricultural cycle. Each of the epochs is a refinement or a more specific form of creation that ensures the continuity and fertility of the Trixano world. Each set of intermediaries was sent down to the earth as a "planting." In turn, each gave order to a more restricted portion of the world, called a "cultivated field," and at "the harvest" of death returned to the heavens so that there would be more fertility on earth. In this scheme, the harvest marks both the end of a cycle and the preparation for the beginning of another, because without the harvest no seed would be gathered for the subsequent planting. The agricultural metaphor likens the planting and harvesting of the agricultural cycle to creation and destruction as well as to birth and death. Initially, in the creation mythology, all living beings were periodically harvested through the destruction of the world. Later, during the epoch of Jesus Christ, each individual was allowed to have an independent life cycle and an individual harvest of death. In both epochs death is necessary for new cycles of birth and fertility.

The Creation of Order from Ambiguity

The creation mythology as a body forms a chronology that moves from the general to the specific: from God to the saints, from the "fields" of the universe to each community, from all living things as an unclearly differentiated whole to each individual. While I suspect that it may have once been told by Indian elders in the form of a single unit, mythology dealing with the creation is now told in short stories, or *cuentos*.[18] Each one of these stories contrasts the unclearly structured universe of the Eternal Father with the subsequent neatly categorized and delineated universe of Jesus Christ. The stories deal with the physical universe, the nature of human beings, and the dynamics of birth and death in the universe.

The first set of stories, as told by a Trixano elder, contrasts the interpenetrating levels of the universe—the seas, earth, and sky—of the Eternal Father's universe with the discrete levels formed by Jesus Christ: "From the time that Christ came, he ordered the world. He separated the waters in some places and put the earth in other places. In ancient times in the epoch of the Eternal Father all was united. There was very little land. One could not walk much because one went along plunging into the pools of water." In ancient times during the epoch of the Eternal Father, the world was an undifferentiated unity because the categories of existence interpenetrated each other. The boundaries of the seas, the earth, and the sky were ambiguously graded into one another. The earth and sea were "united" so that there was little ground for the inhabitants of the world to walk on without falling into the waters. The sky and the earth were also united because God lived in both places, coming to the earth to direct creation and to oversee all that happened and returning to the sky when he was tired from his labors. The Trixanos note that God finally became "bored" with his labors and returned permanently to a spiritual existence in the heavens, marking them off from the physical nature of life on earth. His Son, Jesus Christ, further defined the natural environment through his first act, separating the waters and the earth.

In the two epochs, the nature of the physical universe closely parallels that of its inhabitants. During the epoch of the Eternal Father, human beings, who lived on an earth indistinct from the seas or the sky, were not clearly separated from animals because all living things could communicate with each other through "the spoken word" and lived in peaceful coexistence. Humanity was not divided into races and "neither Jews nor Spaniards" walked the earth because God created only one class of "humble and obedient people." In the forms of the various kinds of persons—elders, youths, and children—God came to visit humans on earth to find out about the behavior of his creations, although he made no attempt to correct or punish bad behavior or individuals. During his visits God also blessed the crops and directed human agricultural labors because people lacked the "intelligence" to proceed independently: "The Eternal Father lived in the sky, in heaven, and only came in person here on earth for a time, a moment. He had to come to become aware of the good and the bad that the people did and for the blessing of the crops. In ancient times there were no ideas like now exist in the [minds of the] people, but rather they needed the direction of someone superior in idea and intelligence." The humans' lack of intelligence meant that they had little knowledge of the world and no volition because good and evil were not clearly distinguished as separate forms of behavior. Behavior had no consequence for the relationship of individuals to God, for the periodic judgment and destruction of the world was inevitable.

Paralleling the division of the physical universe, the second set of stories discusses the creation of clear distinctions between different classes of living beings. In his role as a second creator, Jesus Christ is associated with the division of human beings from animals:

> The animals in the epoch of the Eternal Father were not enemies of the people because they spoke and if they needed something they asked for it. The change succeeded in the epoch of Jesucristo. The Eternal Father watched over the people of his creation and did not want the people who he had created to suffer. When Jesus Christ came, all the animals were deprived of speech because there was much evil in the people. Because of the danger that the animals presented, one remembers that there is a God when one comes face to face with an animal.

Christ separated the spatial domains of living beings so that wild animals would live in the forested wilds and humans and domesticated animals would live in the towns. No longer were animals able to communicate with humans, since humans were the only living beings to retain the capacity to communicate through speech. Nor did the wilds peacefully coexist with the domesticated regions, because, with the division of the towns from the outlying areas, the wilds became the domain of the forces of nature that endangered the settlements. Humanity was further separated into different "races" called the "rich" and the "poor" or "foreigners" and "natives": "Before there was no difference in race because only one class of persons existed. There were neither Jews nor Spaniards, but rather one class of persons who were created by the Eternal Father. God permitted the races to differentiate at the time of Jesus Christ because it was not a bad thing that people were succeeding to know more of the world. The rich were beginning to know and populate different places; and when they came to primitive places, the mixed race arose, a mixture of foreigners and natives." The separation of the races is in some sense analogous to the distinction between wild and domesticated animals, although the latter is much more clearly articulated in the conquest mythology that will be presented shortly.

In the creation mythology, foreigners, who had knowledge of God and of the world through exploration, are contrasted with the native race that was associated with the wilds: "There already existed native persons who perhaps did not know of the existence of God. Here one still sees the remains of the first town of San Andrés that was called Chutinamit [small town] and was located north of the present town. The principal reason why this place was abandoned is not known, but I believe that it was found to be very secluded and was the object of many dangers from the steep gullies and wilds." At the same time that the races were allowed to spread out and explore the world, setting the stage for conquest (a historical action in the sense that it was independent of God's direction), human beings were given the ability to choose between good and evil. The end point of the creation mythology, then, is the recognition of the individual as a moral being with an independent life cycle. To describe this last transition, which deals with the dynamics of the world, the two epochs will again be juxtaposed as they are presented in the *cuentos*.

In the third set of stories, the dynamics of the universe, requiring the periodic total destruction of all living things during the epoch of the Eternal Father, gives way to the particularities of individualized life spans in the time of his Son. The Eternal Father did not let the first creation of the universe stand because, in a world of incomplete order, his "humble and obedient" creations became increasingly disobedient as time went on. This growth of disobedience was a natural tendency of the world and Trixanos offer no further explanation of it. The Eternal Father gave humans a long life of one hundred to five hundred years; but, as evil increased with age, God periodically judged and destroyed the entire world by flood:

> When there was a Holy Judgment, all the people of the world died. All that was in the sea and the birds in the mountains, all died. The seed of different animals and of a few families were kept. I do not know who the person was who kept all this seed; some say that it was Noah, but I cannot be sure. Then those who did not help to collect the seed all died, and the *señor* who kept the seed made a kind of box in which to keep all the animals. On top of all the animals went this person with his family. When the seas covered all the world, these boxes floated. And when the seas receded, the animals went in different directions.

God's cataclysmic judgment of the world is seen by the Trixanos as another agricultural metaphor: the world was God's field in which he harvested humanity through the destruction of the world and used a few people as seed for the next planting, which gave rise to more people.

At the close of the Eternal Father's epoch, instead of commanding the waters of the seas to flood and once again destroy the unclearly formed world, God sent his Son to finish the task of creation. Jesus Christ came to the earth as a representative of his creator-father and of humanity. He was sent to take God's place in the ordering of the world and direction of its inhabitants and to take the place of humanity in the cycle of regeneration through periodic total destruction. Christ brought new order and a new fertility to the world.

In separating for once and for all the interpenetrating levels and categories of the world, Jesus Christ ordained the uniqueness of humans in the realm of living things. Christ's identification with humanity seemed to be incomplete as long as the categories of living things ambiguously overlapped. Thus, one of his first acts was to distinguish humans from animals. Once the separation was complete, however, he assumed humanity's place in the Eternal Father's cycle of the simultaneous judgment and destruction of all human beings to ensure the continuity of life on earth.

Christ was on one level identified with all humanity and on another

with the individual. Trixanos say that Christ was born and later cruci-
fied so that more human beings would die and more would be born.
Rather than allowing all to die so that more would be born, Jesucristo
determined an individualistic cycle: "If a man dies in the morning,
another is born in the afternoon; if a person is born now, later someone dies." The new law of the Son of God was:

> that we die after a short life so that there will not be much evil,
> since the bad are taken back more rapidly. If it were the contrary,
> evil would grow. We would kill each other every moment on earth
> so that we could feed ourselves and get what is necessary. If there
> were no death, our food would become scarce and it would present
> a danger for all. For this reason, Jesus Christ decided that while
> some are born, there is work and planting for the feeding of each.
> For this reason, people continue to die, so that the world is com-
> plete.

Along with the creation of individual life spans, the epoch of Jesus
Christ is associated by Trixanos with the creation of the moral order.
This moral order, which calls on the individual to choose between
alternatives, resulted from an agreement between Christ and his chief
Apostle who tried to usurp Christ's creative powers by imitating and
deceiving him. When Christ asked the angel San Gabriel to punish the
disobedient follower, the Apostle was transformed into a being with
both human and animal characteristics. With each lash from San
Gabriel the Apostle grew a horn and finally turned into Satanás, the
Devil. By refusing to obey the new order, Satanás embodied the old
undifferentiated order in which humans were not separated from
animals. Thereafter, the two agreed that Christ's domain would be
the heavens, the mountain tops, and the town where his followers
lived; and Satanás's domain, the wilds and the underworld.

Trixanos believe that the creation of these two domains meant that
each individual must choose between two paths: one very rugged, narrow, and full of spines that leads to God and the other very wide and
overflowing with differently colored flowers, leading to Satanás. The
spines on the path to God are the individual's sufferings through which
he earns the company of God and eternal rest. Yet life was not to be
all suffering because those who "adore God, behave correctly and love
their fellow men" are rewarded on earth with a long life, many children, and successful plantings and harvests. On the other hand, those
who follow the alternative path and make a pact with Satanás to gain
riches without suffering through hard work will be punished because

this path leads to the wilds and the home of the Devil in the under-world volcanos. There individuals are transformed into human-animals, beasts of burden, which must work eternally without rest. Individuals as moral beings choose between the new order and a spiritual existence after death or the old order in which they become anomalous physical beings at death. Both Satanás and those who make pacts with him assume the form of human-animals, paralleling the lack of clear separation of living beings associated with the premoral epoch of the Eternal Father.

The creation mythology culminates with the separation of the races that began to demonstrate their knowledge by exploring the world and the creation of the individual with a separate biography as a moral actor capable of deciding between good and evil. The conquest mythology takes these separate themes and demonstrates the problematic nature of moral action in a society composed of different races. At the conquest, Spaniards (as one of the "foreign races" exploring the world and bringing Christ's order through their religious beliefs) encountered the native population of what came to be San Andrés. The contact of the Spaniards with the native population produced an ethnically plural, Catholic society dominated by the Spaniards.

The Conquest and Civilization

For some inexplicable reason, the Indians of Chutinamit, the pre-conquest name for the town of San Andrés, were isolated from the last stages of creation in which humanity was separated from nature, the races diverged and began to explore the world, and individuals as moral beings were given the choice between heaven and hell. Trixanos say that the town was secluded in the mountains in the midst of the wilds and the steep gullies instead of being separated from nature. The "tribesmen" were also incompletely distinguished from nature; for they wore animal skins and feathers for clothing and worshipped "deities of stone and roots," in which, it is said, they had little confidence. The tribesmen were unaware of the existence of other races in the world, although other tribes lived in the region, practicing agriculture and waging wars to extend the dominions of their kingdoms. Within the kingdom, Trixanos recount that people lived in peace with little division of labor or disparity in wealth and no distinction between rich and poor. Each family had plenty of land on which to raise crops for consumption and surpluses to exchange for minerals and skins. The king maintained internal order and directed the exploitation of gold, which was formed into coins imprinted with the figure of the king or a god. It is said that the king, along with other officials of the realm, was highly respected because he did not allow social differences but presented himself as an equal to the people of the tribe.

To this scene, according to the mythologies, came the Spaniards from "far away." They "civilized" the native peoples by introducing a school to impart knowledge and a religion centering on the worship of God and the saints so that humans would have a choice between good and evil. Civilization, knowledge, and religion were exchanged for the mineral riches of the kingdom, especially for the gold that had represented the equal distribution of wealth in the kingdom.

The transition from primitive to civilized was accomplished by a striking ritual, having its own *cuento*, in which an initiate was separated from the natural surroundings, including the social order of the tribe, and introduced into the new Spanish social order as a worker (*mozo*):

> Before, there was one kind of primitive people. When the Spaniards came, they brought mirrors, ear rings, and razors. They cut the hair of one of the primitive men and shaved him. When he felt clean, he felt a great change in his personality, because the people of the tribe had been accustomed to long hair and beards and it was difficult to tell the men from the women. They also bathed him. He felt like a Spaniard. However, there was a problem because the rest of the people in the tribe did not like the way he looked and he was forced to work alone for the Spaniards.

This rite of passage, with all of its overtones of purification, produced a radical shift in identification, because the tribesman "felt like a Spaniard" after the encounter. The initial reaction of his fellow tribesmen was to isolate the initiate by refusing to work with him and thereby forcing him to work for the Spaniards. As the Spaniards, however, increasingly dominated the countryside by taking over the lands of the kingdom, all Indians appear to have moved through this transition and become civilized.

The separation of the Indian from nature involved a new identification with the town instead of the larger kingdom. According to mythology and Trixano interpretations, the Spaniards gave the Indians of each town a distinctive kind of clothing to take the place of the traditional dress of animal skins and feathers that had bound the tribe to nature and to the kingdom. The Spaniards also introduced a new religion, which centered on the celebration of God and the saints rather than on the earlier deities of stone and root. To further distinguish each town, the foreigners renamed each one after the saint that became its guardian. Images of the saints were given to the Indians, who were organized into brotherhoods to celebrate the new religion. Although it is said that many Indians were initially ambivalent about the new belief system, as time passed and the domination of the Spaniards increased, they left behind the "idols" and began to work under the supervision of Spaniards and "civilized" Indians in the construction of a huge stone and adobe church still to be seen in the town today. The Spaniards who directed the building of the church are described as firm and demanding, forcing Indians to do such heavy work as hauling large rocks and adobe bricks on their backs from outside the town for the massive walls of the temple. This relationship of the Spaniards as the directors, *patrones*, to the Indians as the workers, *mozos*, continued when the Spaniards formed large plantations and used the Indians as a source of labor.

The Spaniards are remembered as active people full of good ideas that they brought to the tribes in the form of religion celebrated in the churches and education taught in the school; yet, Trixanos point out that in the process of civilizing the tribes, the Spaniards made people suffer and sacrifice themselves "like beasts of burden" for the new religious and social orders. Furthermore, they carried away all the wealth of the town and took over the lands of the people. It is said that only the priests treated the poor well by defending, curing, and teaching them religion. Trixanos conclude the conquest mythology by explaining that the Spaniards returned to their native land after this period of colonization, leaving their descendents, the Ladinos, to order relations between the town of San Andrés and the nation of Guatemala, located in the capital city.

2. Mythology as Ideology in a Bi-ethnic Society

Using the foregoing mythological accounts, I would now like to turn to a comparative analysis of Trixano versions of the creation and conquest in order to discuss the character of Spanish domination and transformation of Indian society. Additional material will be presented to demonstrate that Indians perceive a continuity in domination from the early Spanish period to the Ladino-controlled present. Whereas Chapter One analyzes mythology in its own terms as an expression of Indian world view, the goal of this chapter is to consider the ideological significance of this symbolic form. As well as narrating the process of world creation, mythology embodies models for interethnic relations in the present.

For Trixanos, mythology serves as a symbol system for the presentation of a contradiction (and a resolution) between moral action and domination, between the universalistic, egalitarian value system of the Indian civil-religious hierarchy and the social inequities based on ethnicity of colonial and present-day societies. Differences between the political and social and the religious consequences of the conquest are expressed in mythology through contrasting Ladinos, as intermediaries between the town and external society, to the saints, as intermediaries between the earth and the heavens. In a parallel manner, the wilds that form the dominions of Satanás and the order of nature are distinguished from the town where the law of Christ prevails. In both cases, Trixanos describe a world in which they can exert only a limited amount of control over their own lives because of the coexistence of independent, threatening, and competing systems of power. In characterizing the external control of Indian society, Trixanos associate both Spaniards and Ladinos with Satanás who reigns over the wilds but threatens the town and the cultivated fields around it. Space (as a system of ecological relations) becomes a symbol system in which both ethnic groups and their interrelations are represented in such a way as to suggest that Indians may assert a measure of control over their own affairs even though they are embedded in the more powerful Ladino society.

The belief that Indians may assert a measure of control over their lives despite their subordination is manifested in the two images that Trixanos have of the origin of San Andrés. On the one hand, mythology portrays the Spaniards as the originators of the present form of the bi-ethnic town in which Indians are cast in a subordinate role as laborers for Ladino *patrones*. On the other hand, an alternative series of *cuentos* ignores the conquest in dealing with the creation of the town by the saints and the invention of tradition (*costumbre*) by Indian ancestors independent of Ladino intervention.

These mythological models parallel the alternative sets of conceptions that Trixanos associate with the symbol "community" (*el pueblo*) in the present. In a certain range of contexts, Trixanos speak of community as a bi-ethnic entity in which Indians are always subordinated to Ladinos by ethnic identity. Alternatively, in other contexts, Trixanos speak of community as an exclusively Indian entity that has inherited "blood" (or common "descent") and "tradition" from the first Indian ancestors. In short, mythological models of the origin of society parallel the present dual meaning of community. In this way, Trixanos have elaborated distinct ways of conceptualizing their ethnic identity and distinct models for organizing Indian-Indian and Indian-Ladino relations.

This chapter describes how Trixano belief expresses what I refer to as subordinate and separatist models for ethnic identity and social relations in San Andrés. In addition to presenting a symbolic analysis of the dual images of identity, this analysis will describe which image of identity is deemed appropriate by Trixanos for everyday social interaction in agricultural production, the civil administration of the town, and religious celebrations. Trixanos believe that separatism, which calls for independence from Ladino control, is a valued ideal; yet their ability to maintain separate forms of agricultural production, civil administration, and religious celebration within the social realities of San Andrés varies considerably. In addition to examining the ways in which Indians negotiate toward separatism in the present, this chapter will also present material on the historical responses of the Indian community to Ladino penetration into Indian affairs.

From the Conquest to the Present:
Myth and Models for Social Action

In the terms of Trixano mythology, the Spaniards were a social product of the new order that Christ gave to the world. As a race capable of independent historical action, they explored the world and introduced "knowledge and intelligence" to peoples who lacked both qualities. As moral beings, they brought the new Christian religion that defined the individual as an intelligent, independent being, able to weigh the alternatives and consequences of good and evil. At the conquest, the Spaniards brought to Chutinamit (San Andrés) the two separate themes of Christ's creation: the separation and subsequent encounter of the races and the distinction of the individual as a moral actor who determines the form of her or his afterlife by allegiances and actions in the world. In the hands of the Spaniards, however, these two themes proved incompatible.

To be a moral being, the individual, so Christ ordained, must be distinguishable from nonhuman animals and capable of choosing between suffering in this life that leads to heaven and ease in this life followed by descent into hell. The mythic narrative suggests that Spaniards introduced the concept of the moral actor by converting Indians to Catholicism and then made it impossible for them to actualize the implications of this conception of the individual. The Indian (as well as the Spanish) individual was not allowed moral autonomy as a social actor because of the nature of Spanish domination, which subordinated the individual as an actor to ethnic identity. Indians could not determine the form of their individual lives because the Spaniards defined their place in the new society in terms of ethnic identity as it contrasted with the ethnicity of the conquerors.

According to the Trixanos, Spanish domination of the Indians was accomplished through annexation of their lands and mineral wealth. Subsequently, Indians were forced to work on Spanish plantations, located on former Indian lands, as agricultural laborers for the new social order of the conquerors. Spaniards both continued to associate Indians with animals (domesticated beasts of burden) and failed to allow them a choice between the different forms of life leading to heaven and hell. The construction of the new church building demonstrated the triumph of the new religious and social systems serving as a focal point for the new town of San Andrés, named after the colonial Catholic patron saint. Indians who lost their place in what is pictured in mythology as an egalitarian indigenous society became the source of manual labor for the construction of the church and occupied a position subordinate to the Spanish *patrones* who directed the work. The civilization of the Indian signified subordination to Spaniards in the new social system. Significantly, civilized Indians who worked on the church "felt *like* Spaniards," but did not become Spaniards, although they adopted the colonial Catholicism of the conquerors. Indians could find their place in the new social order, but they had no control over their new ethnic identity or subordinate position as dictated by the new social ideology.

On the one hand, the religion of the conquerors presented the individual Indian with a moral choice that Indians were unable to act upon because of their subordination. On the other hand, religion gave meaning to the suffering of Indians by offering the reward of eternal rest in heaven to those who suffered on earth. In setting up the new social order, the Spanish appear to have stressed the aspect of religion that compensated for the suffering of manual labor and the fixed subordinate status of Indians. Since Indians by the nature of their social position would "receive their rest [in heaven] because one has already come from suffering here on earth," moral action of the individual became a secondary issue to ethnicity and economic domination. Moreover, poverty was to bind Indians more closely to God: "If we are poor, we remember God and we have necessities which make us go to God. If we are rich we do not [remember] because we only have the ambition to have more."

For Spaniards, who had an easier life directing the labors of Indians, ethnic identity also superseded the issue of moral action of the individual. Thus, according to Trixanos, when the Spaniards died, "they had to go to a special place inside the wilds where there is a city for them. But they have to work not as they worked here on earth, but rather the work there is more arduous." By subordinating Indians, Spaniards gained riches without suffering through hard work and, thus, chose the path leading to a special hell. Spaniards and their descendents are associated with Satanás who punishes his followers by demanding that they work eternally as beasts of burden in an underground hell inside a volcano. Spaniards instituted a parallel order in the town of San Andrés by causing Indians to suffer as laborers.

Domination, based on the inflexible and non-negotiable character of ethnicity, would appear to be the worst possible moral transgression in this belief system because it renders inconsequential all other moral acts of individuals. Individual moral acts of particular Spaniards had no bearing on their lives after their deaths because domination and subsequent divine judgment were phrased in ethnic terms that overrode the actions of the individual.

The descendents of the Spaniards, the Ladinos, perpetuated economic domination. After the conquest, the Spaniards returned to their homeland and left Ladinos to mediate the social axis of the new society; that is, the relations between the town and the capital where the Spanish-founded government was located. The descendents of the Spaniards are believed to share both Indian and Spanish blood because they resulted from the mixture of the races at the time of the conquest. The mixture of blood, however, did not unify them with Indians, because Spanish blood is seen to predominate and mark Ladinos off from descendents of the autochthonous population.[19] As problematic as the mixture of blood may seem to be, Trixanos note that Ladinos use blood (or descent) to explain their continuing separation from and innate superiority to Indians. Thus, Ladinos continue to assert dominance in terms of ethnicity, which supersedes the unity called for in the religious order brought by Christ and promulgated by the saints.

The Spaniards converted the Indians and, before departing from the town, set up brotherhoods (*cofradías*) to celebrate saints as mediators between the people and God. Unlike the Ladinos, the social mediators between the town and the capital, the saints as religious mediators between the town and the heavens embody the unifying aspect of Christ's commandment that people "unite, love, respect, and mutually understand one another in doing that which is correct." San Andrés, the guardian saint of the town, has blessed those who follow this code instead of associating themselves with the Devil's domain: "San Andrés has given his blessings for the production of our harvest here in town. San Andrés has not permitted us to suffer with the Devil that exists here, but rather he wants us to work decently. We could be rich if we made pacts with the Devil but our father, San Andrés, does not want this so that his children will not suffer later in the homes of the mountains." In this way, the town-centered religious order of the Indians, who celebrated God and the saints, was clearly demarcated from the hell in the wilds where Spaniards and their descendents were sent after death.

The issue that remains is the way belief systems express the impact of the order of Satanás in the wilds on the order of the saints in the town. These symbols embody conceptions of the impact of Spaniards and their descendents on Indian society. Satanás's underworld is always associated with those forces located outside the town that influence the activities of Indians in town. At the time of Christ, hell for Indians was described as a plantation where those who had avoided suffering in life would work and suffer as laborers after death. For Spaniards and Ladinos, hell is a city in which they must engage in heavy work instead of directing the work of others, as they did on earth. The hells of both the plantation and the city are symbolically located in the wilds (*el monte*) outside the primary domain of Christ and the saints in town. In the heavily forested areas of the wilds another kind of order prevails, one governed by the supernatural laws of nature and administered by the Lord of the Wilds (*el dueño del monte*), another guise of the Devil. A brief description of the Trixano conception of the wilds will show that it is a particularly apt idiom in which to express Spanish and Ladino influence thought to emanate from outside the town, from the plantations and the capital.

According to the Trixanos, the order of nature in the mountainous wilds operates independently of Indians and differs from the human order of the town where "the streets do not have plants or vegetation but rather constructions of houses on flat ground." No one plants trees and shrubs in the wilds; yet they grow to great heights in the naturally fertile ground. No one cares for wild animals by feeding them; yet they are able to find food. In the mountains, wild plants and animals exist without human help.

Yet, where the order of nature penetrates the town, it is viewed as a potential threat to the work of the agriculturalists and their domesticated animals that are kept in the town. Nature obeys its own laws and becomes an antagonist when it brings too much rain, violent storms, and earthquakes endangering crops and the town. Furthermore, wild vegetation and animal life prey on cultivated fields and the town. In the fields, wild plants rob the earth of its nutrients so that the cultivated plants do not completely develop. Wild animals are known to penetrate the town and to rob people of small domestic fowl. Trixanos protect their crops and animals from nature by carefully weeding their fields and pursuing wild animals that endanger their domestic animals. In distinguishing between the concepts "wild" and "domesticated," Trixanos point out that, while wild plants and animals are independent of the town's domesticated order, they threaten and compete with it. In contrast, domesticated plants and animals are dependent on humans for their care and development. As one Trixano noted, "If one gives them [domesticated animals] food, they become tame and humble before their owner. The animals of the wilds pit themselves against man and are his enemy."

Indian agriculturalists maintain a very complicated relation with the natural wilds, which are sources both of new fertility and of destructive threats to Indian life in the town and the fields. Indians believe that they first received domesticated staples, like corn, from the wilds. The mountains also serve as places where firewood is gathered and land is cleared for new fields; yet Indian penetration of the wilds has often been interpreted as a form of trespassing. In this vein, *cuentos* tell of punishments Indians have received from the Devil for entering his dominions without permission to gather firewood.

By projecting threats of Ladino domination onto the wilds that contrast with the Indian community in the town, Indians have been able to characterize Ladino influence as a form of control originating outside the town on the plantations and in the Ladino capital city. Yet a closer look at the community shows that Indians recognize local Ladino control of land and the official municipal government as extensions of the external plantations and the city. As the Devil limits Indian activities in the wilds, so Ladinos, to the distaste of the Indians, have directly circumscribed both Indian access to the wilds for firewood and the extension of new fields through policies enacted by the Ladino-staffed town government.

In acknowledgement of Ladino control both outside and within the town, Trixanos have two ways of talking about their community, or *pueblo*. On the one hand, they speak as if the community were composed entirely of Indians in contrast to an external Ladino society. On the other hand, Trixanos point out that the Indian-Ladino contrast exists within the community itself. The rest of this chapter will deal in one way or another with the issues which result from the alternative ways in which Trixanos conceptualize the community of San Andrés.

Negotiability of Subordination and Separatism

In the face of the wilds that endanger the Indians' domestic plants and animals and the Devil who embodies a different law, Indians have been able to assert a measure of control over their society through the selective adoption of colonial Catholic religion without its external priestly hierarchy. By largely ignoring the official hierarchy of the Catholic Church, Indians have been able to emphasize an Indian organization, the civil-religious hierarchy, which governs the local Indian population, administers the religious brotherhoods, and cares for the *calvario* chapel. Indians have incorporated an egalitarian ideology associated with Christ and the saints as well as the concepts of respect, obedience, and suffering that these divinities are felt to exemplify. The belief system and religious practices of the civil-religious hierarchy are known as *costumbre*, or tradition. They are of fundamental importance to Trixanos who say, "If we didn't do these activities, it would be as if there were no law or order in force. For this reason, it is necessary."

Significantly both *costumbre* and the civil-religious hierarchy are said, in this context, to have been "invented" by the first Indian ancestors (*antepasados*) to worship God and the saints. In talking about religious practices and the civil-religious hierarchy, Trixanos rephrase the creation mythology so that it *omits* mention of the conquest. In this alternative version of the climax to Christ's creations, the most important saints such as San Pedro, San Pablo, San Antonio, and San Andrés accompanied Christ during his life on earth and were witnesses to Christ's suffering and death. God rewarded these Apostles by making them saints and investing them with the power of being intermediaries between God and humanity. Jesus Christ gave each of the saints "a piece of land and for this reason each town has a distinct name and a guardian saint." When the towns were divided among the saints, each took one to be his cultivated field where he would control the planting and the harvest, insuring the fertility of humans and their crops "if the people were correct." Ancestors of the Trixanos were sent by God to inhabit the town given to San Andrés.

The first Indian ancestors who "invented" *costumbre* became models for correct behavior, which was "rewarded by a long life, many children, and successful plantings and harvests." In serving God, ancestors participated in each of the groups that made up the civil-religious hierarchy: the civil government (*el cabildo*), the religious brotherhoods (*las cofradías*), and the chapel (*el calvario*). In addition to activism in these organizations, the ancestors valued peace and tranquility within the family, respected the "sacred quality" of marriage, and acknowledged the position of the elders in the community by "asking their pardon if they passed them on the road of life." God rewarded the ancestors with various forms of fertility and a pardon for their sins because their "ideas and words were good ones."

The Trixanos celebrate continuity with the ancestors by following "their ideas and words" and by replicating the way in which they practiced *costumbre*: "We should act like our grandparents acted, behaving well, believing in God, and adoring him. If we remember God, he will watch over us. Our ancestors lived a long time because they behaved well before God in loving their fellow man. Thus God rewarded them with good plantings and harvests."

The Devil does not disappear from *costumbre* but is felt to coexist with the law of Christ and the saints. If the Indians do not provoke the Devil, then he will not bother the Indians: "We should not criticize the evil of the Devil because this was a contract made with God, not with us. Rather we should follow our Father who always looks out for us. We should not mistreat the evil because it is not proper. Above all, Satanás does not bother us. However, if we mistreat him, yes, he will cause problems. This is because he has power too." *Costumbre* seeks to perpetuate the behavior of the ancestors toward fellow Trixanos and God to gain fertility in this life and heaven in the next. The Devil and the wilds are held at bay by *costumbre*.

Trixanos feel that the belief system and the organization of the civil-religious hierarchy are meaningful only to the descendents of the ancestors, to the Trixanos as an ethnic community. The inflexible and non-negotiable character of ethnicity through which Spaniards justified the subordination of Indians is transformed by Trixanos to serve as the basis for separatism of government and religion. The beliefs that Spaniards first brought Catholicism to the town and that Indian ancestors originated Indian social organization and religious belief may appear contradictory; but holding these contradictory ideas has allowed Indians a sense of continuity and separatism in the face of the domination that followed the conquest. Like the two conceptions of community, the elaboration of separate Indian governmental and religious institutions has permitted Indians to maintain one system of beliefs for Indian-Indian relations and another for Indian-Ladino relations. In pursuing the interrelations of the two definitions of community and the negotiability of separatism and subordination, I would now like to present material on Trixano perceptions of economic, legal, and religious institutions in San Andrés.

Ladinos continue their domination of Indians, although Trixanos maintain a separate social organization and ideology. Domination is most direct in the economics of agriculture. Ideally, Trixanos value the maintenance of separate farms, calling on kin and friends to assist the nuclear family during labor-intensive periods in the agricultural cycle. In this case, work involves labor exchanges within the Indian community. Trixanos note, however, that, in actuality, lack of land forces Indians to work as laborers for Ladino landholders. On large plantations or smaller Ladino farms, the ethnic division of labor fixes Ladinos as owners and supervisors and Indians as laborers. In contrast, the subtle interplay of domination and separatism is successfully maintained in the legal and political organization of the bi-ethnic community. In the municipal government, Indians have maintained a separate legal system, based on *costumbre*, that governs Indian affairs so long as they do not impinge on the codified national law administered by Ladinos. Cases involving either national law or local Ladinos are adjudicated by the Ladino mayor. In the context of law, then, community may be defined in either of two ways: as an Indian entity with its own customary legal system as opposed to the Ladino community external to Indian law or as an ethnic entity subject to Ladino law. It is, however, only in the ritual activities of the religious brotherhoods, where members are ranked by social age and the interdependence and unity of the generations is celebrated, that separatism seems to take a nearly complete and independent form and community is defined exclusively as those who trace descent from the first Indian ancestors. I would now like to go into detail about Trixanos' perceptions of their involvement in economic, political, and religious institutions in San Andrés.

The social and economic subordination of Indians to Ladinos, justified in terms of ethnicity, continues to define Indians as laborers and Ladinos as *patrones*. One Trixano laborer summarized the ethnic division of labor in the following terms: "One works here [in the fields of the plantation] because it is the work of the Indian. If I were not an Indian, I would be a *patrón*. But as I am an Indian, I have to work under the command of a *patrón* or chief." In work that brings together both ethnic groups, Indians assume the subordinate role, whereas Ladino landholders direct, or find an assistant to oversee, the work of the laborers in the fields. Supervisors make sure that adequate numbers of laborers are recruited for plantings, weedings, and harvests of the staples of corn and beans and the cash crop of wheat. They also check to see that laborers have completed the stipulated amount of work, generally spatially measured as a *cuerda* (approximately one-fifth of an acre) a day, and pay the Indian laborers or subtract earnings from debts owed to the *patrón*.

The division of labor associates Indians with the tools of manual labor, physical endurance, the ability to bear the vagaries of weather, as well as with special knowledge of the agricultural cycle. On the other hand, Ladinos are associated with the tools of literacy, less arduous working conditions inside an office, and knowledge gained through education. Two Indian laborers described the differences in the following words:

> [First Informant:] Ladinos' work is less arduous in an office and under a roof where they find themselves in front of a desk writing. We Indians dedicate ourselves to the fields with a hoe, machete, and axe. We must bear the sun and the rain.

> [Second Informant:] From the beginning the Ladino father is interested in his son's studying whereas we take children to the fields

so that they will learn how to work. If there were a Ladino who did not study, I am sure that it would be difficult for him to do the hard work that we do and he would die of hunger. The Ladino of ten or fifteen years of age only thinks of the pencil and pen, not of the hoe and the axe. For this reason, they know how to read and write and we know only hard work to earn a living.

Categories of work are generally mutually exclusive. If Ladinos were forced to work as agricultural laborers, it is said by Trixanos that they would starve. If Indians were educated, they would become lazy and incapable of supporting themselves.

Work for Ladino *patrones* of the town or with their counterparts on the coastal plantations is a necessity because few Indian agriculturalists own enough land to subsist on. Most Indians own some inherited land; but few are able to harvest enough corn and beans to feed their families until the next round of harvests. In order to supplement insufficient harvests from their own lands, Indians rent additional land from Ladinos or work as full-time laborers on larger farms. Complete independence from *patrones* is an ideal that is rarely actualized. More often, Indians must supplement income by doing outside work, always of a manual nature, compromising the efficiency of their own work: "One cannot do his own work well if one has a *patrón*, because one has the duty to finish the work of the *patrón* first and then one gets behind in his own work. For this reason, it is better to be independent, telling oneself what to do. In contrast, with a *patrón*, one has to do what he commands, and *patrones* are often bad." Dependency on Ladino landowners who demand priority for plantation work sets off a cycle of increasing dependence. If the agriculturalists get behind in their work, the harvest will be small, forcing them to borrow money and to seek more work with the *patrones*. As one Indian explained, "We must work as laborers as a custom, or a vice, because we cannot stop doing it if we are poor." Separatism has not been possible in the realm of economics because poverty only ties Indians more closely to Ladino landowners who give agriculturalists land to cultivate and pay laborers a daily wage (fifty cents a day in 1971). In addition, the Ladino strengthens the bonds between *patrón* and laborer by loaning the Indian money for festivals or family crises, such as sickness; by becoming godparent for Indian children; and by favoring the Indian's side in minor disputes.

The *patrón*-worker relationship is both hierarchical and non-negotiable. Ladinos employ only Indians, but Indians do not employ Ladinos as field hands. Nor do Ladinos mark subordinate relations to Indians by seeking them out as godparents for Ladino children or by borrowing money from them. Indians may employ other Indians for help in the fields, especially during the frantic pace of the harvest. A staggered exchange of labor on each other's fields is the usual arrangement between Indians, even if payment is offered to the laborers. Furthermore, Indian employers work in the fields at the same tasks as laborers and are not considered to be *patrones* or supervisors who merely direct the work of others.

One might expect that a more equitable distribution of land would allow for a greater development of separatism for Indians in economics; but, empirically, this situation has never arisen in the last hundred year or so, and Indians think of themselves as laborers for the *patrones* within a "community" of both Indians and Ladinos. In the legal systems of the municipal government, a greater flexibility in the definition of community is evident.

In the past, asymmetrically distributed and partially separate sets of municipal officials following distinct legal codes governed Ladinos and Indians. This administrative system, which will be described in some detail from Trixano accounts, continues to the present, albeit in a slightly modified form. The mayor (*alcalde*) is the highest civil official in the municipality. Almost always he has been a Ladino. The mayor is assisted by a nationally appointed secretary and other specialized Ladino officials who take care of communications between the town, the neighboring state capital, and the national capital. Together these officials represent the town (including both Ladinos and Indians) to higher levels of government, maintain the formal register of the population and its tax records, and implement governmental policy and national law on the local level. Under these officials, the municipal government divides into separate ladders of councilmen (*regidores*) for Ladinos and Indians. Ladino councilmen take care of local-level Ladino affairs, including the planning of specifically Ladino festivals, whereas Indian officials administer the civil-religious hierarchy and local Indian affairs.

The legal system parallels the administrative, governing structure of the town. Court cases involving both Ladinos and Indians, as well as serious cases within the scope of national law among the Indians, fall under the jurisdiction of the Ladino mayor who acts as a municipal judge: "Before, there were two mayors together in the municipal government. The first mayor was a Ladino and the second an Indian. A problem among the Indians first appeared before the Indian mayor, and, if the case was serious and he was not capable of resolving it, the case passed on to the hands of the Ladino in order to see if the person should be fined here or had to go to a larger jail in another area." This hierarchical system of dual government, in which Ladino officials take care of intergroup relations, continues to exist today, although the Indian mayor is now called the first councilman, a title which more clearly marks his subordination to the Ladino mayor as well as the Ladino mayor's more centralized jurisdiction.

In the past, the Indian mayor took care of cases that did not require "much care" but instead required a knowledge of the *costumbre* of the town and the inner workings of the civil-religious hierarchy. With assistance from elders of the Indian community, the chief Indian civil official recruited new members for service in the religious brotherhoods and the *calvario* chapel and made sure that Indian municipal officials were doing their jobs. The Indian mayor was given the post by Ladino officials in consultation with Indian elders, who chose a person with experience in the civil-religious hierarchy, knowledge of his own people, and familiarity with their traditional activities. His duties were to give immediate attention to those under his jurisdiction and "to act in benefit of all Indians."

When problems arose in the Indian community, the Indian mayor decided the appropriate course of action within a system of customary law *distinct* from the codified regulations of the Ladinos: "The law was not found in any book. Rather he [the Indian mayor] acted through rules of conduct or morality to decide what was good and to punish bad conduct. On the basis of his own experience and his sense of what was proper, he punished or absolved a case of difficulties among people." Customary law that the Indian mayor enforced was not a specialized knowledge of national law but rather of the rule system implicit in *costumbre*, which will be dealt with shortly. Indians preferred to be judged by the Indian mayor because he was viewed as being more flexible than the Ladino, who was felt to enforce written national laws strictly, levying fines or imprisoning Indians who worked for the municipal government in order to pay off fines. In contrast, the Indian mayor "showed a greater consideration of the people" by allowing an Indian fined for minor offenses to return to his or her family so that they would not suffer from the absence of a wage earner. After accumulating the necessary money, Indian offenders paid their fines to the government.

From the Indian point of view, duties of the Ladino mayor were outward looking, dealing with the community as a whole and its relation to the national government. Because the Ladino spoke Spanish and was literate, he had access to the "articles of discipline" (the formal legal code) and acted "in benefit" of the town in the bi-ethnic sense as its representative to the national government in the capital. The duties of the Ladino mayor, then, were to represent the community to the outside and to advise the Indian mayor, who was generally illiterate and only partially fluent in Spanish. In turn, because the Ladino did not understand the Indian language, he was dependent on the Indian to transmit information to that portion of the community.

In the present, the Trixanos' ability to maintain judicial separatism varies within the municipal government, depending on the Ladino mayor's assessment of who has jurisdiction in a particular case. In general, the Indian mayor, or first councilman, works for the Indian community. Additionally, in cases involving both Indians and Ladinos he may represent Indians, acting as an intermediary between the two groups in the wider community.

The note of self-depreciation of the Indians in bi-ethnic affairs apparent in one of the earlier quotes ("For this reason, they know how to read and write and we know *only* hard work to earn a living.") also appears in the descriptions of the two mayors in the municipal government: "The Indian mayor did not need much intelligence [much knowledge] because he only took care of the problems of the civil-religious hierarchy. He did not have to be educated because he occupied the post only by his experience of knowing the people. Because the Ladino mayor knew how to read and write, he had a better way in which to resolve problems." It would appear that when Indians are in contexts that are ultimately defined and controlled by Ladinos they internalize invidious distinctions made by Ladinos. Since the relative positions of the two groups are rigidly defined in terms of ethnicity, it is not surprising to find a note of resignation in Indian accounts dealing with direct comparisons of respective civil officials.

Finally, religion is the third major context in which different models of community and identity are negotiated by Indians within constraints imposed by Ladinos. In the celebration of *costumbre* by the religious brotherhoods, ethnicity is again used to justify the appropriate model of community. In this case, ethnicity is the basis for the separatist stance of the religious section of the civil-religious hierarchy. Indirectly, all of the civil-religious hierarchy is under the jurisdiction of the municipal government. Yet, from the Trixano point of view, the distinction between Indian brotherhoods and the civil government allows them to stress the perceived independence of the brotherhoods.

Costumbre of the brotherhoods, say the Trixanos, is a system of beliefs and traditions first practiced by the ancestors to guide their lives and to honor God and the saints. *Costumbre* unites that which is separated: bilaterally reckoned kinsmen with their ancestors as well as individuals with their fellow Trixanos in San Andrés. All Trixanos are the "children" of the guardian saint in that they celebrate the same "ancestors" and thus share Trixano blood. Living on the saint's lands, Trixanos respect their guardian and in turn are protected by him. San Andrés has commanded his children "to unite, love each other, and express mutual understanding" by joining together to serve the community. This commandment is fulfilled through cooperation and common effort among members of the civil-religious hierarchy who are in charge of ritual observances as well as the everyday administration of Indian civil government.

Blood, land, and a code for conduct that values respect and understanding between generations are core symbols of unifying *costumbre* for kinsmen and fellow Trixanos alike.[20] Trixano descendents are united with the abstract and undifferentiated category of ancestors through commonality of blood, inheritance of land, and continuity of values that guide behavior. The code of *costumbre* emphasizes respect for authority gained by experience and directs elders to care for and counsel their children. In the nuclear family, *costumbre* organizes the interdependence of generations through the joint expression of "union and mutual understanding" manifested in cooperative work in the household and fields. Blood, a substance which gives life to the body and character to the child, is passed from both sides of the family to the children of a couple. Land inheritance follows the same pattern since all children receive land from the combined holdings of the parents, although there is a great deal of variation by sex and birth order in the proportions they receive.

Community unity is expressed through common "origin," visibly and audibly signaled in town-specific traditional dress and the town's dialect of Cakchiquel. Origin has two dimensions: temporal continuity of descent from Trixano ancestors and spatial unity of residence as exemplified by ownership of a homestead and land in San Andrés. Origin is described in similar terms for religion, ethnicity, kinship, and town residence. Within these domains of identity, the code for conduct of *costumbre* and the natural identity of blood are closely associated, for to have Indian blood implies that one will act like an Indian in accordance with *costumbre*. In this vein one Trixano commented:

> So that a child might be an Indian, he is dressed like his grand-
> father and many [people] use the name of the grandfather or
> father for him so that the child will be like them, a pure Indian.
> They teach him only *lengua* [the town-specific Indian dialect]
> and say to him, "We have given you the name of your grandfather
> because he was an excellent person. As you look a little like him,
> we want you to be the same as he was. You will be a brave Indian
> and you should behave well as your grandfather did." This is the
> form of transmission, telling him that he is of the race of his
> grandfather who was brave and correct.

Continuity of blood in terms of descent and race and continuity of a
code for conduct that defines the "correct" behavior of the grand-
father are exclusively tied to the town. According to mythology, ever
since the first ancestors were sent from God, both blood and *costumbre*
have marked the town as the boundary of the Indian community and
the highest unit of Indian social organization. The following comment about the brotherhoods can be extended to the other sections of
the civil-religious hierarchy: "Brotherhoods [*cofradías*] perform the
costumbre of their town, the *costumbre* of our ancestors. Each town
does its *costumbre* in its own manner, just as *costumbre* should be
done. For this reason, the brotherhoods cannot go to other towns." The
sets of offices or *cargos* in the civil-religious hierarchy bring together
all families to form the Indian community. They extend the context
for the expression of *costumbre* from the family to all Indian townspeople through public recognition of important transitions in the life
cycle of family members.

Composed of adult heads of nuclear families, the sections of the
hierarchy bring religious and civil officials together to represent the
community in major celebrations of the highest-level divinities, such
as Jesus and San Andrés. Through these celebrations, "respect, union,
love, and mutual understanding" are presented as guiding principles
for social action. These core values are diffuse. They are not directed
toward any specific instrumental goal but should be manifested in all
social interaction. They are enduring because they pattern relations
throughout life as each new generation is sent from God, ascends the
hierarchy, and returns to God as ancestors. They are solidary in that
they join together all families in the unity and concern for the well-
being of the community.[21]

The values of respect, union, love, and mutual understanding are bound together and expressed through the civil-religious hierarchy in social recognition of transitions in the life of the individual and in the ranking of positions in the hierarchy. Although these transitions in the life cycle are marked, they are not the focal points of individualized ritual, unlike baptism, marriage, and burial. Instead, they are part of major community celebrations during which all offices within the municipal government and the chapel caretakers, or within a brotherhood, are transferred to new occupants for a year's tenure. For some, assumption of office is an indicator of adulthood; for others, moving to higher levels, it marks the status of elder. A man is recognized as an adult—that is, capable of doing his own agricultural work and supporting a wife and their offspring—by being invited to participate in the hierarchy for his first one-year post, a position of responsibility on the lowest level as the last assistant (the lowest *mortomo* of a brotherhood, the *chejal* in the church, or an *alguacil* in the town government). For certain rituals, especially in the brotherhoods, the wife is her husband's counterpart in the *cofradía* kitchen or in processions as a candle or censor bearer.

After this initial post, the individual is expected to accumulate economic surpluses from his agricultural labors during a period of several years of "rest" (*descanso*) and to invest them by holding office at a slightly higher level where the contribution for candles, incense, liquor, and staple foodstuffs for ritual meals is greater. The mainstream of the adult's life, spent in agricultural production, is typically punctuated every five years or so by community service. At these times he spends much of his time serving the town by office holding and contributing his savings for major community religious celebrations. Alternating religious offices in the brotherhoods and *calvario* chapel with positions in the local government, the Indian finally reaches the highest post (as *cofrade* in the brotherhoods, *piscal* in the *calvario* chapel, or first *regidor* in the government) at which time he is recognized as an elder of the community. After serving at the highest level, he is permanently retired to the rank of *principal,* or one of the body of overseers for the entire hierarchy. These transitions are simultaneously recognized at the investiture of all officeholders because their significance does not reside in the transition of a single individual to a specific post as much as in the structural relation of all hierarchy offices to each other and the roughly parallel association of officeholders in the three sections of the hierarchy. The ancestors were the first to express the principle behind the social organization of the civil-religious hierarchy: ranking, based on age, of interdependent generations.

The exemplary ancestors showed respect for their elders. They believed that with age came experience in life, knowledge of *costumbre*, and authority both in the highest posts of the hierarchy and in roles as mothers and fathers of families and as elder neighbors. The ancestors expressed respect for age and the unity of elder and younger "by greeting elders as they passed them on the path of life," by observing the serving order of ritual meals, and by taking their place in the files of celebrants in religious processions. The ritual meal most clearly spells out the principles of ranking. In this "small meal" (*refacción*) the officials of the hierarchy are seated according to rank in a counterclockwise direction along three walls of the shrine facing the altar of the saints. The seating order defines and reflects *social* age, since each man begins to participate in the hierarchy at the same stage of life and ascends the hierarchy at the same pace. In these rituals, the highest-ranking officials of the municipal government and the participating brotherhood or their ritual guides (in both cases elders) exchange discourses, and a ritual meal is served by the junior members of the host brotherhood. The principle of respect for social age is obeyed in the order of services, which proceeds counterclockwise. In addition, the ritual meal expresses the principles of unity and egalitarianism because each member receives the same amount of food and drink that is then consumed only after the lowest member is served.[22] At the close of the meal the speakers exchange abbreviated discourses of thanks and a procession is formed for the transfer of brotherhood saints to the *calvario* chapel for the community celebration—be it Holy Week, the Saint's Day of the town, or a minor celebration that interrelates major festivities. In the processions, the order of rank is observed by those who accompany the saints as they parade through the town.

So far, this chapter has described the alternative images that Trixanos have formulated for their community and the contexts in which either or both images serve as models for behavior. Although ethnicity is a component of both images, it has a different significance for the models of subordination and separatism. The ethnicity of the Spaniards and their descendents, the Ladinos, is used, on the one hand, as a basis for the ethnic division of labor and the domination of the Indians who become workers in the bi-ethnic community. On the other hand, the ethnicity of the Trixano ancestors and their descendents is used to justify separatism of the Indian community that practices an egalitarian *costumbre* in which "we are all equal before God" and rank is defined by social age.

It is very clear from this examination of economics, political organization, and religion that Indians see the possibility of either subordinate or separatist identities being expressed in each of these contexts. Nevertheless, as we have seen both in the case of plantation economics and in the overall civil administration of San Andrés, Trixano negotiation of identities does not involve a choice between equally accessible alternatives. Rather, Ladino control of land and the civil administration of the town limit or constrain Trixano success in negotiating toward the valued alternative of separatism from Ladinos.[23]

In short, Ladino domination stands above and encompasses Indian separatism in community institutions linked to the external Ladino world outside San Andrés. The judicial system is the clearest example of the embeddedness of separatism in subordination. Indian officials may use various strategies for attempting to settle a court case involving Indians within the separatist Indian community; yet the final decision as to whether the case will be dealt with in terms of Trixano *costumbre* or national law rests with Ladino officials. Separatism is most clearly achieved in the realm of religion. There Indians celebrate a world view that stands at the center of an Indian identity independent of Ladino values and control. Yet even in the case of religion, Ladinos have an indirect source of control over Indian religious officials who are nominated by the Indian civil administration and subject to the Ladino civil officials for confirmation.

Strategies for Marking Separatism from Ladino Control

I have already argued that the Indians' strategies for separatism are structurally embedded in wider patterns of ethnic domination. Ladinos ultimately define the success that Indians have in negotiating a separate identity. In the face of consistent institutional subordination to Ladinos, Indians have chosen to stress separatism wherever possible. Yet we know from oral history accounts that the twentieth century has been marked by varying degrees of Ladino encroachment into Indian affairs and a weakening of the possibilities for the expression of separatism.

Because Ladinos monopolize all commercial establishments and large landholdings in San Andrés, separatism in economics has been nearly impossible for Trixanos. Trixanos blame the period of forced labor (*el mandamiento*) early in the twentieth century for the precipitous decline in Trixano landholdings:

The government of Manuel Estrada Cabrera [1899–1920] brought bad treatment. There were the poor who sold their lands and others who became rich because they took advantage of the bad times to buy more property.

Cabrera's law caused great poverty among the people [i.e., Indians] who had to comply with forced labor. They were not left with time to cultivate. Many looked for [local] *patrones.* They stayed and worked for these *patrones,* who took advantage of them by asking for more work from those who did not go [to the coast] for the *mandamiento.* This is the reason for the poverty of the families in town. Afterwards this was a poor town because the majority of the people sold their lands at a low price for their necessities.

While Indians accept a subordinate status in economics, the separatism of independent small-scale farming is a valued ideal. Yet since the growth of Ladino population in the town during the early part of the twentieth century, few Indians have been able to maintain or achieve economic independence. In response to subordination in plantation economics, Indians have shifted emphasis away from separatism and toward the ideal of finding "good" *patrones* who are not unjustly demanding and will see laborers through personal crises.

Separatism in law and religion has been more readily achieved from the Indian point of view. In court, the overriding authority of the Ladino mayor has been emphasized by reforms that demoted the highest Indian civil official from the position of Indian mayor to that of first councilman (*regidor*). In negotiating legal affairs from a subordinate position, the Trixano first councilman must be able to evaluate cases in terms of *costumbre,* and this ability depends on his knowledge of the inner workings of the bi-ethnic political system. The councilman is in a bargaining position to the extent that he may present cases to the Ladino mayor so as to insure that they will be settled according to *costumbre.* Alternatively, in cases judged to fall within the bi-ethnic definition of community, the Indian councilman acts as an intermediary between Indian defendants and Ladino authorities. In either event, the ability of the Indian councilman to settle disputes follows from his knowledge of the local administration of national law as well as his familiarity with the application of *costumbre.*[24]

In religious matters, the brotherhoods (*cofradías*) are closely aligned with the civil section of the hierarchy. The first Indian councilman is in charge of recruitment of new members for the brotherhoods and is invited to represent the municipal government in all ceremonial meals and processions. Since the first councilman is under the authority of the Ladino mayor, the brotherhoods are indirectly tied to the Ladino administration of the town. Indians, however, stress the separatism of the brotherhoods, which maintain the celebration of *costumbre*, the code for conduct that gives meaning to separatism. As with the council-man in politics, the success of negotiation is based on knowledge of religion in the bi-ethnic community. In the most important religious celebrations of the town, during Holy Week and the titular feast of San Andrés, the brotherhoods take part in processions that include representatives of the bi-ethnic community such as the priest and the Ladina catechists, self-appointed women who function as directors and representatives of the *calvario* chapel. Separatism is carefully marked off from the bi-ethnic aspects of celebrations by shifting responsibility for the images from brotherhoods to the Ladina catechists when they are brought to the bi-ethnic celebration at the *calvario* chapel and by having Indians unaffiliated with the brotherhoods carry the images of the saints in processions representing the bi-ethnic community.

Perhaps the clearest challenge to separatism has come with the oc-casional participation of Ladinos in the brotherhoods. At the turn of the century and during intermittent periods in the late fifties and sixties, a few Ladino leaders in the bi-ethnic community took positions in the brotherhoods. Indians explain these penetrations into separatist organizations in terms of the bi-ethnic mythology that states that the Spaniards took positions as directors in the religious brotherhoods when the organizations were first introduced into the town at the time of the conquest. Although the motivation for the more recent Ladino religious activism is not clear, both periods of Ladino membership were marked by relatively peaceful relations between *patrones* and laborers in the town. During the intervening years when relations between Ladinos and Indians were felt to be more tense from the Indian point of view, Ladinos were forcefully excluded from brother-hood ceremonies and shrine dances: "In 1915 or 1920, Ladinos stopped being leaders in the *cofradías*. They only went to dance in the house of the brotherhood. In subsequent years, they decided to celebrate a separate fiesta and had their dance in the salon [at the school]. They did not frequent the brotherhoods, only going to watch. Ladinos wanted to have a separate fiesta because of the bad treatment that they gave to their laborers [*mozos*]. For this reason, laborers fought them during fiestas. Ladinos decided not to join the brotherhoods so that they would not have to suffer these fights." Indians seem to be more protective of separatist organizations when their ability to negotiate separatism in economics or law is severely undercut. At the same time that Ladinos retired from the brotherhoods because of violence during the drunken dances of the titular feast, Indians were subject to forced labor: "The Ladinos made themselves superior. The patron demanded double the work and the laborer who did not finish was beaten and even thrown in jail. The Indian was not heard or given importance. Moreover, they [the *patrones*] paid very little [in wages] and it was total suffering for the Indians. They had no success with the municipal government because Ladinos had an understanding among themselves." Violence became a way to assert the right to negotiate separatism, but only in the context of the ritually marked *cofradía* dances, celebrated twice a year during Holy Week and the titular feast of San Andrés.

The incorporation of Ladinos into the brotherhoods during periods of relative interethnic calm has been accomplished in such a way as to preserve symbolically the contrast between separatism and subordination. Ladinos have chosen to serve in the brotherhood of San Andrés, which is considered to be the most important brotherhood in the town and requires the greatest monetary outlay for ritual meals, processions, and several nights of dancing during the festival of the guardian saint. Indians suggest that Ladinos wish to participate both because of the excitement of the celebration and because the dance and other commercial activities (which are beginning to draw tourists) allow them to make money during the festival.

The multivocality of the symbols during brotherhood celebrations allows for either separatist or subordinate interpretations. Symbols used to decorate carrying platforms for the saints include feathers, which allude to the preconquest Indian dress, and mirrors, which were brought by the Spaniards at the time of the conquest. Both feathers and mirrors surround the saints as they are carried in procession through the town. The saints have come to represent "the civilization of the Indians" at the time of the conquest. Alternatively, there is a separatist exegesis for the same symbols that are said to represent souls in heaven and stars in the sky. This interpretation refers to the creation of the heavens at the time of Christ and to San Andrés's subsequent creation of the separatist Indian town. Ladino participation in the brotherhood acts to bring to the foreground or emphasize references made to the conquest in Trixano interpretations of ritual. Even in this event, contrasts between Indian subordination and separatism are maintained through the relation of the titular feast of San Andrés celebrated in November to Holy Week ceremonies held at Easter time. While the festival of San Andrés may become a bi-ethnic celebration, Holy Week has been maintained as a separatist Indian celebration in the brotherhoods. Perhaps it is significant that Holy Week ceremonies re-enact the last segment of the creation mythology, dealing with the creation of the moral order through separation of good and evil, the town and the wilds.[25]

Variation in the extent of Ladino enforcement of a bi-ethnic definition of community is met with responses that uphold the possibility for the negotiation of Indian identity toward separatism. Varying levels of positively sanctioned violence during brotherhood dances signal demands for religious separatism in reaction to the intensity of domination in economics and politics. Violence in religious contexts seems primarily to support religious separatism, rather than effectively to challenge economic or political domination. In addition, the expression of separatism is negotiable, ranging from the activities of all sectors of the civil-religious hierarchy to finely drawn distinctions in ritual decoration or the well-timed shifts of carriers of the saints in procession. While this flexibility of the means of negotiation has allowed Indians to continue a separatist identity and to assert the importance of the values of *costumbre*, it has also acted to perpetuate the structural relation of Ladinos and Indians.

3. Images of the Person:
Will, Destiny, and Ladinoization

Throughout earlier chapters, we have seen that Trixano belief presents the individual as the ideal locus of moral choice. Ethnic subordination, however, has deprived individuals of ultimate moral choices, according to Trixano belief. This chapter continues the analysis of Trixano world view by further examining the way in which belief systems are used by Trixanos to organize their conceptions of the person.

The Trixano concept of a person contrasts an individual's "will" (*voluntad*) with his "luck-destiny" (*suerte*). Will is exercised through an individual's ranking of valued alternatives in everyday behavior. Will, however, does not involve the kinds of moral choices spelled out in creation mythology. Rather, this aspect of the person reflects the Trixano belief that each individual "thinks in a different way" about the set of alternatives embodied in *costumbre*. These alternatives that individual wills rank in their own way, as well as the separate experiences of each individual, are shown to be drawn from *costumbre* by one set of ritual intermediaries. These "ritual guides" of the civil-religious hierarchy represent the positive direction of will toward the unifying principles of *costumbre*. They celebrate the individual's connectedness with other individuals within the Trixano community through discourses and prayers given in brotherhood ritual.

The second dimension of the Trixano conception of the person is expressed by the concept luck-destiny. Luck-destiny is an immutable quality that individuals are born with and cannot change. Once again individual moral choice is not an issue. Some Trixanos have the "luck-destiny" to make pacts with Satanás; others, to pursue nonmanual occupations successfully. This analysis will point to the interpretation that luck-destiny represents an explanation for the behavior of individuals who pursue ladinoized alternatives outside the bounds of the ideology of *costumbre*. This aspect of the person is also represented by a set of Trixano intermediaries who have the luck-destiny to become sorcerers. Unlike the ritual guides of the civil-religious hierarchy, sorcerers operate in the wilds, celebrating rituals dealing with individual deviations from *costumbre* and with interpersonal conflict caused by "envy" (*envidia*).

Ritual guides and sorcerers are the two most important religious intermediaries in Trixano society. Both are "guides or interpreters" of the words of supplicants during rituals in which they officiate to communicate between the sacred and social realms. Both are respected for their ritual knowledge; yet, the sources of this knowledge and its applications distinguish them. Ritual guides serve as intermediaries in the social order of the community, where they stress the unity and equivalence of individuals. The ritual guides work to maintain the correct relations between the social order and the divinities so that the entire community will be blessed with fertility by God and the saints. In contrast, the sorcerers deal with accidents or sickness that have singled out individuals as victims of envy or they deal with an individual's ambition to seek unusual material wealth and personal fertility.

By having two kinds of intermediaries (the ritual guides and the sorcerers) who operate in distinct symbolic domains (the town and the wilds) and represent distinct aspects of the individual (will and luck-destiny) and of the individual's relation to society (through unifying tradition and divisive envy), Trixanos treat the maintenance of society as an issue separate from problems between individuals. An important implication of this belief system is that social change in the Indian community is individualized and projected onto the wilds away from the civil-religious hierarchy in the town. Furthermore, change in the direction of ladinoization is portrayed by this belief system as being beyond institutional and individual control.

The Guides of the Civil-Religious Hierarchy: Unifiers of Diversity

The ritual guide (*camol beij*) is respected by the community by virtue of his age, experience in the civil-religious hierarchy, and knowledge of traditional mythology. He achieves this position through years of service to the community in which he follows the path of the ancestors promoting the inheritance of *costumbre* and achieving recognition as an elder of the community. He specializes in the narration of ritual discourses in civil-religious ceremonies when the three sections of the hierarchy are brought together to celebrate key periods in the ritual cycle. As the members of the hierarchy change each year, the guide has the responsibility of directing the new groups so that they will continue traditional ritual, including shrine meals and processions of the saints. He is not a formal member of the groups he serves, excluding himself from contributions that members make to finance ceremonies and from nonceremonial civil and shrine duties. Rather, the ritual guide speaks for the sections of the hierarchy, greeting representatives of the municipal government, the church, and the brotherhoods as they assemble for rituals. He guides the ritual through the medium of discourses.

The subject of these discourses is the description of *costumbre*, a paramount code for conduct, that guides social behavior. The code represents the commandment of God, as reiterated by San Andrés, to "unite, love each other, and express mutual understanding." This code for conduct sketches the Trixano notion of community by outlining the forms of bonds between individuals as family members, kin, and fellow townspeople and by stating that all relations should be governed by two principles: cooperation with and respect for social elders (called "elder mothers and fathers"). Rituals of the civil-religious hierarchy are the paradigmatic expression of these guiding principles as they direct the cooperation of all townspeople, while ranking them according to social age in a way that crosscuts particulars of specific affiliations with family, kin, and townspeople. Broadly speaking, all positions in the three wings of the hierarchy can be assimilated into two levels under the direction of the *principales*, or retired members of the hierarchy: the elders who act as administrators of the wings and the adults who act as servers. Together these officials work to fulfill the model of society envisioned and first enacted by the ancestors, who represent an undifferentiated category of Trixano antecedents and are thus the symbol for unity and continuity of blood and land.

The ancestors' model of society is reflected in *costumbre*, which directs cooperation and respect by identifying the individual with the community and with the life cycle of interdependent generations of "elder fathers and mothers" and "younger sons and daughters." Discourses given during brotherhood ritual by the ritual guide elaborate a series of contrasts between positive and negative models of behavior toward kin and townspeople. Key contrasts elaborated by the ritual guide during the shrine rituals are virtually identical from ceremony to ceremony with the exception of a brief mention of specific saints to be honored.

At the beginning of the discourse, the guide of the municipal government greets the head of the host brotherhood by rhetorically in-

quiring about the health of the host and of all those with whom he has
social relations: his family and kin (including bilaterally reckoned
grandparents and grandchildren), his assistants in the brotherhood,
and his fellow townspeople in the community. After making similar
inquiries of the assistants, the guide proceeds to point out that it is
possible that these relations may be tranquil and the health of these
individuals good, and if this is so "a happiness, a contentment on
earth." He also says, however, that the opposite is possible, that relations may be troubled and individuals sick. In this event, the guide
continues, it is not only the family that bears "the worry or hardship,"
but "all the world shares the sorrow." Because an individual's sickness
is not an isolated event, all the world shares its consequences.

The same theme of the relation of the individual's health to the
community is returned to once again at the close of the discourse when
the death of a member of a family is described as the loss of the entire
community, which should pray for the deceased, asking God's pardon
and care:

> When we hear the ringing of the holy bells on the earth, the
> dominions of the Apostle San Andrés, we might say, "Ah Dios,
> who might this mother be, who might this father be who goes
> back, who returns before God? God, that you pardon him; God,
> that you take care of him." This is what we would say if we were
> good Christian souls. But perhaps we do not have good souls, be-
> cause ours is another generation. Perhaps we are happy, we laugh
> at the death of our fellow man, the return of our father, of our
> mother. But this is not what God commands. He has told us to
> come together, to love each other like brothers. We lack the
> presence of our first fathers, our first mothers of the past day of the
> past hours, who had better words, better expressions and be-
> havior before a king, before a justice, before a guardian of the
> church, before a brotherhood.

Although the ancestors are not physically present as models for the
community, their legacy, *costumbre* as celebrated in ritual, represents
the rule system against which the present is measured. Clearly, to be
"good Christian souls" is to follow the model of the ancestors, to
identify an individual's worry with the suffering and hardship of the
world and to identify the loss of a member of a family as a loss for the
entire community.

The second major theme of the discourses re-emphasizes the interdependence of the generations. Discourses describe the respect that the

ancestors showed for their own elders, a respect which was rewarded by a long life and attainment of the status of elder. These positive actions of the ancestors are contrasted with the disrespect of the present generation for their elders, leading to punishment and an early death. As the passage opens, an ancestor is addressing an elder on "the path of life":

> "Excuse me father, excuse me mother. Permit me to pass before you, to pass behind you," they said and this was the indication of their words. And it is possible that their day grew and their birth grew because they did not push aside or expel their elder father or mother on this path, on this earth. They asked their pardon and their peace. For this reason their day and their birth grew. They were given more life by God, they became white-haired, they became bent over and walked with canes on the earth.
>
> Perhaps for us, the elder father or mother is not important when we encounter him at the crossroads of a path or of life. Perhaps we only push him aside or expel him. Perhaps he comes bent over with his cane, from a worry or a punishment. "Ah Dios, you are my grandchild, my son, and this is what you do in my path and my life of suffering. But that it might not be this day that you harvest my worry or my punishment." Perhaps he might say your day, your birth. This day arrives or does not arrive—our departure, return to the feet of God, all because of the weight of our sin.

Once again, behavior of the ancestors is contrasted with possibility of deviation from this model in the present.

Elders say that by the very enactment of *costumbre,* it is evident that they are adhering to the model of the ancestors. The present elders note that the contrast in valued and devalued forms of behavior was as important in the past as it is in the present. In following the ancestors, one shows respect by acknowledging the presence of the elders and by acting with reference to them in daily life. Such behavior is rewarded as the individual's length of life is extended by God until the respectful become the respected, supported by canes as they become physically weakened by age. In contrast, lack of respect is reflected in ignoring the elders by failing to take them into account. In addition, disrespect is shown by casting elders off the "path" (that is, denying their roles as reference points) and by refusing to empathize with their sufferings. The length of life for those who show no respect for the elders is cut short as a punishment. In brief, to become an elder is to have respected one's elders.

In addition to dealing with respect, the discourses point out the interdependence of the generations. The individual is asked to identify with the life cycle of interdependent generations through an image of an old person, bent over with age and supported by a cane, walking the path of life. Trixano interpretation of this image notes that the elders are guides because of the knowledge and ideas acquired through a life of suffering for their families and sacrificing to leave their children land. In their waning years the elders are supported by canes, their descendents, who work under their direction to support them. The youth are referred to as both the canes of the elders and their "flowers, buds, and fruit." They both support the elder generation and are the product of the fertility of their elder mothers and fathers. To deny the elders is to deny the continuity of blood, land, and *costumbre* that is inherited from them.

As I commented before, *costumbre* as a synthesis of an abstract code for conduct does not rigorously establish concrete priorities for individuals' behavior as long as they show some form of active concern for the community. In other words, the ordering of alternatives demonstrates that an individual's commitment to the values of *costumbre* is flexible and the acting out of commitments is open to multiple interpretations. In theory, priorities for alternative forms of activism in community organizations are not formally codified in the Trixano world. Nevertheless, in practice, there are certain situations in which the consequences of the Trixano maxim "each mind is a world" create problems in the civil-religious hierarchy. In this eventuality, Indian authorities are forced to rank commitments and to argue that certain members of the community have a duty to show a higher degree of activism than others.[26]

The ritual guide is a prime example of a person who directs his will toward social ends in a community in which collective and individual interests may be divergent from the individual's point of view. In guiding the wings of the civil-religious hierarchy, the ritual guide brings together the heads of families for celebrations that stress cooperation between family members, kinsmen, and neighbors in the community. The guide represents continuity in the midst of (*a*) the variability of individual wills and (*b*) an annual turnover of hierarchy officials.

The constant reference to community unity in ritual discourses betrays a preoccupation with that which is most problematic in the Trixano world, the forging together of individuals with different wills into a community and the achievement of some level of consensus that will lead to collective action. This task is not easy since Trixano society is not thought of as being coercive and each individual is thought to evaluate alternatives for individual behavior or to act out commitments to *costumbre* in a slightly different manner. As one elder ritual guide put it:

> Each person has a distinct *voluntad* because we think in distinct ways. For example, he who wants to drink will drink, and he who does not want to, will not. He who wants to plant enough will plant, whereas he who wants to have little harvest will plant only a little. He who wants to go to a fiesta will go and he who does not, will stay in his house. This is *voluntad*. He who has the *voluntad* to do something can do what he proposes. He who does not want to do something, who does not have the *voluntad*, will not do it.

Such variability of individuals' will is accepted rather than being simply tolerated, for it is an implication of the statement "each mind is a world." It is assumed that each individual will evaluate his or her own circumstances in a slightly different manner. Evaluation signifies the individual's establishment of priorities within a conventional set of commitments. Thus, will or lack of will explains variations within an accepted range of behavior. It implies that an individual's action or inaction in a particular context results from the personal ranking of a larger set of valued alternatives.

Will, however, is not used to explain behavior which deviates from conventions. This concept describes why a Trixano plants a little or a lot, or why he plants lima beans in addition to corn and beans. It is not used to explain why a youth refuses to follow his father to the fields and wants to study or become a bus driver. To aspire to nonmanual employment or to work outside the town lies *outside* the set of conventional alternatives. Nontraditional choices are explained by a concept that contrasts with *voluntad*. Such choices are believed to be manifestations of another aspect of the individual, his luck-destiny.

The goal of community groups is not to challenge different wills or to force consensus, but rather to create an environment in which individuals with different *voluntades* may "unify and understand each other." First, the belief system does not demand strict compliance to a set of highly detailed obligations. Instead, it presents a broad range of alternatives through which commitments to the code for conduct of *costumbre* can be expressed. For instance, in fulfilling community service a Trixano can choose from a large number of positions with different duties and different time schedules in any of the three sections—the brotherhoods, the church, and the municipal government. It is assumed that motivations for selection of a particular wing will vary and explanations for choices are not generally elicited. Second, the belief system of the brotherhoods allows for individualized blending of religious traditions within the broad outlines of *costumbre* rather than for taking of a dogmatic stance of orthodoxy. Third, open confrontations between different interpretations of belief are avoided by highly stylized ceremonial behavior mirroring the Trixano concept of respect. The flexibility of individual commitments to *costumbre* reflects the principle "each mind is a world" and its corollary that "each person has a distinct *voluntad*."

As stated before, an individual's will is not seen as something to be manipulated or coerced. Socially valued behavior is not the product of being forced to conform, but rather flows from the individual's desire to cooperate actively in town affairs. Trixano society, then, presents only a few hard and fast obligatory rules for its members. For each Trixano inhabitant of the town, the highest-level obligation is to serve the town periodically in one of the three sections of the hierarchy; that is, to reaffirm the code of conduct of *costumbre*. In this way, each member of the town must recognize that he is part of the larger social whole, the Indian community.

At times, however, there is a lack of interest in serving the community through the hierarchy. Significantly, this is when *voluntad* (will) is opposed to *buena voluntad* (good will). In this case, *voluntad* explains each individual's ranking of commitments, where *buena voluntad* explains the more valued (at least from the point of view of the committed town leaders) combination of self- and community interest.

The locus of will, or the willingness to act in a particular situation, lies in the individual. Strategies for actions are thought to be diverse and difficult to pin down: "Some serve in the religious brotherhoods as *mortomos* [ranked assistants to the head of the brotherhood] because they are *devotos* [devotees to the particular saint celebrated in the brotherhood], others because they obtain rights to communal lands and still others because they do not want to serve in the municipal government where they will lose a great deal of time." In commenting that an individual has the will to serve in the brotherhoods, it is unusual for the issue of motivation to come up. In the case of brotherhood assistants (*mortomos*) all those serving would be said to have the will to do so, although their reasons for serving range from the fulfillment of personal promises made to the saint to the economic advantage of access to communal lands offered to the landless in exchange for service. Others prefer the religious brotherhoods because duties are light in comparison to those of the municipal government. Will emphasizes the contrast between action and nonaction, leaving behind the specification of motivation. Generally, motivations are only discussed at times of difficulty when the lack of will has diminished the ranks of those willing to perform community service. In this event, pressure is put on those who benefit most directly from service, those with communal lands, to participate. Thus, inaction may lead to a scrutiny of motivations.

Just as there is an assumed diversity of motivations for behavior, so there is also an accepted pluralism of belief within the general outline of *costumbre*. In many cases members of the religious brotherhoods have only the vaguest conception of the significance of particular ritual symbols and their relation to mythology, leaving the direction of ritual and the discourses to the ritual guide. Often there are differences of opinion over which of the divinities is most efficacious. For instance, each individual will have preferences as to which saints to supplicate in times of personal need. Some of the townspeople, especially older individuals from the isolated hamlets outside the town, believe that general fertility is associated not only with God, but also with the World-Earth. In stressing diversity that is unified, the religious brotherhoods represent such variation in belief during shrine rituals. As one *cofrade* said, "There are many who invoke only the World-Earth, others only God. For this reason, in the discourses, both are mentioned. The discourse is not to divide people; it says something for each person."

Confrontations about differing interpretations of behavior or belief are studiously avoided both within and outside the civil-religious hierarchy. Decision making is not a public affair and counsel between generations, although ideally valued, rarely takes place because it may lead to a confrontation of wills. In the event that a judgment or evaluation of others is called for, people almost inevitably preface their assessments of a situation with a statement, such as "this is only my opinion," that carries with it the idea that others have different opinions; and the speaker will limit the scope and force of his opinion, at least in public. Such behavior attempts to avoid open criticism of others and possible disagreements that would be interpreted as an expression of envy. Other expressions used are "I don't know if this is correct or not" and "only God knows." The last of these qualifiers is an invocation to the abstract God, one who can evaluate in an absolute way, but who, because of his remoteness, does not make his judgment known to man. Much of the stylization of public encounters and the rigid structure of ritual performances avoids the potential of a confrontation of varying opinions or interpretations. The ritual guide fits in here as a man who is a specialist in the diplomacy of bringing individuals with different wills together to achieve some sense of common purpose.

The flexibility of the civil-religious hierarchy and *costumbre* confronts and perpetuates the difficulty of cooperation and common purpose within a community built up of individuals who think in different ways. Despite such ideal flexibility, however, there are, in actuality, occasions in which members of the civil-religious hierarchy publicly rank alternative ways of showing allegiance to *costumbre*. In some cases, good will has been contrasted with will. Heads of the hierarchy may state that some wills, especially those directed toward community service, are valued more highly than others that exhibit only self- or family interest. In a second case, benefits accruing to possible candidates for posts have been given priorities by the elders, and those with communal lands have been required to give service to the community. Access to communal land, a right given to landless Indians, obligates them to serve the community. I would suggest that contexts in which *buena voluntad* is held up as a model and Indians with communal lands are told that they should serve the civil-religious hierarchy occur with greater frequency when the code for conduct of *costumbre* is threatened by religious competitors. These competitors, be they new orthodox Catholic or Protestant groups, present new codes for conduct and alternatives for the expression of commitment to religion. Such redefinitions, and the circumstances in which they have grown in importance in San Andrés, are the subject of Part Two of this study.

The ritual guide, then, does not represent the subordination of individual to community, but rather the possibility of cooperation between individuals who perceive a parallel between their personal needs and those of the community. The guide's will is directed toward activism and collaboration in community groups so that *costumbre*, or the code for conduct which presents the commitments each person orders in an individual way, will be perpetuated. By bringing people together, the ritual guide acts as a guide rather than a leader, translating the different thoughts of each individual into the correct expressions of *costumbre* in order to address God and the saints and to gain blessings for the social order. Outside the social order, however, lies the *monte*, the wilds, in which a different set of mediators, the sorcerers, guide people in a way opposed to that of the ritual guide.

Sorcerers and the Devil:
Shapers of Conflict and Change

Unlike the ritual guide, the sorcerer is independent of larger institutions that bring individuals together in community-wide celebrations. Sorcerers work as independent intermediaries in the order of nature dealing with symbols of luck-destiny (*suerte*) and envy (*envidia*) that order discontinuities in the lives of individuals and division and antagonism between them. Sorcerers play out different luck-destinies that lead them to be adversaries of each other and to attribute a similar relation to supplicants.

The "sorcerer of the day" (*ajg'ij*) has been given power by God to interpret misfortunes that may be caused by townsmen seeking vengeance through the "sorcerer of evil" (*ajitz*) who draws power from Satanás. Both sorcerers define the success of some in the community as contingent on the failure of others and both perform rituals that seek redress in order to equalize success and failure. In addition, the sorcerer of evil assists those who have the luck-destiny to make pacts with the Devil.

In the case of the sorcerer of the day, recruitment to the position of intermediary takes place in a way which contrasts with the achieved social recognition of the ritual guide, as well as with other traditional agricultural occupations. God gives an individual the "gift" (*el don*) to become a sorcerer. This gift is not inherited, although sorcerers sometimes come from the same family. Instead, it is given to a particular individual who is singled out by God for this position. As an old sorcerer of the day commented: "[Sorcerers can] predict through dreams or the casting of stones or beans if a person is suffering a punishment from God or an evil from another person. This is the *suerte* that one has found or owns. *Suerte* cannot be bought or desired or copied from another. It is a way to earn one's daily bread. One comes to the facility or the gift to predict something through *suerte*. It [the prediction] is a sign that one has *suerte*." The luck-destiny that is revealed to the sorcerer and gives insight into the supernatural forces of nature makes sorcery stand in opposition to other traditional occupations, which stress continuity between generations as father teaches son and elder instructs youth by example during long periods of apprenticeship. One sorcerer explained that sorcery differs from the work of the agriculturalist who takes his child at an early age to the fields if only to bring water or the noon meal. As this child grows older, he begins to assist and watch the way in which his father accomplishes the tasks of the agricultural cycle, learning to form the raised rows of earth in which seed is planted, to weed the crops as they grow, and to harvest the crop when it matures so that it can be stored and seed selected for the next planting. The result of this training is that "after a while the child likes the work in the fields [*el campo*] and learns to perform the tasks because from the beginning he has helped his father." Unlike the agriculturalist or ritual intermediaries of the town, who learn their occupations by following in the footsteps of the older generations, the luck-destiny of the sorcerer of the day is given directly from God as a gift. Such luck-destiny can be neither rejected nor denied nor changed "just as it is impossible to change a person's manner of being, character or behavior." The sorcerer of evil is recruited in a similar way, although in this case power comes not from God but from the Devil.

The sorcerer of the day uses insight gained through the gift of luck-destiny to aid individuals and their families in times of trouble when sickness, accidents, or poor harvests threaten their well-being. Assistance of this sorcerer is only called upon when misfortunes seem to single out individuals; generalized disasters that jeopardize the community are handled within the town by the civil-religious hierarchy. The *ajg'ij* makes misfortunes meaningful by showing that they have a cause, which is the envy of others in the town, and that there is hope to ameliorate the misfortunes by appealing to higher authorities. Like other intermediaries, the sorcerer acts as a translator of diverse forms of experience into ritual formulas. The role of the sorcerer of the day and its similarity to other forms of mediation are described in the following way by a sorcerer:

> In the event that a person is bothered by another, the sorcerer can be like a lawyer who goes humbly to express the desire of the [affected] person. Especially if the person is unable to express himself or is unable to do so because of sickness. The sorcerer asks if there is any way for the person to re-establish himself. For instance, if a person is sent to jail under the authority of the mayor and he cannot express himself, his friends or family look for a fellow townsman to intercede for him, to explain that the problem is

not serious, and to supplicate the mayor so that the person can leave or pay a small fine. This is like the work of the sorcerer who only guides or interprets the words of another.

This intermediary defines the situation for a client by using the system of laws governing interpersonal relations. Like the lawyer who understands the system of law and the nature of authority invested in its representative, the sorcerer understands the supernatural laws of nature through which a person's welfare can be first threatened and then regained. Mediation does not involve a solution of the problem between the two human parties in conflict. Rather, the intermediary appeals cases to higher authorities who will sit in judgment and rectify the state of the affected, allowing the sick to regain health and the prisoner, freedom. The unanswered issues in this account are the relationship between the two human parties and the nature of the higher authority to which the sorcerer appeals. To address these issues we must look at some material on the sorcerer's domain.

The domain of both types of sorcerers lies outside the town and beyond the cultivated fields in the wilds. In this region, special saints (called "lords of the wilds") represent the forces of nature such as the Wind, the Sun, and the World-Earth. In addition, the wilds are the home of Satanás who controls the underworld.[27] Human intermediaries also parallel these distinctions, for the sorcerer of the day serves as a guide for those who want the assistance of the lords of the wilds in their guise as saints and special guardians of fertility. The sorcerer of the day, however, is often thought really to be a sorcerer of evil, one who performs ceremonies for vengeance, causing accidents, infirmities, and poor harvests for individual farmers. In addition, the sorcerer of evil may act as a go-between for individuals seeking assistance from the Lord of the Volcano (*el dueño del volcán*) or the Lord of the Wilds, these being other names for the Devil.

Through the sorcerer of evil, those who are motivated by envy of the successes of others with sexual conquests, material acquisitions, or good harvests can tap the malevolent powers of Satanás or misinform God or the ancestors so that their adversaries will be punished. To counteract these powers, individuals who have problems in their families or plantings seek out the sorcerer of the day who will divine the cause of the difficulties and suggest recourses, often involving ritual sacrifices, to neutralize the work of the sorcerer of evil.

Both sorcerers define a person's problems as resulting from acts of others in the community. Symbolically, these individual battles are fought outside the community. Events that single out individuals in either success or difficulty are attributed to acts of individuals against the well-being of others. One person's gain is defined as another's loss and the loser is thought to redefine envy into vengeance with the help of the sorcerer of evil. The object of vengeance who feels singled out for an unjust punishment seeks the help of the sorcerer of the day. Punishment is unjust if the individual "knows in his conscience that he has not acted badly, robbed, or killed." The sorcerer of the day divines the cause of the punishment by casting stones or through dreams, in order to find out who has been motivated by vengeance to harm the family, and then acts to rectify the unjust punishment.

The interdependence of the two sorcerers is best demonstrated by sketching an example in which sickness and death within a family were interpreted as the result of an envious adversary acting through a sorcerer of evil. The family of don Antonio, as they will be called in this account, emigrated from another highland town to San Andrés, bringing with them new forms of dress, agricultural innovations, and forms of artisanry that had not been practiced in San Andrés. The town's reception of the new family was ambivalent, although their industriousness, facility in dealing with people, and activity in the civil-religious hierarchy were felt to be exemplary. Here is their grandson's account of the family's arrival:

> They brought new things to the town and always presented new ideas. They were superior to the townspeople because they were acquainted with new means of employment not only in the fields, but also in artisanry. At first they were not liked. But as they had better ideas for their own people, the Indians, they were accepted over the years by the town, but not by everyone. They cultivated a great deal of land and had more contact with Ladinos. Their crops produced well and their presentation distinguished them. They were successful both in a more comfortable life and in more privilege with women. These successes gave rise to envy which resulted in an evil act on the part of those who did not accept them.

Don Antonio stood out from other members of the community not only because he came from another town, but also because of his unusual material successes, the result of bountiful harvests and employment in nontraditional occupations of tilemaking and carpentry. Along with economic success and a more comfortable style of life, don Antonio occupied high positions in the civil-religious hierarchy, ultimately as the head of a brotherhood. He also pursued romances with women of the town and surrounding hamlets. On the one hand, the family felt accepted as other townspeople imitated their successful economic strategies. On the other hand, the family believed that some of the townspeople did not accept them and were envious of their successful emigration.

Don Antonio felt that the envy of individuals in the town crystallized when members of the family began to see anthropomorphic shadows that entered the family house. Later his wife became gravely ill with pains throughout her body, high fevers, and visions in which a man laughed at her sickness. When his wife screamed out the name of the man, it was clear to don Antonio that his wife's illness was not natural, but rather caused by the vengeance of an adversary, by someone who had become embittered by don Antonio's successes.

The adversary had felt that don Antonio's successes were his own loss in a zero-sum world. Envy caused the adversary to feel that he had been personally harmed by don Antonio. This harm was traced back to an earlier disagreement over a girl friend. To rectify this, the adversary is said to have contacted a sorcerer of evil to punish don Antonio by calling on Satanás, who sent spirits in the forms of wild animals and shadows to bring sickness. In turn, the family of the victim called on the sorcerer of the day to perform curative ritual and, later, to diagnose don Antonio's own sickness brought by malign cats and toads sent by the sorcerer of evil. The ritual of the sorcerer of the day was to no avail, and don Antonio died soon after his wife, leaving the family impoverished because of the expenses of enlisting sorcerers and paying for the various local medical treatments that they tried. As in this example of don Antonio, sorcerers give meaning to phenomena seen as symptoms of interpersonal conflict by clarifying motivations and dealing with them outside of society in the wilds. Society as embodied in the civil-religious hierarchy seems to be unable to deal with these kinds of conflicts.

Significantly, the outcome of the interplay of the two sorcerers is an overall leveling of individual differences in economic wealth and other signs of fertility. Don Antonio's early success was the result of introducing innovations from outside the moral community. He was also felt to have unusually strong ties with Ladinos. On the level of the community, Trixanos explain that sorcery, in effect, neutralized don Antonio's advantages resulting from ladinoized strategies for success. Such leveling would appear to feed back into the value system of *costumbre* in which poverty, suffering, and the equivalence of Trixanos are stressed. Furthermore, *costumbre* rewards individuals with fertility in this life for following the model of the ancestors, not for adopting ladinoized strategies for success. With don Antonio's family, sorcery is used to explain the injustice of early deaths in the family despite their eagerness to work hard and contribute to the community through activism in the brotherhoods. In addition, sorcery explains for the descendents the sudden, and seemingly arbitrary, impoverishment of a wealthy family.

While vengeance is expressed through the sorcerer of evil by those who envy the successes of others, the individual can also reach for sources of material success with the help of the sorcerer. The intermediary assists supplicants in making pacts with the Lord of the Volcano, the Devil. To make a pact, the sorcerer of evil brings the supplicant to the mouths of caves where the home of the Lord opens up to the wilds. At the mouth of the cave the sorcerer petitions the Devil, offering the service of the petitioner after death in exchange for material success and fertility of family, domestic animals, and crops. Not just anyone, however, can successfully petition the Devil, only those with the appropriate luck-destiny. As in the recruitment of the sorcerers, luck-destiny explains discontinuities in the individual's life that lie outside his and society's control. Sudden wealth in the community is often ascribed to luck-destiny involving pacts with the Devil, and townspeople express a great deal of ambivalence about the *pactados* (pacted individuals).

Those who have made pacts cannot reveal the source of their wealth or their newly found allegiance to fellow townspeople, who have accepted the necessity of suffering in this life to please the divinities and to be assured happiness and ease after death. Nor can the pacted avoid their destiny after death: to be returned to the Devil and transformed into wild animals to work as slaves for eternity. Clearly, siding with the Devil is a betrayal of community ethos, inverting the relation stating that this life is to suffering as the next life is to eternal happiness. For the pacted, then, this life is one of sudden ease and material success, whereas in the next life they are eternally punished as the benevolent Lord of the Volcano becomes a cruel master and the pacted become wild animals that suffer with eternal work.

Luck-destiny often carries a negative connotation because, in dealing with nontraditional commitments, it is a quality causing individuals to deviate from the model of the elders, such as the ritual guide. Luck-destiny implies change which, from the Trixano point of view, is out of human control and occurs on the individual, rather than the institutional, level. An examination of changes brought about through luck-destiny shows that change occurs in one direction: toward economic success through becoming like members of the other ethnic group, the

Ladinos. The playing out of luck-destiny most often involves nontraditional occupations. If children learn the work of their parents but see another kind of work and imitate it, luck-destiny is said to cause this deviation. Those who successfully attend school, continue their studies outside the town, and aspire to nonmanual occupations have the luck-destiny to do so, for without it they would be unable to learn to read or write. Just as some Trixanos have the luck-destiny to turn away from their parents' work as agriculturalists, others have the luck-destiny to make pacts with the Devil, exchanging eternal suffering after death as a laborer in the underworld for material success in this world. Significantly, successful Indian landowners who are wealthy enough to employ Indians as permanent laborers are often said to be pacted to Satanás. Their supervisory positions mark them off from other Indians who are independent agriculturalists or who work for Ladinos as laborers.

Turning toward nonagricultural employment, gaining literacy in Spanish, employing laborers as a *patrón*, and valuing material wealth as an indicator of prestige are alternatives outside *costumbre*. They are not, however, external to traditional commitments in a random way. Instead, they are building blocks or key facets of the concept of Ladino identity as seen by the Indian. Ladinos monopolize nonmanual occupations, mediate the town and higher levels of integration through the medium of the Spanish language, control large tracts of land on which they employ Indians as laborers, and value the display of material wealth as a prime indicator of prestige. Ladinos mediate another set of domains standing outside those encompassed by *costumbre*.

As intermediaries, the ritual guide (*camol beij*) and the sorcerers (*ajitz* and *ajg'ij*) represent a set of fundamental oppositions dealing with Trixano identity as reflected in conceptions of the individual, relations between individuals, and formation of society. As an individual and member of the community, the ritual guide exhibits the positive direction of will (*voluntad*) toward participation in and perpetuation of key community institutions. The ritual guide does not deny that "each person thinks in different ways," but instead demonstrates that individual priorities can be aligned with ongoing activities of community organizations, bringing social recognition for community service. As a ritual intermediary, the guide brings together kinsmen and neighbors, who express will through active participation in the civil-religious hierarchy to celebrate the unity and tradition of the town and to gain God's blessing for the entire community. Unity is expressed in the Trixano maxim that states that people are sent from God as a planting to insure the well-being of their families and communities by ascending the civil-religious hierarchy and by returning to God at the harvest of death so that more people will be born. Thus, in directing will toward community activity, individuals secure blessings for themselves, their families, and fellow townspeople and acknowledge that individual ranking of commitments is a particular expression of the code for conduct expressed in *costumbre*.

In opposition, sorcerers are singled out not by devotion to the community, but by luck-destiny that causes them to stand outside the community and the civil-religious hierarchy in the order of nature. As intermediaries, the sorcerers explain that sickness, accidents, or crop failures affecting a specific individual rather than the entire community are not the result of a misalignment of the individual's commitments with those of the code for conduct. On the contrary, they are symptomatic of the fundamental incompatibility of separate individuals' striving for similar goals. Sorcerers reinforce a divisive aspect of the individual, the individual's capacity to envy others who, for seemingly inexplicable reasons, succeed while many fail. Sorcerers talk of a zero-sum universe in which one person's gain is another's loss, although the scales may be tipped in the supplicant's favor.[28] Thus, in the symbolic wilds, the individual may attempt to subordinate the interests of the community and fellow townspeople to personal material success.

Maximization of self-interest that flows from envy is de-emphasized in society as the dark side of the individual in San Andrés. For this reason, it is difficult to get Trixanos to talk about sorcerers and envy; and, while two men in the town are known as sorcerers of the day, no one will admit to being a sorcerer of evil. Even less accessible is information on pacts with the Devil, although private accusations are not uncommon; and a series of *cuentos* is told about the adventures of those who have stumbled on the Devil or his animals in the wilds and others who have successfully transacted pacts. None of the sorcerers' activities are mentioned in a positive or a negative way in public ceremony, perhaps because they are felt to be dissonant with the core tenets of *costumbre*. Moreover, *costumbre*, which is based on intergenerational continuity, does not have a vocabulary with which to talk about change that occurs outside its conceptual scheme.

Change, then, is associated with the powers of Satanás. One becomes like the Devil, that is half man–half animal, if one assumes the characteristics of the class of people whom the Devil represents.[29] The Devil, then, becomes an ambivalently conceived symbol of the external powers controlling that which society cannot, the luck-destiny of the individual and the forces of nature. Luck-destiny, the maximization of self-interest, and ladinoization are discussed in the same symbolic idiom as being outside the control of Indian society, as being arbitrary and inevitable, and as leading to the decline of Indian *costumbre*.

Change for the Trixanos does not imply that the individual becomes a Ladino because ethnicity in terms of blood cannot be changed, but rather that change denies the strong association of blood and *costumbre* inherited from the ancestors. Those who have the luck-destiny to make pacts with the Devil maintain Indian blood but subordinate this symbol of the unity of the Indian community to a ladinoized code of conduct. On the one hand, *costumbre* defines the equivalence of Indians within the Trixano community. On the other hand, this analysis suggests that Indians who imitate the Ladino code for conduct by becoming *patrones* or gaining literacy and training in nonagricultural employment are in the position of subordinating other Indians in the Trixano community. In short, the pacted threaten to replicate the domination of the bi-ethnic community *within* the separatist Indian community by subordinating Indians to fellow Indians. The pacted fail to follow the *costumbre* of the ancestors that directs respect for social age, the interdependence of generations, and the unity of the Indian community. Instead of identifying with the suffering of others in the separatist community, the pacted may cause suffering through positions as *patrones*. Nor do they acknowledge the elders as reference points for their lives, because they do not support the code for conduct of the ancestors or follow the implications of descent from them. Those who have the luck-destiny to follow the Ladino code for conduct invert the character of Indian life because they do not suffer in this life. As a consequence, they merit eternal punishment after death because of their domination of others; yet they remain distinct from Ladinos because of their Indian blood. The pacted are sent to a special hell, not in the Ladino underworld city, but rather on an underworld plantation where they must work as subordinates for all time in the employ of the Lord of the Wilds, the Devil.[30] That this luck-destiny is outside the control of the Indian community once again points to a subordination of the Indian community to the external influences of the Ladino society in which it is embedded.

PART TWO

Neither Devils nor Ancestors:
The Revolutionary Beginnings
of Catholic Action

4. Anticlericalism and the History of Catholic Action

This chapter continues the analysis of ethnicity in San Andrés by presenting material on the founding of a new religious congregation, Catholic Action (Acción Católica), in the town. Ironically, the developments of both the civil-religious hierarchy in the nineteenth century and its later challenger Catholic Action in the twentieth were fostered by reactions to Guatemala's long tradition of strong anticlericalism. During the colonial and early republican periods, the Catholic Church was very active in Indian communities. This central religious role was ended by a second wave of liberalism, which, under the direction of Miguel García Granados and Justino Rufino Barrios, who led the provisional government in 1871, adopted a militantly anticlerical stance toward the Catholic Church. Church properties and investments were confiscated, foreign clergy were expelled, religious orders were disbanded, special treatment of clergy in the courts ended, priests were not allowed to hold political office, and religious schools were nationalized. In short, the Catholic Church lost its financial and political power bases as well as much of its formal social organization and means of perpetuating sufficient numbers of priests and sisters. Activities of the remaining clergy were restricted to narrowly defined devotional duties. It is significant that among Indian populations, religious celebrations and activism thrived after the decline of the Catholic Church. Increasingly, Indian religion developed independently of the Catholic Church's guidance and administration, crystallizing in the civil-religious hierarchy (Holleran 1949:173–199; Adams 1970:278–280).

The liberal, anticlerical stance of national governments was continued from Barrios in the late nineteenth century to the revolutionary governments of Juan José Arévalo from 1945 to 1951 and Jacobo Arbenz from 1951 to 1954. Jorge Ubico's administration from 1931 to 1944 was the only exception to this trend, and even he demanded that the national Catholic Church refrain from formally commenting on political or social issues and avoid political activity. None of these governments pursued a policy opposing Catholic theology or sacramental participation. Rather, liberal governments opposed the resumption of the institutional Catholic Church as an independent power holder with great wealth and influence as had been the case during the colonial period.

With the revolution of 1944, the Catholic Church saw its chances for a continued loosening of liberal restrictions disappear with Ubico. The constitution of 1945 incorporated a strongly liberal stand, banning monasteries and convents and prohibiting clergy from involvement in politics or issues relating to labor (Silvert 1954:16). It was in this anticlerical environment that the archbishop of Guatemala promoted the mobilization of orthodox lay Catholics into study groups called Catholic Action (Rossell 1946). On the one hand, these organizations were intended to compensate for the scarcity of priests, especially in rural areas where the Indian civil-religious hierarchy continued to direct religious activity. On the other hand, Catholic Action can be interpreted as the archbishop's response to the politics of the revolution.

Explicitly, the Guatemalan Catholic Church worked through Catholic Action to create new groups of community leaders committed to Catholic orthodoxy and to lay evangelism on a local level. By organizing decentralized groups tied to parishes and small settlements within parishes, the Guatemalan Catholic Church has hoped to weaken and ultimately destroy unorthodox religious beliefs and rituals of the Indian brotherhoods (*cofradías*). In many cases Catholic Action reinforced trends of declining authority in the civil-religious hierarchy. The civil-religious hierarchy had suffered losses of civil power when Ubico began appointing the highest municipal officer in rural communities. During the revolutionary period Indian elders were often successfully challenged by parties seeking to organize electoral politics. Thus, the training of catechists and the formation of local Catholic Action groups introduced an additional dimension of factionalism into Indian communities (Adams 1957a, 1957b, 1970; Mendelson 1957; Colby and van den Berghe 1969).

In addition to religious goals, the head of Guatemala's Catholic Church looked to Catholic Action as an organization that would direct Indian activism away from radical politics. In Guatemala, Catholic Action was first promoted on a wide scale in 1948 by Monsignor, later Archbishop, Mariano Rossell y Arellano, who exercised considerable power over the national Catholic Church from 1939 to 1964. From the beginning, Catholic Action was organized as an opposition to philosophies that were perceived as competing with Catholic orthodoxy: "humanism, Protestantism, rationalism, autorevelation, historical materialism, and laicism" (Adams 1970:295). In Guatemala, early experimentation with groups of orthodox lay catechists was instituted to counteract the successes of Protestant missionaries (Rojas Lima 1968). In the late forties, however, the opposition was communism. By the time of the counterrevolution in the midfifties, the archbishop was able to observe: ". . . our small Catholic Action was one of the greatest comforts in those hours of enormous distress in the presence of the Marxist advance that invaded everything" (Rossell 1955).

Archbishop Rossell spoke powerfully and passionately in pastoral letters and other published messages to the faithful about his opposition to the growth of communism in Guatemala during the revolutionary period.[31] Rossell warned that revolutionary politics, as infiltrated by "Soviet-directed international communism," would destroy both the moral and social orders in Guatemala. Communism would undermine religion, destroy family solidarity, and would promote class and ethnic antagonism. He believed that Indian populations were especially vulnerable to communist propaganda and manipulation: "Today [the Indian population] is a tame and long-suffering lamb, but it is very easy to turn it into a cruel wolf, or a ravenous lion, or a poisonous snake" (Rossell 1949). The archbishop argued that impoverished, exploited, ignorant rural populations would be fertile ground for the spread of communist ideology. He described situations in which rural agitators were said to have fomented ethnic hatred, offered peasants the return of their lands, and manipulated Indian brotherhoods in order to promote and even to force compliance with their cause (Rossell 1955).

His commentaries on the revolutionary period may seem extreme today; certainly their portrayal of a monolithic conspiracy is inaccurate. Today, many analysts label the revolutionary period as one of limited, urban-directed bourgeois reforms. National governments began important experiments with agrarian reforms and the political organization of rural areas; but in many cases these experiments did not have enough time to penetrate the highlands seriously. Nor did these governments have adequate time to articulate and test a comprehensive rural development policy. Political parties competed for membership in rural areas, but the impact of political ideologies and new organizations on Indian communities is currently the subject of debate in the social sciences.[32] Apparently the archbishop, however, was deeply threatened by such preliminary experiments in directed social change and party politics.

In fact, while the revolutionary governments did not seek out the Church as an ally, neither did they persecute the Catholic faith. During the revolutionary decade, the number of diocesan and regular priests increased from 114 to 195. This number grew even more rapidly, however, after the counterrevolution, reaching 242 in 1955 and 517 diocesan and regular priests in the late sixties (Turner 1969:135–136).

Despite the fanatical tone of the archbishop's commentaries, they should not be understood as idiosyncratic. Rather his stance reflected the dependent position of the Guatemalan priesthood that strongly identified its political interests with antirevolutionary elites. Certainly part of Rossell's strong reaction to the revolutionary political regimes was his total identification with the Catholic Church as a formal institution. The archbishop saw the national Catholic Church, as an institution, as ideally standing above particular governments or political parties, yet playing a central role in the social and moral life of the nation. Rossell believed that the Catholic Church should be able to exercise ecclesiastical autonomy, hold property, regulate marriage, and care for the spiritual life of all citizens, as well as organize charitable, educational, and welfare services (1945, 1948*a*, 1954*a*). Rossell wanted the national Catholic Church to be a powerful and economically independent institution that would not be restricted by anticlerical governmental policy.

The archbishop believed that all political groups that promoted the exclusion of the Catholic Church as a formal institution from a central role in Guatemalan national life were to blame for the revolutionary threat. For this reason at the same time as he denounced "atheistic communism" he also sharply criticized both liberalism and conservatism. Each of these political ideologies, in its own way, directly limited the role of the Catholic Church or made impoverished masses receptive to antireligious ideologies. Rossell stated that the enemies of the Catholic Church were not only those who opposed its theological doctrines, but also those who in the eighteenth and nineteenth centuries stripped the Catholic Church of its role as the protector of the Indians from exploiters who robbed peasants of their lands. The marginal economic position of rural populations that resulted from this history of exploitation only made Indians more receptive to communist rhetoric in the present. In addition, the archbishop criticized "false anticommunists," who did not pay workers just wages or who charged inflated prices for basic commodities, because they also contributed to the discontent and potential radicalization of workers (Rossell 1948*a*; 1954; 1955; 1958).

The archbishop's attitude toward Guatemalan laborers remained paternalistic throughout the revolutionary and counterrevolutionary periods, although his concept of necessary social reforms broadened significantly. At the time of the revolution, he held that the role of the

Guatemalan Church was to "awaken the feeling of charity" among the rich and to encourage "Christian resignation" and hope among the poor (Rossell 1945:5–6). Apparently this position, with the concept of resignation, was challenged by workers who complained that the Church failed to identify with the needs of the masses in favor of its ties to capitalists. The archbishop responded that the international Catholic Church had a history of providing relief for the poor, helping workers involved in disputes, and promoting organizations such as co-operatives, syndicates, and schools. As further evidence for the Catholic Church's concern with workers, he noted that Church teachings instructed employers and landowners to pay their workers on time and not to defraud them. The archbishop continued to believe that the rich should act as "stewards and parents" to the less fortunate through acts of charity (1946:9).

By 1948, however, Rossell phrased his argument in broader terms that asserted that radical ideologies were most attractive in societies where there was a highly visible gap between the small wealthy elite and the masses at subsistence level. He asserted that in order to slow the advance of communism, elites must act not only out of compassion and charity, but also out of a sense of "social justice." He argued that those employers who defined their duties to workers narrowly would only increase tensions. Others who assisted a worker "to better his life socially and morally, physically and spiritually" would be contributing to social justice. He suggested that *patrones* invest in institutions that would serve workers such as hospitals, maternity wards, and schools. To workers he had a different message: that they demand their legal rights but not be influenced by agitators who could not fulfill their promises for a transformed society. In the event of a communist revolution, he held that both rich and poor would be subject to a dictatorial social order (1948a:9–12). To avoid such a result, the archbishop advised activities aimed at achieving social justice, to promoting harmony rather than conflict between social classes and ethnic groups.

By the time of the counterrevolution, the archbishop had broadened the scope of valued reforms arguing that "good salaries, wages, and gifts are not enough for the peasant if he does not properly own his just piece of land" (Rossell 1955:19). His solution, however, was not a program of broad land reform through redistribution or through communal ownership because Rossell held that the concept of private property was sacred. Rather by the early sixties, he came to advocate increased international economic aid, programs of migration from overpopulated regions, the introduction of modern technology to increase national productivity, the creation of production and consumption co-operatives, and the establishment of savings and loan banks for rural areas (Rossell 1962).

Rossell was powerful because he had ties with conservative Guatemalan elites and represented the bishops to the government. His central position arose from his apparent ability to monopolize control over national Church affairs from his archdiocese, which included the capital city. Actually no direct authority over other bishops was conferred upon him by the structure of the Catholic Church's hierarchy. Rossell's position benefited from the lack of internal organization of the national Catholic Church and from the fact that there were few dioceses in the country (Adams 1970:283–285).

The counterrevolution, which was greeted with enthusiasm by the archbishop, had paradoxical effects on his position. Carlos Castillo Armas' regime ended the long anticlerical slant of national policy, which had lasted since the late nineteenth century. Certainly, the Guatemalan government understood the potential of religious organizations and a strong national Catholic Church to refocus the political energies of young Indians who had been involved in political parties, peasant leagues, and agrarian reform committees during the revolutionary decade. The Catholic Church began to enjoy a position of new privilege and was formally granted new legal status in the 1955 and 1966 constitutions. In the sixties, the Catholic Church was allowed once again to hold property, was exempted from certain forms of property taxes, and was given titles to properties that it had held in the past (Adams 1970:259–260, 310–311).

In postrevolutionary Guatemala, the national Church joined a set of political interest groups that included the landholding elites and the military in domestic affairs and the Vatican and the U.S. government internationally. These groups shared a common commitment to halting the development of socialism and to stemming communist influence in Guatemala. They agreed that a strong and active national Church would help to combat communism. These national and international groups, however, had very different stances on the scope of necessary social reforms to promote welfare and deal with social inequality in Guatemala. More comprehensive plans for economic development in rural areas were advocated by international agencies that lacked strong ties to Guatemalan elites and controlled their own sources of funding (Calder 1970:178–186).

The return of the Catholic Church to prominence was followed by decentralization, undercutting the archbishop's control of the affairs of the national Church. The Vatican authorized new dioceses that were directly responsible to Rome through the country's papal nuncio. In addition, Castillo Armas opened the country to larger numbers of foreign clergy who represented a greater diversity of national backgrounds, political stands, and concerns with social development than had been common before. Especially in the case of the U.S. diocesan priests and missionary orders, foreign personnel have brought with them broader, independent sources of funding that have allowed them to complement sacramental activities with small social welfare projects. Postrevolutionary priests and sisters have worked increasingly in rural areas that had been virtually ignored in earlier years. They have been concerned with promoting local development projects, including savings and loan cooperatives, agricultural cooperatives, health care facilities, radio schools, special advanced schools for Indians, linguistic work with Indian languages, as well as groups of Catholic Action to foster sacramental activism and religious education. Still, many towns lack resident priests or sisters and have not been touched by development projects sponsored by the Catholic Church. The national Catholic Church is still concerned that economic inequities in Guatemala will limit people's commitment to modern Catholic orthodoxy and will make radical politics an attractive option for the masses (Adams 1970: 283–285; Calder 1970:37, 48–55).

Chapters in Part Two of this book focus on the religious belief system, social ideologies, activities, and political implications of Catholic Action in San Andrés. Catholic Action as a group and Indian catechists as individuals describe their religious work in the following way:

> The role of Catholic Action is to be an apostle, to give good action to the non-Christians. What is good action? It is to clarify for them that after this life there is another and that in this life we have to avoid that which God does not want. This is the mission of Catholic Action in town. Catholic Action is the collaboration of laity with the hierarchy, from the pope to the last priest. But the priest does not get to the hamlets. Thus, the laity as catechists collaborate by taking the message of the priest to the people that the priest does not get to.

Catholic Action is a critical link to orthodoxy in San Andrés since the town lacks a resident priest and receives visits from the parish priest stationed in neighboring Panajachel only once a week for an early morning mass.

The early history of Catholic Action in San Andrés caused the group to take on more than an intermediary role between the community and the formal priesthood. This analysis will argue that Catholic orthodoxy has been extended by Indian catechists to serve as a vehicle for a major and rather sudden shift in the cultural identity of Trixano Indians. In the last twenty-five years, Indian members of this congregation have formulated a social ideology that denies the Trixano association of blood with the code for conduct of *costumbre* as the core symbols for identity.

Catholic Action ideology, as it has been elaborated by Indian converts in San Andrés, asserts that spiritual membership in the universalistic Catholic Church should supersede ethnic identities; singles out local Ladinos as the major stumbling block for the actualization of economic equivalence for all individuals; and proposes ladinoization as a means to achieving social and economic equivalence of Indians and Ladinos in the broader society. The impact of Archbishop Rossell's attempt to depoliticize the rural sector has met with very mixed success. These chapters will discuss the ways in which Indian converts' experiences with other groups in the community, including the civil-religious hierarchy, have contributed to a local reformulation of Indian models of society and identity. This analysis will also examine the impact that the social ideology of Indian converts has had on interethnic relations, Indians' perceptions and analyses of ethnic subordination, and Indians' responses to postrevolutionary rural development projects.

The Establishment of Catholic Action in San Andrés

San Andrés has been the object of missionary action since the 1920s; yet groups such as the Assembly of God, the Mormon church, the Jehovah's Witnesses, and the Baha'i have never succeeded in gaining more than a handful of often temporary converts. The first religion to present a serious alternative to the civil-religious hierarchy was the Central American Mission, a nonsectarian fundamentalist sect from Texas. The initial converts to the Central American Mission were members of a local Ladino family who were brought into the religion by evangelical relatives from the capital in the late 1920s. While early converts showed interest in local evangelization of both ethnic groups, membership throughout the 1930s and 1940s remained extremely small and unstable. Over time, Ladinos dropped away and the group took on an Indian character, focusing on one extended family in town. Undoubtedly, the presence of the Central American Mission influenced the reception that Catholic Action met in the town, if only to demonstrate the near impossibility of establishing a congregation in which ethnicity is not a central issue.

Apparently, at the entrance of Catholic Action into the town in 1952, it was not strongly associated with the other nontraditional religious group, evangelical Protestantism, in the minds of the Trixanos. At that time, Catholic Action converts sought to strengthen ties with the wider Indian community, including the civil-religious hierarchy, by stressing the commonality of Catholicism, whereas the evangelicals had initially adopted an extreme form of isolationism from Trixano religious beliefs and social institutions. Later, Catholic Action was forced to adopt a separatist stance; but only after they had gained a substantial group of new members. Catholic Action experienced continual growth throughout the 1960s and now shows membership of eighty men and women and their families. Ironically, the Central American Mission has been a beneficiary of Catholic Action success to the extent that their membership also increased in the 1960s, although it remains significantly smaller than that of Catholic Action.

Following oral history accounts of the town's Indian catechists, we can see that the initial Trixano contact with the new Catholic movement was strikingly fortuitous. One day early in 1951 a member of a prominent San Andrés Indian family visited the nearby Cakchiquel town of Tecpán to transact some business and fell into conversation with an Indian catechist and member of the Tecpán Catholic Action group, who questioned the Trixano about religious practices in San Andrés. The Trixano replied that religious devotion in San Andrés centered on the celebration of the saints by the brotherhoods that brought together the sections of the civil-religious hierarchy. The Indian catechist countered with a critique that the brotherhoods celebrated a "pagan" form of Catholicism mixed with *costumbre*; he argued that such religious practices ignored the hierarchy of the universal Catholic Church and the celebration of the sacraments. Trixano *costumbre* demonstrated a lack of awareness of the obligations of the "good Christian" as enumerated in the Catholic catechism. He continued explaining that without these forms of direction the Trixano brotherhoods had come to confuse the "spiritual" and the "material," honoring the images of the saints as if they were gods and reveling at fiestas where drunkenness and sexual license prevailed. The catechist offered to follow up this critique by bringing several of his "brothers in Christ" to San Andrés to teach the orthodox Catholicism and to organize a group to study the doctrine of the Catholic Church.[33]

When the catechists from Tecpán arrived in San Andrés they organized a small group of interested Indians to study the catechism in a private house. At that time, they predicted problems if the meetings were held in the town's bi-ethnic chapel, called *calvario*. From the beginning catechists stressed understanding of the doctrine of the Catholic Church, the ability to explain beliefs, and the implications that beliefs had for daily life. Unaccustomed to this form of teaching, the new converts were uncomfortable when asked to explain what passages from the catechism meant: "At first the catechists offended us by asking for explanations of points from the catechism. No one could respond. Then they explained the meaning of words from the catechism in Cakchiquel. They told us to continue the group, explaining the religion, working in the town, and behaving well as an example for others in the Church." Thus, from the beginning the converts were exposed to the role of the catechist who explained such religious distinctions as the "material" and the "spiritual" aspects of life and required precise explanations and applications of these core principles to daily life.

The catechists emphasized that belief in the commandments and the teachings of the Catholic Church entailed obligations such as the recognition of the formal hierarchy of the Catholic Church, participation in the sacraments, and education of others. Commitment to the new belief system required conversion through the sacraments of baptism, confirmation, and marriage in the Catholic Church. It also involved voluntary exclusion from practices that conflicted with doctrine, such as immoderate drinking and the general excesses of the brotherhood-sponsored dances. Such exclusion implied that the convert was asked to define religious membership as a positive adherence to orthodox Church teachings as well as as a negative association with the practices of the brotherhoods. Such a contrast called for a framework within which to study comparative religion. As will be shown in the body of this chapter and in the next, Catholic Action not only developed such an analytic framework, but also extended it to interpret interethnic relations. Once marked off from the old religious practices, the Christian had a duty not to avoid nonmembers but instead to increase the size of the congregation through "expressing love and concern for his fellow man and by giving him good counsel." If offended by another, the convert was enjoined not to despise the offender but rather to work to bring the person into the religion.

The small study group grew and began to take over leadership from the Tecpán catechists who were only able to come to the town once a month. With the assistance of the bishop of a neighboring state and the priest from a nearby town, the group was formalized as a local branch of Catholic Action and a directorate was elected and installed. At the same time, sixteen Indian couples were baptized, confirmed, and married and told that they should make the necessary efforts to carry the word of God to all the people of the town as "apostles." Literate converts who had studied the Bible and catechism in depth became catechists with special duties to direct meetings and instruct new converts.

When Accommodation to the Civil-Religious Hierarchy Failed

The group continued to attract new members and in 1956 a decision was made to move to the town's *calvario* chapel because it had larger facilities. The move from a private house to the public chapel was made with the knowledge of an early warning from the Tecpán catechists about potential conflict with the civil-religious hierarchy. Catholic Action was asking to be defined as an integral part of the Indian religious community at the same time as it was unsure of the exact nature of its role in the *calvario* chapel. The Indian converts to Catholic Action planned to complement existing brotherhood activities with religious study groups and masses.

Armed with a loudspeaker to broadcast their meetings, Catholic Action catechists clearly planned to speak out to the wider community and to begin evangelization from the onset of their tenure at the chapel. Immediately, they instituted weekly sessions of prayer, song, and study of doctrine. They coordinated these meetings with the activities of the priest, translated into Cakchiquel his sermons given at infrequent masses, and talked about the implications of the message for daily life. The Indian catechists also continued catechism classes to prepare young Indians for confirmation. From the beginning they found themselves embroiled in conflict with both the civil-religious hierarchy and the two Ladina women who served as catechists in the chapel.

The Indian converts planned to present an orthodox alternative to the pagan practices of the brotherhoods. They found that religious intentions were quickly reinterpreted in a political light because, I will argue, they challenged the separatist and subordinate models of the Indian community.

A closer examination of the activities centered at the hillside chapel will make this analysis clear. Before Catholic Action moved to the chapel, three groups had participated in chapel activities: the brotherhoods, the caretakers, and the two Ladina catechists. The Trixano brotherhoods and caretakers had maintained clearly defined relations with the self-appointed Ladina catechists. These two women encouraged brotherhood activities, helped to maintain the chapel with the assistance of occasional Ladino contributions, organized special masses and processions, and gave catechism classes from time to time. The Ladinas saw no contradiction between the practices of the Catholic Church and the brotherhoods.

Furthermore, activities of the Ladina catechists were easily translated into the two models that the traditional Indian belief systems portrayed for San Andrés. The Ladinas did not interfere with brotherhood practices at Indian shrines located throughout the town in the homes of brotherhood elders. In the context of shrine activities, then, the separatist model was honored. At the shrines the images of the saints were prepared for processions, discourses honoring the ancestors were recited, and ritual meals for the civil-religious hierarchy were held. Only when processions for the major fiestas filed up the hill of the chapel did the Ladina catechists take over, as directors of the chapel's caretakers and as representatives of the dominant segment of the bi-ethnic community. Once the brotherhoods delivered the saints to the chapel, the Indian caretakers (who form the *calvario* wing of the civil-religious hierarchy) took over jurisdiction of the images, which were paraded through the town in a special procession at the high point of the celebration. At the close of the fiesta, the images were transferred back to the brotherhoods who returned them to the shrines. Only during the period of the festival when the caretakers took possession of the saints did the Ladina catechists direct religious activities by supervising the caretakers and recruiting carriers for the procession. Thus, in every major celebration, there was an oscillation between the separatist Trixano and interethnic aspects of the community.

With the entrance of Catholic Action into the chapel, the new Indian catechists found that they were at odds not only with the brotherhoods, but also with the entire civil-religious hierarchy, which had a commitment to separatism precluding direct ties to the hierarchy of the Catholic Church. In addition, by replicating some of the functions of the Ladina catechists, the new orthodox converts were challenging the models of Ladino domination in bi-ethnic affairs. Up until this time, the Ladinas had monopolized the roles of directors and catechists in the chapel and relegated Indians to the subordinate role of care-takers and image bearers in processions.

In principle, Catholic Action was not opposed to the existence of the civil-religious hierarchy. They argued that Catholic Action was not introducing a new religion as much as revitalizing an old one. From the Catholic Action point of view, the first heads of the brotherhoods during the colonial period celebrated the fiestas of the Catholic Church in a Christian way. Although these *cofrades* did not study the Bible because "as new Christians they were not able to interpret the word of God," brotherhood officials did follow the guidelines of the cate-chism. Through time, Catholic Action explained, practices of the brotherhoods began to deviate from the Catholic Church's teachings, mixing Catholicism with traditional preconquest Indian beliefs. Catho-lic Action's plan, then, was to convince others to leave behind old Indian beliefs and to learn to use the Bible to "teach and correct the life of the Christian." As teachers, Catholic Action catechists began clearly to explain their knowledge of the Bible and to formulate com-mentaries and interpretations of sacred literature under the direction of the priest. In this way, Indian catechists hoped to redirect brother-hood practices and beliefs.

In attempting to work alongside the civil-religious hierarchy, mem-bers of Catholic Action found themselves in conflict with the brother-hoods over the nature of town celebrations. Catholic Action argued that there was no reason to spend money in holding offices and partici-pating in the often costly celebrations of the brotherhoods, which often called for large expenditures for alcohol and for the marimba that played at the brotherhood dances. Phrased in economic terms the argument made sense to increasing numbers of brotherhood members. Many saved for months just to enjoy the brotherhood celebrations and these savings were rapidly spent in a few days of drinking and dancing that often led to "fights and adultery." It is significant that Catholic Action phrased its original argument in neutral economic terms in-stead of directly attacking the form of brotherhood ceremonies and dances. Only later, when they had been forced to separate from the civil-religious hierarchy, did Indian catechists try a frontal assault on the belief system behind the rituals.

While criticism of the Indian brotherhoods was phrased in economic terms, the converts more directly attacked the traditional bi-ethnic chapel by challenging the two Ladina catechists. For years the Ladinas had informally coordinated the activities of the brotherhoods and the *calvario* officials in the chapel, taught the children of both Ladinos and Indians the outlines of Catholicism, and organized rosaries and processions for important holy days. The activities of the Ladinas had always carefully complemented those of the brotherhoods and had represented the interests of nonpracticing Ladinos in the bi-ethnic chapel. In fact, the Indians of Catholic Action had been first taught the catechism by these two women. In looking back on the experience, the converts to the orthodox movement felt that the Ladinas had not stressed understanding of the teachings for Indians who were sometimes unable to comprehend the recitation of the catechism in Spanish and more often unable to read it. Lessons were memorized and there was little explanation of their content. As one Indian commented, "Although we could repeat the catechism to all the world, we did not understand it."

Disagreement with the Ladina catechists was not restricted to pedagogy but also included inappropriate interpretations of the Catholic religion and the expression of belief. Foremost in the criticism was the emphasis placed on the material, over spiritual, aspects of religion. Catholic Action held that the Ladina catechists believed that the image of the saint was the saint itself. In contrast, through their studies the Indian converts found that the saints had a spiritual existence in heaven. Thus, there was no reason to cross oneself in front of the image of a saint, because they were only "representations"; and, furthermore, the converts should turn to God, not to the saints, for help.

Catholic Action found itself in an increasingly awkward position as it tried to evangelize from within the already existing religious community. Ideologically, they rejected the syncretism and separatism of the brotherhoods as well as the incompetence and domination of the Ladina catechists. Their ultimate goal was to reorient Indian belief toward the sacramental orthodoxy of the Catholic Church and to bring the brotherhoods within the authority of the official Catholic priesthood. Yet, as newcomers to the bi-ethnic chapel, they were forced to accept the rights that the brotherhoods, the *calvario* officials, and the Ladina catechists had in defining the nature of religious activities. The rights of both Indian traditionalists and the Ladinas were backed up by the relation of traditional religious officials to groups controlling land in the wider community. The brotherhoods and Indian caretakers were part of the civil-religious hierarchy that was administered by the Indian leaders (*principales*) of the community who gave out communal lands to impoverished Indians; and the Ladina catechists represented the Ladinos in the community who controlled virtually all large landholdings and commercial establishments and made up the nationally recognized government.

At this time Catholic Action still felt that evangelization from within was an option if some kind of accommodation with the existing bi-ethnic chapel organizations was possible without compromising their work. In this light, converts accepted an offer from the Ladina catechists to form another kind of religious brotherhood, called an *hermandad*. The terminological distinction was important because *cofradías* are Indian religious societies, whereas *hermandades* are Ladino religious organizations. In suggesting the formation of *hermandades* the Ladinas were recognizing differences between the new Indian converts to Catholic Action and the traditional Trixano brotherhoods. They were also acknowledging the Indian converts' concern with values, such as literacy and scholarship, that were traditionally associated with Ladinos. Furthermore, the *hermandad* was dedicated to the recitation of the rosary, an act associated with the more orthodox celebration of Catholicism yet consistent with the Ladinas' form of worship. Nevertheless, the old uncertainty as to the position of Catholic Action in the bi-ethnic chapel's chain of command survived this redefinition of the group as an *hermandad*.

Shared disagreements between Catholic Action on one hand and the brotherhoods and Ladina catechists on the other did not come to a head through direct confrontation. Instead, in 1958, a Ladino from a neighboring state came to the town and, by volunteering to repaint some of the images in the hillside chapel, was drawn into the controversy. At first he sided with the Ladina catechists against the Indian converts but later found that differences in belief forced him to take issue with the Ladinas' judgment of the importance of Catholic Action in the town. The Ladino subsequently became active in the affairs of Catholic Action as well as in the chapel where he took care of the images and prepared the altars for masses. The members of the *calvario* section of the civil-religious hierarchy reported his activities to the municipal authorities saying that the "outsider" was working at night in the chapel building and had plans to rob it. Immediately, he was cited by the civil authorities in a meeting in which both the civil-religious hierarchy and Catholic Action were present. Words were exchanged and the first Indian councilman (*regidor*) decided that the

Ladino should leave the bi-ethnic chapel. Catholic Action interpreted the dismissal as an action calling for their separation from the bi-ethnic chapel. When the priest and bishop came to the aid of Catholic Action's rights to hold meetings and masses within the chapel building, they too were barred from the chapel.

Catholic Action felt called upon to defend itself and definitively separated its spiritual activities from those of the civil-religious hierarchy and the town. The Indian converts decided that since they were no longer welcome in the bi-ethnic chapel, they would withdraw all support from its activities including participation in masses, decoration of the chapel for important holidays, and monetary donations to support activities. Furthermore, they decided that the action of the municipal government implied that the new group was not part of the town. In response, they decided to withdraw from all community activities and from any form of service to the town through the civil-religious hierarchy.

After being excluded from the bi-ethnic chapel, Catholic Action began to clean up the old colonial church building that had been destroyed by an earthquake and later used as a garbage dump. In 1958, Catholic Action began the reconstruction of the old colonial church in the main plaza and, after cleaning it out and restoring the adjoining meeting room, began to hold their sessions and masses there. Initially, there were problems for and persecutions of the new group, such as destruction of the altar cloth and defilement of the church plaza, that were thought to be perpetuated by Ladinos who sided with those active in the bi-ethnic chapel.

Later, reconciliation was attempted by the bishop and priest who felt that there would be more difficulties if peace were not established between the two groups. So a mass was said in the bi-ethnic chapel for the assembled members of Catholic Action and the Indian *principales* of the town. The priest offered to give the mass when the civil-religious hierarchy requested, if they would leave Catholic Action alone. He also declared that members of the groups might attend masses sponsored by either religious group as they pleased. Following this reconciliation, the town calmed, although bitterness between the two congregations continued for years and masses were voluntarily segregated.

During its early history, Catholic Action tried out a series of ultimately unsuccessful positions in the community. Because Catholic Action converts saw their first goal as dealing with Indians in the town in attempting to revitalize brotherhood religion from within, they were forced into the separatist-subordinate mold. Thus the *hermandad* came to be a new variation on the old brotherhood theme. As was the case with the Trixano brotherhoods, the separatism and subordination of the *hermandad* was ultimately based on ethnicity. It was only when the orthodox converts "left" the community that they could form a unit with clear boundaries to which others could be converted through a meaningful moral choice. Such conversion involved not only separation from the practices of the civil-religious hierarchy, but also acceptance of a new concept of the person. The analytic categories for this new concept of the moral actor, "the good Christian," were drawn from distinctions made by the Catholic Church.

Separation and the Significance of a New Choice

At the center of Catholic Action's analysis of the differences between the brotherhoods and the orthodox Catholic community was the concept of "disorder." When Catholic Action talked of disorder, they emphasized the belief that certain aspects of the celebration of *costumbre* "did not fit or agree" with religion as they conceived of it. For converts to orthodoxy, this lack of fit involved the failure on the part of traditional Indians to recognize a set of fundamental distinctions that the new converts used to describe the person as a member of the Christian community of the faithful. From the Catholic Action point of view, the person had two conflicting natures, the body and the soul, manifesting belief in both internal and external ways, in both the spiritual and material domains of life. Catholic Action did not deny the body, external celebration of belief, and the material aspects of life; rather, they held that one must stress the soul, the internal, and the spiritual to regain and maintain, through the sacraments, a state of grace. This grace in turn showed itself in the body and external activities in the material life of the individual. To follow the commandments of the Church as set out in the catechism was to show one's allegiance to God. To deviate from the Christian path and primarily to stress the body, external belief, and the material aspects of life was to show allegiance to the World. According to Catholic Action, the brotherhoods failed to understand the pivotal importance of grace and consequently showed allegiance to the World. In so doing, they were strongly associated with sin and the Devil as far as the converts were concerned.

By not distinguishing the soul from the body, the brotherhoods were characterized as celebrating the body through the "drunkenness, fights, and impurity" of the dances. The "doctrine" of the brotherhoods became the expression of conflict between individuals and families because Indians awaited the brotherhood dances to bring up problems that they were usually unwilling to express. Along with ritual meals, processions and masses, brotherhood-sponsored dances marked high points in the ritual cycle at Easter and the titular feast of San Andrés. In the tightly packed dancing hut where the marimba played long into the night, youth no longer looked to the authority of the elder, wife no longer took heed of the orders of her husband, and the Indian no longer deferred to the wishes of the Ladino. In the celebration all were free to challenge or ignore those who usually defined their lives. Sons fought with their fathers, neighbors aired old grievances, wives left the dance hut to initiate affairs, and Ladinos became involved in altercations.[34] To the brotherhoods, who recognized this variation from the nonritual social order, it was an important part of the gaiety and excitement of the religious celebration. They went no further than *costumbre* to explain the significance of brotherhood rites. For members of Catholic Action, however, this part of the celebration was the antithesis of religious worship, becoming one of the chief enemies of the soul and a place where the Devil tempts man to sin.

The disorder of the brotherhood celebrations was also thought to exemplify an imbalance between internal and external manifestations of belief as well as between spiritual and material aspects of life. The brotherhoods relied on external manifestations of belief such as the celebration of saints in processions and the decoration of altars and tombs with flowers without paying attention to the internal forms of celebration such as meditation and mental prayer. Catholic Action noted that when the members of the brotherhoods did pray—that is, recognize a spiritual aspect of belief—others in the processions were "making noise and scandal" so that their fellow townspeople did not hear the prayers. Converts held that such audiences with God should have commanded the attention of all present.

According to the new orthodox converts, by failing to consider the difference between the spiritual and material domains of life, the brotherhoods emphasized the material pole. They were concerned with the immediate material benefits of the ritual, which from Catholic Action's point of view conflicted with such other important commitments as the family. The brotherhoods had become commercial ventures demanding large contributions to cover the expenses of liquor and hiring a well-known marimba. As one Indian catechist put it, "I can't pay the contributions to the brotherhoods and use the same money for the personal needs of my family."

These three sets of contrasts—body-soul, internal-external, and spiritual-material—gave Catholic Action a single analytic framework within which to discuss the individual as well as religious groups in the community. To be a moral actor was to choose both to recognize these distinctions and to struggle for a balance between them. The separation of Catholic Action from the religious community of the bi-ethnic chapel was felt to give Trixanos the choice between allegiance to the World or to God. The choice was no longer between the pagan brotherhoods and a competing *hermandad*, because Catholic Action had discovered that both forms of brotherhoods were embedded in the larger institutional structure of a town ultimately regulated by Ladinos. For this reason, Catholic Action left the community of San Andrés, not just the *calvario* offices and the bi-ethnic chapel. One consequence of the separation, then, was to sever Indian converts from a series of subordinate relations to Ladinos in the community.

Implications of the Separation for Indian-Ladino Relations

The separation of Catholic Action from the bi-ethnic chapel was more than the creation or recognition of religious factionalism in the community. I would argue that it foreshadowed a rejection of the traditional model of Indian-Ladino relations, likened by one Trixano to the "head and the hands." The head, or the Ladino civil authorities, took care of all extra-town communications, as well as unobtrusively regulating all Indian groups in the town. The hands carried messages for the salaried governmental officers, maintained the chapel, and carried the saints in the brotherhood processions. The Indian civil officials, the caretakers of the chapel, and the brotherhoods were not autonomous institutions but rather were subordinate to Ladino civil officials on the local level (cf. Chapter Three).

In dealing with the brotherhoods and *costumbre*, the Ladino mayor and civil government usually gave free reign to the highest Indian civil official who saw to it that new recruits were solicited for the sections of the hierarchy and that the civil section was represented in brotherhood ritual. Ladino authorities often invited themselves to civil-religious ceremonies and, when it was convenient, attended the most important ones. The Ladino position in the community was reflected in the ceremonial seating order, where Ladino officials were placed ahead of the members of the hierarchy. If they chose not to eat the ritual meal at the shrine, the servers of the brotherhood carried it home for them. In this manner, Ladinos could define the extent to which even brotherhood ceremonies expressed Indian separatism.

The bi-ethnic chapel was under the jurisdiction of the Ladino government. Since Ladinos also visited the chapel, further representation of the ethnic group was manifested in the presence of the Ladina catechists who saw that the chapel was well maintained for specially requested masses and for the nonbrotherhood processions at Christmas, when images of St. Joseph and the Virgin Mary stopped at *posadas* set up in Ladino houses, and at Easter, when Ladino families set up altars for the *Via Crucis*.[35] In these processions, Indians carried the saints and prayed at Ladino altars.

In actions if not in speech, Catholic Action left the formal community institutions that were controlled by local Ladinos with their separation from the town. They refused to participate in the civil government where Ladinos nominated Indians for the civil section of the hierarchy. They did not welcome Ladino leaders of the municipal government to their meetings and made it clear that Catholic Action would operate independently of the Ladina catechists and processions that stopped at Ladino houses. In isolating themselves, the Catholic Action converts gave up the concrete rewards of service to the town; that is, they were not given rights to communal land, administered by the municipal government. Apparently this loss has been offset by the decline in required expenditures for membership in Catholic Action as opposed to the brotherhoods.

Catholic Action did not primarily interpret the separation as an avoidance of all voluntary forms of subordination to Ladinos, although this point became important in their ideology in later years. Nevertheless, they did accord the Ladinos a role in the separation. Specifically, they noted that the Ladino mayor knowingly absented himself the day of the municipal hearing dealing with the intention of the Ladino visitor to rob the chapel. In this way, by leaving the disposition of the hearing up to the Indian councilman, he was thought to be favoring the brotherhoods. The reason for this favoritism was framed in economic terms. Ladinos benefited from brotherhood celebrations because they brought with them a great deal of commercial activity. Ladinos put up the money for visiting marimbas and charged participants for each dance and also ran commercial establishments that sold fireworks, candles, and liquor to Indians. In addition, the Ladinos often made relatively substantial loans, sometimes in the form of advances, to workers who were participants in the brotherhoods. Thus, in attacking the economic aspects of the brotherhoods and their celebrations, Catholic Action was undermining the commercial interests of local Ladinos, who, I feel, have both economic and political reasons for favoring the continuance of *costumbre*. The company-town nature of local economics perpetuates the dependence of Indians on the large landholders.

It is clear that Ladinos were angered by the separation of Catholic Action from the bi-ethnic chapel. Catholic Action was the first major Indian group that was not directly under their local jurisdiction and that did not express its subordination to local Ladinos. Indians active in the separation were called "promoters" (an equivalent of "upstarts") by the Ladinos who are rumored to have retaliated by defiling the renovated plaza church.

Converts to Catholic Action were also aware of the challenge they presented to the Ladinos. In this vein, an Indian catechist commented that Ladinos were unhappy that Indians now "were capable" of reasserting the Catholic Church's rights over lands surrounding the colonial church building, although the Indians had no intention of pressing the issue, which would have endangered Ladino house sites on Catholic Church lands. Catholic Action's strategic position in the community came from its independence of the local-level institutions in the community and from its ties with the formal hierarchy of the Catholic Church, which backed the converts during decisive periods like the separation.

Catholic Action does not seem to have extended its social analysis of the belief systems celebrated in the bi-ethnic chapel to the wider bi-ethnic community in a systematic fashion at the time of the separation. In action, however, they were clearly and quite consistently moving away from hierarchical relations with Ladinos in the community. Later, Catholic Action was to extend this analysis of brotherhood religion to the bi-ethnic economic and political systems of the wider community. This further-reaching analysis was developed to point out ways in which Indians had been dominated and to propose alternatives to existing social and cultural systems based on the concept of ethnicity.

Before showing at length how the consequences of the separation and the subsequent period of adjustment and success have influenced Catholic Action's belief system and social analysis, I would like to introduce another side of the separation controversy. So far only Catholic Action's version of the separation has been presented. In turning to the account of the civil-religious hierarchy, I will be demonstrating how the traditional belief system allowed for the incorporation of the orthodox converts into the community and how the traditional hierarchy conceptualized the growing threat of Catholic Action to *costumbre* and to the existing separatist-subordinate models of the community.

The Civil-Religious Hierarchy's Perspective on the Separation

Catholic Action's initial plan to promote their activities by stressing a revitalization, or in their terms "a return" to old brotherhood practices, appears to have encouraged the view that the group presented an acceptable variation of the celebration of *costumbre* that directs townspeople to unite and show respect for social elders. The association of the new group with Trixano values is exemplified by the comment of two elders in the brotherhoods who likened Indian catechists to Trixano elders and the officers of Catholic Action to the hierarchy of officials in the brotherhoods. It would seem that the flexibility of the traditional belief system, including its acceptance of differences in expression of commitments and avoidance of confrontation of differing interpretations, made it difficult for traditionalist Indians to fend off a new religious group as long as it appeared to adhere to the tenets of tradition. As one Trixano elder said: "We are free, each one here on earth, to choose the true path that he believes will carry him to salvation. May the Catholics follow the path that they take and we also follow our path without bothering them. We are free each one of us." This comment shows that even after separation, Catholic Action was not classified as a manifestation of luck-destiny (*suerte*) outside of the control of individuals and the civil-religious hierarchy or of ladinoization leading to the domination of fellow Indians. That Trixanos were said to have the will (*voluntad*) to join Catholic Action points to the civil-religious hierarchy's attempt to accommodate the new religion as another variant of *costumbre*. The two groups present different means (paths) toward the same goal (salvation) from the point of view of the brotherhoods. (As we will see in a later presentation of the orthodox Catholic belief system, Catholic Action does not concur in this statement because they believe that there is only one path; and, furthermore, they define salvation in very different terms from those used in the brotherhood view.)

A closer examination of the brotherhood's justification of the separation, however, points to the anomaly of Catholic Action within the traditional classification of alternatives as being considered manifestations either of will (if they are considered to be within the system) or of luck-destiny (if they are outside the system of traditional commitment).

Catholic Action was initially accepted into the town as a variation of *costumbre*. When it became apparent that the group was challenging the elders of the town and the brotherhoods, the officials of the civil-religious hierarchy began to look for a way of dealing with the new group that, it seems, they categorized as an unspecified threat. With hindsight, the brotherhoods talk about the separation in terms of a disagreement over the timing of processions: "The separation occurred with the initiation of Catholic Action because they were not in agreement with the tradition to delay the time of the processions. When they separated, the people were allowed to decide for themselves if they wanted to follow. Catholic Action only believes in one God, all-powerful, and downplays the saints. Everyday, people are congregating to the religion. The [orthodox] Catholic religion remembers God, does not drink liquor, prays daily, and says the rosary. They are not doing evil things." On the surface this would appear to be a minor difference; but, on closer inspection, we can see that timing is related to the differences in sources of models for celebrations.

In events leading up to the separation, the brotherhoods cited the tradition inherited from the ancestors as the reason to hold the dramatization of the crucifixion at three o'clock, whereas the Indian converts cited the Bible in suggesting that the acts should be held at noon. In effect, the brotherhoods were saying that Catholic Action was not really returning to the old traditions because it was deviating from the very source of knowledge on which *costumbre* is based, the passing of a tradition from ancestors to descendents. Converts, however, were documenting their beliefs with the Bible and catechism and further suggesting that there was a correct interpretation that orthodox Catholics as catechists could derive from an acknowledgedly profound and ambiguous text. Expressions of commitment were rapidly becoming subject to evaluations by a new set of religious specialists.

The elders talked about the diffuse threat that Catholic Action presented to the brotherhoods in the following words, "There wasn't a precise motive for the separation, although it nearly came to a fight; but, because a primary motive did not exist, there wasn't a fight." Perhaps the inability of the elders to formulate a clear-cut reason for the events that led to the dismissal of Catholic Action from the chapel resides in the anomalous character of Catholic Action. Catholic Action's initial willingness to work within the organizational framework of the bi-ethnic chapel and their historical notion of the development of *costumbre* appear to have placed the group within the range of acceptable variation of the expression of commitment to religion as practiced by the ancestors. At the same time, the source of orthodox Catholic beliefs made it clear that validation came from a literary tradition outside the town. This view was further reinforced by the appeals of Catholic Action to the Catholic Church hierarchy of priests and bishops, rather than to the elders of the town, for advice and support as well as for ritual guidance. For the civil-religious hierarchy, there appears to have been no way to frame the attributes of this threat, which violated the conceptual scheme for dealing with the boundaries of society and social change. To "return" to Indian religion, the orthodox Catholic converts were becoming like Ladinos through literacy and their ties with institutions outside the town. They were neither Devils nor ancestors, but a little bit of both; and they were institutionalizing this anomaly. For the civil-religious hierarchy, the problem was finding a concrete strategy for dealing with a problem that they could not quite define. Thus, the actual confrontation did not involve an articulated debate over conflicting interpretations of the source of knowledge; rather, the civil-religious hierarchy found a focal point for an indirect confrontation, a visiting Ladino.

Accusations, which served as a pretext for the separation, redirected the tensions between the civil-religious hierarchy and Catholic Action toward a Ladino visitor who became a well-chosen scapegoat for the indirect confrontation of the two groups. I will argue that he was a particularly appropriate symbol to attack. The Ladino was an outsider who was meddling in the town's religious affairs by taking over the care of the chapel just as Catholic Action was a group introduced from outside the town that had come to dominate religious meetings and masses in the chapel. On the one hand, the Ladino became like an Indian serving in the chapel and it is said that he aspired to be the head of the *calvario* wing of the Indian hierarchy. On the other hand, converts were becoming like Ladinos in the sense that they were usurping the position of the chapel catechists that had always been occupied by Ladinas. Thus, the anomalous qualities of the visiting Ladino and the converts were inversions each of the other; and, so, the visiting Ladino was a near-perfect symbol for pinning down the confusing nature of the new Catholic group.

Although I am not interested in pushing these parallels too far, it would seem that the civil-religious hierarchy felt that the Ladino's intentions were to rob the chapel of the images of the saints, just as Catholic Action was, from all points of view, eliminating the central role of the saints from religion by suggesting that one should adore God, not the images of the saints. From this perspective also, the Ladino was a well-chosen symbol, one that gave the civil-religious hierarchy an opportunity for expressing their reactions to the Indian converts. The converts understood the hierarchy's message, for when the Ladino was told not to enter the chapel, the converts interpreted this warning as a dismissal of the new religious group. Moreover, the qualities ascribed to the visiting Ladino also fit the religion of the converts: "He was an unknown man who was not from the town. They didn't know his qualities, if they were good or bad." Thus, on an unarticulated level, the Ladino can be interpreted as embodying the anomalous characteristics of Catholic Action and the major differences between the two religions. In excluding the Ladino from the chapel, the civil-religious hierarchy both literally and figuratively excluded the Indian converts from the old religious system and the Trixano hierarchy.

Drawing on oral history accounts from representatives of both Catholic Action and the civil-religious hierarchy who were instrumental in the separation, this chapter has presented an interpretation of the early history of Catholic Action in San Andrés. For the converts, the first eight years of Catholic Action's presence in the town was a period of continual attempts to refine their self-definition in response to the commitment to evangelize and the reactions of both the civil-religious hierarchy and local Ladinos to the new religious activism. In concluding this chapter, I will try to demonstrate that the shifting goals and alliances of the converts were largely an attempt to reconcile Indian and orthodox Catholic identities. The resulting tension between the particularism of the Trixano concept of blood and the universalism of the orthodox Catholic conception of soul is evident from the beginning of their stay in the bi-ethnic chapel.

The dual goals of revitalizing brotherhood religion and catechizing the townspeople of both ethnic groups brought to the forefront a series of dilemmas concerning the position of blood and soul in the new world view. Orthodox Catholicism rests on the ability of the new converts to offer the individual the choice of an identity that stressed the soul and the spiritual unity of the universal Church, instead of the traditional identities which centered on the concept of blood. In action, however, the new belief system was increasingly compromised by the ethnic-based ideologies of both Indians and Ladinos.

The spiritual universalistic emphasis of orthodox Catholic ideology threatened both the separatism of the brotherhoods and the super-ordinance of the Ladina catechists. Yet, because Catholic Action evangelized within an institutional framework that reflected the ethnic basis of community, they were initially forced to fit into the molds of separatism and subordination. On the one hand, converts made a concession to the separatism of the brotherhoods in presenting the new religion as "a return" to the religious practices of the ancestors. This accommodation to *costumbre* was not total because the Indian converts spoke of *historical*, not mythological, ancestors as models for religious action. They did not view historical ancestors as symbols of separatism in terms of blood and *costumbre*. On the other hand, Catholic Action compromised their challenge to the pedagogy and beliefs of the Ladina catechists by founding an *hermandad* that was subordinated to the Ladino control of the bi-ethnic chapel in much the same way as the civil-religious hierarchy had been structurally subordinate to Ladino civil officials. In short, the converts were maneuvered into a position from which they could not offer the choice between allegiance to God or to the World as long as they worked within the bi-ethnic chapel.

The subordination of the moral actor to her or his ethnic identity is a theme discussed in traditional Trixano mythology as well as in Catholic Action's early history in the town. That the two belief systems deal with the problematic place of the Indian in a bi-ethnic Catholic society leads to the conclusion that history for the modern orthodox Catholics is the counterpart of mythology for the civil-religious hierarchy. The ways in which the two symbolic systems treat this theme vary significantly. In Trixano mythology, the individual is offered the choice between good and evil during the epoch of Jesus Christ. In the *cuentos*, the moral actor is subordinated to ethnicity after the arrival of the Spaniards (according to the bi-ethnic version) or since the division of the world among the saints (in the separatist version). In both accounts, the concept of a universalistic soul loses all significance as a core symbol for Indian identity. Instead, blood becomes the core symbol for both separatist and subordinate identities, allowing Indians to maintain one system of beliefs for Indian-Indian relations and another for Indian-Ladino relations. Both cultural identity and social organization stop at the boundaries of the town for the Indian who defines ethnic identity, religion, and town citizenship in the same terms.

In contrast, the negotiability of the orthodox Catholic identity rests on the belief that ethnic and religious identities are distinct, one being defined by blood and the other by the universalistic soul. As long as Catholic Action was subordinated to the Ladina catechists who ran the bi-ethnic chapel, the orthodox Catholics could not play out the contrast between religious and ethnic identities. Nevertheless, even during this period, the unstressed universalism (which was manifested in the application of distinctions such as that between the material and the spiritual) was used to criticize both the practices of the brotherhoods and the teachings of the Ladina catechists. The gap between the ideal and actual practices of orthodox Catholicism was narrowed when the converts were forced out of the chapel and defined themselves as being outside the community.

Once conceptually outside the community, converts placed new stress on symbols that transcended identities associated with the town. In so doing they clarified distinctions between religious and ethnic identities. Historical ancestors of the Trixanos were de-emphasized as models for the correct expression of orthodox Catholic belief. The converts began to teach that the ancestors were also subject to God's judgment, and only those living up to the teachings of the Catholic Church were admitted into heaven.

In place of the ancestors, Catholic Action put forward Christ's Apostles as the spiritual ancestors of the new religion and the models for valued behavior. They declared that Christ's followers became Apostles because they showed a commitment to God's spiritual kingdom not to "specific territories or towns on earth." Furthermore, while the Apostles were models for behavior, a person's most significant spiritual relationship is with the transcendent God. Thus, after the separation, the new converts reaffirmed the judgment that they were like neither the ancestors nor the Ladinos (just as the brotherhoods had symbolically concluded). Instead, they were orthodox Catholics because they felt that they could offer the choice of an identity not based on or subordinated to ethnicity.

5. Social Implications of a Reinterpreted Orthodoxy

This chapter deals with the way Indian converts to Catholic Action conceptualize the social implications of the postseparation Catholic belief system. The events that led to Catholic Action's departure from the bi-ethnic chapel showed converts the extent to which a belief system can be compromised in practice. Within Catholic Action the models for moral action and the expression of faith were clearly codified in the catechism and in the celebration of the sacraments. In contrast, the external relations of orthodox Catholics to the civil-religious hierarchy proved more problematic. The converts felt that their mission was to reorient Indian beliefs toward the sacramental orthodoxy of the Catholic Church and to bring the brotherhoods within the authority of the official Catholic priesthood.

Feeling that they had encountered no ready-made answers to the issue of their position in the community with regard to the long-established brotherhoods, the new converts experimented with a series of different possible stances toward the brotherhoods in their early attempts to evangelize in the town. The missionary zeal of Catholic Action, however, met with opposition not only from the *calvario* officials and the brotherhoods, but also from the heads of the civil-religious hierarchy and local Ladinos. The history of this experimentation, though painful, was to give the Catholics a new perspective on the relation between religion and social organization in the town. Initially, the first converts formed a small study group within the larger community. Later, they moved to the bi-ethnic chapel hoping for peaceful coexistence with the civil-religious hierarchy and a return of brotherhood beliefs and practices to what they believed to be a more orthodox form of Catholicism. Although their attempts to introduce orthodoxy failed, Catholic Action left the community of San Andrés with a knowledgeable nucleus of converts who had learned a great deal from the conflict of orthodox Catholic and Indian identities within the monolithic power structure of the town.

The early history of Catholic Action influenced the internal belief system and subsequent forms of evangelization. As I will show in this chapter, Indian catechists have elaborated an interpretation of the

1. The bi-ethnic township of San Andrés Semetabaj overlooks Lake
Atitlán at 6,385 feet in the western highlands of Guatemala. Agriculturalists from San Andrés trade surpluses with towns to the north of
the lake, such as Panajachel and Sololá. Indians value special cultural
affinities with Cakchiquel towns to the east, such as Patzún and Tecpán.

2. The community of San Andrés is the administrative center and focus of communal life for the township of the same name, serving some 3,500 inhabitants of the community, surrounding hamlets, and nearby plantations. One quarter of the central community's population is composed of Ladinos, an ethnic group that traces descent from Guatemala's Spanish colonists. Three quarters of the population is composed of local descendents of Cakchiquel Indians, who form the second largest Mayan linguistic group in Guatemala.

3. The main plaza is ringed by the offices of the municipal government, a new clinic, the elementary school, the agricultural cooperative, and the plaza Catholic church. The wheat growers' cooperative and the plaza church pictured here have been key forums for social change in Indian identity in the last twenty years.

4. Townspeople wait in front of the offices of the bi-ethnic municipal government. The local government includes separate hierarchies of Ladino and Indian officials. Indian town councilors are members of the civil-religious hierarchy that links the Indian civil administration to religious brotherhoods and caretakers of the *calvario* chapel. In the past, all adult Indians were expected to serve the community through posts in the civil-religious hierarchy.

5. Commercial establishments and homes of the Ladino population of the town surround the central plaza. Generally, Ladinos engage in non-manual forms of employment as owners and overseers of plantations, proprietors of stores and taverns, teachers, and local representatives of national bureaucracies.

6. Indian homes lie outside the commercial core of the town. Married brothers often build homes in their parents' compound, sharing the same central courtyard. Indians work as peasant agriculturalists, as agricultural laborers on nearby plantations, or as wage laborers outside the town on road and construction crews.

7. The *calvario* chapel overlooks the town plaza. This chapel is a focal point of Indian and Ladino folk Catholic celebrations at Holy Week and the festival of the town's patron saint in November. The civil-religious hierarchy and two Ladina women organize processions, masses, and ritual dramas at the chapel during festivals.

8. Images of the saints are carried through the town in processions sponsored by the Indian religious brotherhoods and the *calvario* chapel. Festivals begin with the assembly of civil-religious officials in brotherhood shrines located at the homes of their chief sponsors. After ritual discourses brotherhood members carry the saints to the *calvario* chapel. During community festivals, processions leave the chapel and circulate through the town where they are joined by files of towns-people.

9. After community processions, the saints are returned to the chapel. In the 1950s, the civil-religious hierarchy and Ladina catechists shared *calvario* with Indian converts to Catholic Action, a religious movement organized by the national Catholic church to promote orthodox religious belief. Because of ideological differences, Catholic Action later moved to the plaza Catholic church that they renovated and made the center of sacramentally oriented Catholicism for the town.

10. Indian bearers carefully lower carrying platforms into the *cal-vario* chapel. Later they will be returned to the brotherhood shrines. Declining interest in serving in religious brotherhoods, which are financially supported by members, has forced their consolidation. At present, the Indian community sponsors brotherhoods dedicated to San Andrés, the Virgin of Dolores, Jesús Nazareno, the Virgin María, and San Nicolás.

11. A cave shrine is located in the wilds outside the town. While the civil-religious hierarchy specializes in communal rituals in the town, Indian sorcerers petition divinities for individualized blessings in the wilds. At the mouths of caves and at hilltop shrines, pine needles are spread on the ground and candles and incense burned at altars during prayers offered by sorcerers to special saints of the wilds on behalf of Indian petitioners.

12. Children prepare for their confirmation mass at the plaza church. Weekly masses and rosaries as well as instruction in church doctrine are organized by Catholic Action's Indian catechists. Members of this pro-orthodoxy group refrain from participating in brotherhood rituals in favor of a more sacramentally and universally oriented form of Catholicism.

13. Tractors and other agricultural machinery are available to Indian and Ladino members of the wheat growers' cooperative. Development agencies have worked to increase rural standards of living through capitalistic cooperatives. With centralized instruction in new farming techniques, the distribution of high-quality seed and fertilizer, and the availability of modern storage and marketing facilities, these national and international agencies hope agriculturalists will increase local production and gain autonomy from exploitative middlemen. Access to land, however, is still the critical problem for peasant agriculturalists.

14. Despite the machinery available through the cooperative, agriculture is a labor-intensive enterprise. Indian peasants use machetes, wide-bladed hoes, and digging sticks to grow subsistence crops of corn and beans. In many cases, peasants must walk substantial distances to

reach small outlying fields. Large extensions of relatively flat land near the town are monopolized by Ladinos who hire laborers and plant cash crops. The agricultural cycle begins with the clearing and burning of dried corn stalks left from the previous year. Then, using a hoe, agriculturalists form raised rows of earth that are planted with corn and bean seeds saved from the last harvest. Planting is timed so that the young plants will be watered with the first spring rains in April.

15. New corn plants break ground early in the spring. Beans are planted so that they will grow up the developing corn stalks for support. While the corn plants mature, fields are weeded twice by hand. Over the years, new fields have been cleared and forested lands, from which fire wood is collected, are now restricted to the tops of mountains.

16. After maturing, corn is left to dry on the stalk. In January, ears of corn are harvested by hand, dried in the sun, carried back to town by peasants, and stored for later sale or consumption.

17. A plantation laborer brings cows through town from outlying pastures to a nearby dairy farm. While Indian agriculturalists prefer to work as independent farmers, many work as day laborers on local plantations, earning fifty cents a day in 1972.

18. Women in San Andrés use the same techniques in cooking as this woman from another Cakchiquel town. Tortillas are a staple eaten at every meal. They are made by softening dried corn in a lime solution, rinsing and grinding the corn, forming tortillas from the dough, and cooking them on a platter resting on three stones. Milling machines now save women considerable time and effort in grinding corn.

19. A weaver stretches and aligns the warp lines on a winding frame. The thread will later be transferred to a backstrap loom. Women work the double day in San Andrés. In addition to taking care of children, maintaining the home, and assisting in agriculturalists' tasks, women weave clothing for their families and for sale in nearby markets and tourist centers. In the past, clothing styles were specific to each town. Now regional styles are emerging and many fabrics are commercially produced.

20. A young Indian girl works as an assistant at a Ladino business. Assistants learn to wait on customers in stores and restaurants, earning between six and eight dollars a month. Employment opportunities for those young women who must supplement their family's income are very limited in the town.

21. Indian women in San Andrés sell agricultural surpluses in the local weekly market, much like the one in this view of a neighboring town. Long-distance trade is monopolized by men who visit the town during festivals, selling clothing, household goods, and liquor to celebrants.

22. The regional market is in Sololá, the capital of the department where San Andrés is located. Indians from lake communities sell vegetables, grains, and fruits. Inside the market, large-scale traders with fixed stalls sell clothing, dry goods, and meat. Souvenirs are also sold to tourists who have had a substantial impact on the region's economy.

relation between belief and social action that systematically contrasts "person," "community" and "society" in orthodox Catholic and non-orthodox contexts. Orthodox Catholics as converts, evangelizers, and apostles in the wider society strive for a consistency between intention and action in sacred and secular contexts that reflects the predominance of soul over blood. Through the development of a social ideology based on these contrasts, Indian converts have begun to emphasize changes in the broader community. These changes would open up the possibility of social equivalence of individuals in the bi-ethnic, material world, to parallel the universalism of the Catholic Church. As this chapter will demonstrate, the pursuit of this goal had led to an analysis of Ladino domination and to the belief that Indian progress rests on ladinoization.

Body and Soul: The Orthodox Catholic Conception of the Person

The orthodox Catholics believe that the individual is composed of two interdependent and conflicting natures, the soul and the body. The soul is the spiritual aspect of the individual that comes from God and through which the individual lives and understands the world. The material aspect of the individual, the body, is formed directly in the womb of the mother. The body is dependent on the soul, for without a spiritual component the body is dead.

Tension between these two natures of the individual is continuous because that which the soul desires is not reinforced by the will of the body and that which the body wants is not the will of the soul. The goal of the Christian is to balance the opposing forces of the body and the soul so that the will of the soul predominates. To do so is to achieve a state of grace, or spiritual unity with God. Jeopardizing grace are the ever-present temptations of the World, which upset the balance of the body and soul and lead the Christian into a state of sin. The individual may regain grace through a cycle of rebalancing the stress between body and soul. First, the Christian acknowledges his or her sin by repenting. Then the Christian shows personal understanding of the relation between internal intention and external action by confessing to the priest to gain God's pardon. Finally, the Christian is reconciled with the brothers and sisters in Christ in order to cease being a detrimental model for the Christian community.

The saints are individuals who successfully resolved the tension between the two natures of the individual. One catechist describes these exemplars in the following way: "The saints came to be saints because they fulfilled all that God commanded. They were obedient until they mortified their bodies; they sacrificed themselves in order not to perform vices; they did not accede to the desires of the body. Through mortification, they became saints and gained the battle over the World." Catholic Action honors the triumph of those who became saints and imitates the doctrine that they preached so that they, too, will gain admission into heaven after the purification of purgatory. As orthodox Catholics mirror the model of the good Christian, they become living counterparts of the spiritual saint.

Standing in the way of the Christian's allegiance to God and an earthly version of sainthood is the power of the Devil. The Devil is associated with the evils of the World, the will of the body, and the enemies of the soul. The Devil puts obstacles in the way of the Christian so that she or he will sin or, in other words, will follow the will of the body and favor the material over the spiritual aspects of life. With the goal of deflecting the individual from religious commitments, the Devil works through others in the community who give the Christian "false ideas and bad counsel." The Devil values liquor, money, and the "pretty girl," which lead to conflict and envy between persons. Material temptations—along with the inherent weakness of the body which causes the Christian to be too tired to go to mass and participate in the religious community—lead the Christian away from the spiritual life and internal grace with God.

The Christian is caught between the exemplary saints and the temptations of the Devil and must continually reaffirm his or her choice because the battle never ceases. As a result, many Christians lose the fight. Catholic Action has a series of stories about members who first participated in the brotherhoods and then realized that they had made a "vain" expenditure in the material world. Although they subsequently converted to Catholic Action, they lost the battle in the end because they wanted to "serve two masters; they wanted to serve the World and God." When they heard the marimba playing in the brotherhoods, they were drawn into the service of the civil-religious hierarchy, turning their backs on religion and seeking material gain.

Even those who express their commitment to God and spiritual life sometimes fall into sin. Like the individual, the Catholic Church also has a body and soul. To belong to the soul of the Catholic Church is to achieve union of the soul with God through baptism, which gives grace to the individual. Later the individual loses the baptismal union with God and membership in the soul of the Catholic Church as a consequence of sin, which leaves the individual only in the external active membership of the body of the Catholic Church. Through repentance, confession, penance, and the sacrament of communion, the soul of the Christian regains grace and returns to the soul of the Catholic Church.

As I will show in the following pages, the concept of grace is the key to a set of distinctions that members of Catholic Action use to describe the "Christian person." While the converts do not suggest that they can read the minds of others, they do believe that internal thoughts and feelings generally show themselves in behavior. What the converts aim for is consistency between personal evaluation and social behavior. Drawing from this model of the person, an individual's internal, spiritual state becomes a social fact, and those who are exemplary in Catholic Church activism can be judged to be in a state of grace. Just as communion brings the body and soul back into their proper balance, an individual's self-examination and confession of sin reorients the internal and external aspects of the person. Such self-analysis does not occur only after the fact because Catholic Action encourages members to meditate on their relations with others and to consider the relations between intention and action. Lack of proper intent is just as serious a sin as misbehavior.

Grace is an internal and spiritual gift to the individual from God through Jesus Christ who gained salvation for man. In this way, the concept of grace takes on a social dimension, which Catholics discuss in terms of the relation between the internal state and external actions of the individual. New Catholics believe that there is a match between the internal state and the external social actions of the individual, a match which allows others to gauge the individual's personal thoughts and interpret the intensity of religious commitment. Outward manifestations of grace include being friendly, respectful, and enthusiastic; teaching other converts the doctrine; and carrying the message of the word of God outside the religious community. The Christian actively expresses the state of grace through prayer and song. Internal union with God is externalized in public communication through preaching, prayer, and song with the end of being supportive of other converts and extending the message to the wider community. In this manner, the converts draw nearer to the model of the saints.

Not surprisingly, Indian converts extend this view of the person to secular contexts, believing that the individual reveals an inner self in his daily activities. Although ultimately only God knows what man thinks, converts believe that they can come to know the internal state of an individual by the form of her or his life and work. "By his fruits you will know a man," the converts declare. An individual's preoccupations are mirrored in the content of conversations, for "what a man keeps inside is revealed in the way he expresses himself." Because thoughts come out in actions and conversations, one is able to judge if a person is good or bad and if he is "concerned with women, agriculture, or religion."

Members of Catholic Action link external manifestations to internal states by saying that one must be frank in interactions with others. Ideally, a trustworthy and complete Christian says what is on his or her mind because the Christian knows that it is not good to keep something burdensome to oneself. Externalization of problems leads to their resolution and, if one has sinned, to repentance and confession. Sincere repentance involves the recognition that one's behavior is undesirable and reconciliation with God and the other members of the orthodox Catholic community. The individual must be reconciled with God because God pardons the fallen Catholic who expresses repentance "with his heart, not only with his lips." Confession is followed by a change in the internal state of the individual and her or his external actions towards others. At the end of the cycle the orthodox Catholic must be reconciled with the faithful brothers and sisters of the congregation, recognizing that a bad example has been presented to the congregation and has given rise to criticism of the religion and of the brothers and sisters in Christ.

Confession of sins to the priest and reconciliation with the Catholic Action community involve the realignment of internal and external aspects of the individual. Here the issue of the relation between intention and action comes to the fore. Christians examine their consciences, confess to the priest by accusing themselves of the sins, complete penance to cleanse themselves, and participate in communion. Both intentions (or strategies for behavior) and actions (or the playing out of intentions within an often-compromising societal context) are objects of this self-analysis. Attempting to beat the system shows that the internal and external aspects of the individual Christian are seriously out of alignment. If one intentionally sins knowing that confession is always possible, there is no remission of sins.

The stage of reconciliation with God and Catholic Action is marked by special behavior. The individual who has regained grace shows special outward symptoms of a renewed obedience to God's commandments by humbling oneself before the religious community. Those who are truly repentant will be infused with activism in Catholic Action, yet will show humility by not seeking to direct the group: "The person attends the meetings but does not preach or teach the doctrine. It is not that this is not allowed but that the person feels that, with his act, he does not have the right to direct the faithful. Then, if he continues to fulfill his duties as a Christian, after six months or so, he returns to share in the teaching and preaching." During this period, especially, regular attendance at the meeting is necessary; for, if one stops going to the meetings for even a short time, one becomes impoverished in faith and forgets obligations. A return to the religious community does not allow for noncontinuous membership or a division of loyalties because they betray a lack of consistency between intent and action. Thus, when one catechist became a *cofrade* in the civil-religious hierarchy, he was expelled from Catholic Action.

While the confession cycle directs the individual to demonstrate reassessment of the past in present action, meditation through mental prayer requires the Christian to form a judgment of the present in light of potential future action. The proper relation of thought to action is achieved by the good Christian through mental prayer consisting of meditation on one's own relations with God, others in the Christian community, and fellow humans. Meditation complements action in that, if the good Christian "always thinks and meditates on God, acting well, we [orthodox] Catholics are sure that he will go to heaven." On the other hand, action that does not follow from correct thought and intent is negatively sanctioned because sin is thought to include both thought and desires as well as actions or omissions against God and one's fellows.

According to the orthodox Catholics, the masses occasionally sponsored by the brotherhoods are not valid. The intention of such masses is contradicted by Indians' behavior in brotherhood dances (*parrandas*) where the Ten Commandments are flagrantly violated. As one catechist said in discussing the masses of the brotherhoods, "If one of my children gives me a nice shirt and his behavior is bad, will I be satisfied with this gift?" Clearly, one would not, because of the inconsistency between intent and action. In a similar way, to follow a mass given to God with "scandal" is to deny that the spiritual nature of the sacrament has relevance for behavior:

> Christians distinguish themselves by being clothed in grace
> through baptism and confirmation and should not involve them-
> selves with nonbelievers because they will fall into sin deserving
> eternal punishment. If Christians are involved in the dances of

the brotherhoods [*parrandas*] and the hour of the final judgment
or the hour of the personal judgment of death comes, they are lost
because they have found there are liquor, fights, and impurity. I
have been to the *parrandas* before and what happens is that if I
see a pretty girl that I like I invite her and after a few drinks the
assignations come.

The goal of Catholic Action is to direct both thought and action toward God and away from the World. Activism in the sacraments is
complemented by the mental role-playing of meditation in which the
Christian relates the doctrine of the Catholic Church to life:

Now I am working; but I imagine that tomorrow I will assault
someone who has money. If I die soon, with what thoughts do I
die? Where will I go? These are the questions that I ask myself. In
contrast, if I think that tomorrow I will preach the doctrine or
form a chorus and I die, I had a good thought and this is what we
need. Just as the cornfield does not grow alone and one must work
and give it fertilizer, so it is with our soul. One must feed it all the
time to give it life and one must be conscious and sure in the religion so that one does not lose oneself. We have a nearby enemy,
the Devil, who wants to take us to eternal perdition each moment.
Thus, it is important to have our meetings and our mental prayers.

God's judgment following death may freeze the individual into a compromising position at any time. Death lends meaning to an otherwise
uncertain future through contrast with the present in which the individual may still choose strategies and strive for consistency between
thought and action.

Now I would like to turn to a series of external constraints that
Catholic Action recognizes as influencing the actualization of the model
of the Christian person. Converts live in the context of a larger society
that operates with different rule systems for social behavior. In some
cases, such as elopement and the defense of others, converts may be
forced to sin in order to be good Christians. The wider context makes
different commitments incompatible. These contradictions are resolved
by classifying certain actions as "involuntary sins," in the event that
they result from conflicting orthodox Catholic and nonorthodox definitions of a particular social encounter. In other cases, converts have
redrawn the boundary between the spiritual and material aspects of
life so that the religious community can exert control over issues formerly under the jurisdiction of the wider community. In this way,

widely different interpretations of a conflict are minimized because of general disagreement over the evaluation of commitments within Catholic Action.

For the converts who live in accordance with the doctrines of the Catholic Church as opposed to those who live outside of Catholic orthodoxy and those who "serve two masters," the primary cause of sin is conflicts in social values. For instance, in a marriage between an orthodox Catholic and an evangelical Protestant, the orthodox Catholic boy has often to abduct the Protestant girl (with her cooperation) because her parents stand in the way of the union, knowing that the girl will convert and follow her husband in Catholic Action. "Robbing" the girl involves taking her away without parental consent and living with her until the parents recognize the union. Such elopements are an old practice among the Indian youths who find that family feuds often hold up the already protracted negotiations for a traditional marriage. For converts, though, the issue is not squabbling families, but religious differences that block the growth of the congregation and the young person's right to choose a spouse. (The overabundance of men in the endogamous community only adds new intensity to the controversies involving these marriages.)

The good Christian has the obligation to marry and raise a family; yet members of the wider community frown on the idea of giving up a daughter to the orthodox Catholics as a wife and inevitable convert. As a result, interreligious marriages may involve illicit robbery and cohabitation without benefit of ceremony until the nonorthodox parents acquiesce. The situation is rectified in the eyes of Catholic Action when the couple is married in the Catholic Church.

Another example of involuntary sin is the case in which an individual must come to the defense of another, is drawn into a fight, and must defend himself. Here protection and defense of the weak may bring out devalued physical violence. In these examples, the individual is not thought to have intentionally sinned. Rather the context forced him to sin because it invoked the acting out of incompatible commitments.

When dealing with interpersonal disagreements within the group, Catholic Action has attempted to redefine the boundary between religious and secular issues in order to extend its right to adjudicate disputes. Members of Catholic Action emphasize that they have dealings only with religious issues and, in so doing, are independent of the religious sphere of Ladino-controlled institutions on the local level. This desire to maintain autonomy on the local level has led to a redefinition of a "religious issue" and a further redrawing of the distinction between the religious-spiritual and the secular-material areas of life.

Catholic Action draws a line between material and spiritual laws, citing as an example Christ's refusal to judge on a Saturday a sinner who had transgressed. Catholic Action holds that Christ's refusal emphasized that his "kingdom was not of the World" but rather belonged to the "spiritual kingdom in heaven." The converts use this story in an interesting way so that it justifies the definition of certain problems in the community of the faithful as outside the bounds of the municipal authority. As Christ restricted his judgment and implied that the Pharisees should do likewise, so members of Catholic Action think that the municipal authorities should limit their influence over certain aspects of the orthodox Catholic community.

When there is a problem within the body of the local Catholic Church, it is handled by the directorate of Catholic Action in order to avoid the intervention of the town authorities. If the difficulty is serious, assistance is sought from the priest. For instance, if there are domestic problems in an orthodox Catholic family and the wife abandons the home, she is expected to go to the directorate of Catholic Action to explain the difficulty, not to municipal authorities who handle Indian affairs or to the body of the Indian *principales* of the town. The directorate calls the couple and their parents together to look for a solution to the problem so that the couple can return together to their household. (I might add that this is a very different solution to problems between individuals from the traditional one of the sorcerers, who do not bring adversaries together for a confrontation of different views.) Members of Catholic Action who feel that they have been wronged do not appeal to higher authorities to rectify aspects of the problem that affect them personally but rather attempt to correct the relationship between both parties involved in the problem.

Within the religious community, orthodox Catholic conversion has not meant that all members have internalized the new world view as part of the nature of things. On the contrary, older members seem to have had serious difficulties in making the transition from *costumbre* to orthodox Catholicism. In looking at the community of brothers and sisters in Christ, I will present material on how Catholic Action leadership classifies its membership with regard to an understanding of the new belief system and how it explains the lag between conversion and understanding. Since Catholic Action interrelates these internal difficulties with its view of the wider community, this section will serve as a preface to the examination of the bi-ethnic society.

Divergent Concepts of the Person within
the Catholic Action Community

There is evidence that Catholic Action has had difficulty in coming to grips with the traditional conception of the person and society that some of its older members bring into the new religion. Catechists divide their congregation into three kinds of members by the way in which they react to explanations of the doctrine from their brothers and sisters in Christ. First, there are those who understand explanations because they have studied religion and through this preparation can isolate the major themes of religious discussions and apply them to their lives. The second kind only half understands the discussion of doctrine and tends not to be able to achieve the continuity of behavior valued by the group. These Christians are said to swell the ranks of the congregation during the times of the year when there are few forms of recreation in the town and to wander away in the fall and spring when the town is in festival. The third kind "hears the explanation of the doctrine and understands the contrary." Although these members of Catholic Action are felt to be religious, they misinterpret talks given in the congregation because they fail to understand the nature of a religious explanation based on the new world view. It is this last segment of the congregation that bothers the seasoned catechists the most because it is composed of the older members who have faith without understanding and respond negatively to classes in doctrine.

The older members attend the meetings of Catholic Action because they believe that God exists and that disobedience to the word of God, or the Christian religion, will be punished in hell. They seek the salvation that the Catholic Church offers to the faithful but practice the forms of belief by simply copying the behavior of others. "They come only because they see that others do the same and if one is married in the Catholic Church, they also do the same." For the orthodox Catholics ritual forms are important, but they must be accompanied with an understanding of the reasons that stand behind external acts of worship. As one catechist explained: "For the Christian life, it is important to study in order to be able to have more faith in religion, to work well, and to stay clear of evil. Explanations of religion are necessary in order to widen our knowledge of religion. Instruction in the catechism is like schooling to learn how to separate good from evil." The difficulty that older members seem to have is in understanding an abstract code of religious regulation that both fixes the priorities of commitments and makes final judgments of a moral nature. In the belief system of the brotherhoods, there is no ultimate judgment of the individual who has operated within the traditional belief system because all Indians regardless of their individual wills return to God at death. Only those with the luck-destiny to make pacts with the Lord of the Wilds fail to return to God. As I have noted before, these pacts are not the result of a moral act of choice from the Indian point of view since the individual does not control his luck-destiny.

Older Indians in Catholic Action seem to be operating within the traditional conception of the person that holds that each mind thinks differently and explains variation within an accepted range of behavior through different wills reflecting a personal ranking of a larger set of commitments. Generally, there is a wide range of alternative ways in which commitment to *costumbre* can be expressed, and the brotherhoods place emphasis on activism rather than on understanding or ability to articulate beliefs. Pluralism of belief is accepted by the brotherhoods, which focus on the unification of diversity rather than on the confrontation of different interpretations. Furthermore, within the traditional conception of the individual, the issue of motivation—that is, which factors have caused a person to express or fail to express his will—only comes up occasionally. Justification for behavior in public often takes on an after-the-fact quality pointing to factors that caused a person to act in a given way.

Catholic Action operates with a very different model of the person, one in which external action matches up with internal belief and good actions come to nothing if they are not accompanied by correct intentions. For the converts, intention is a product of clarifying the relation between the teachings of the Catholic Church and the life of the individual through meditation and prayer. Intention gives the actor an active role in future behavior and is not intended to be a *post hoc* explanation of behavior. This is not to say that Catholics fail to see the influence of external forces on their lives; rather, they see some ways of dealing with these factors as preferable to others. For example, solutions to the impoverished economic circumstances that they find themselves in are multiple. Members of Catholic Action have declined to accept communal lands that place the Indian under the jurisdiction of the civil-religious hierarchy and the municipal government but have favored activism in the town's agricultural cooperative where they can play out the apostle role as well as farm independently of Ladino *patrons*. Furthermore, converts recognize the influence of external forces on the life of the Christian through the concept of involuntary sin that holds that there are some situations where the intentions of the Christian are compromised by external forces outside of individual control.

The presence of the older generation in Catholic Action appears to lead to confrontations of the two models of the person. The catechists see the problem in the following way: "The problem is that they do not understand and they miscomprehend the issues. Religion teaches and corrects the Christian. Those who misinterpret feel that they are being indirectly contradicted; that is, they feel that the explanation is directed straight to the person, criticizing him. This is when one misinterprets and criticizes his religion. If the person has his religion and at the same time another belief, or a vice, the religion must correct this. When a better form of behavior is explained to correct the faults of the sins, they misinterpret." Unlike the brotherhoods, Catholic Action does not permit pluralism of belief and feels that Christians must confront their beliefs and actions with the commandments of the Catholic Church. The older members see this as personal criticism and some leave because they do not understand that members of Catholic Action have a way of coping with the inevitable discontinuities of behavior through repentance and a sacramental reconciliation with God. "Because they don't understand this, they feel that they are nothing before God."

Catholic Action explains that the older members of the group have difficulties in understanding explanations because they did not have access to education when they were young, either because the school did not exist or because their parents did not allow them to attend the school. For this reason, they are not used to the idea of being taught and they are unable to study the catechism directly. Furthermore, the catechists are very different from the traditional intermediaries of the town. Traditional intermediaries, such as the ritual guide of the hierarchy and the sorcerers, relate the diversity of individual experiences to the common vocabulary of ritual models by interpreting and guiding the words of supplicants. The ritual guide brings individuals with different wills together for brotherhood ritual, in order to promote the continuance of *costumbre*. He acts as a guide, rather than a leader or teacher, by translating the different thoughts of each participant into correct expressions of *costumbre* in order to address God and the saints and to gain blessings for the social order. The sorcerers, on the other hand, define the source of an individual's problems as external to that person and as a part of the social context. They work to determine the social source of affliction and to restore the supplicant's well-being.

In contrast to intermediaries who practice *costumbre* inherited from town-specific ancestors, catechists are teachers of a universal doctrine that originates from outside the town and is tied to the hierarchy of the Catholic Church. Christians measure their lives against this doctrine and any deviations from the commandments are a sin that the Christians must recognize by verbalizing these shortcomings to the priest at confession and by reconciliation with the brothers and sisters in Catholic Action, because the deficient Christians have presented devalued models to the community. Individual orthodox Catholics are responsible for their own actions and must speak for themselves rather than being represented by intermediaries. They must internalize the regulations of the Catholic Church so that they can evaluate their own behavior. Converts achieve recognition in Catholic Action for activism in the group, participation in the sacraments, evangelizing, and carrying the Christian model into secular areas of life, such as the agricultural cooperative. Recognition is not based on age as in the civil-religious hierarchy, where elders are accorded the role of administrators. Rather, leadership positions are rewards for exemplary behavior and knowledge of the doctrine learned through catechism classes and self-instruction that, in turn, is passed on to others in the community.

It is no surprise that elders have a difficult time adjusting to orthodox Catholic beliefs and that many leave the congregation to return to the brotherhoods. As the foregoing discussion of Catholic Action's view of its older members indicates, the orthodox Catholics have redefined the religious symbol system and the means by which actors express commitment to it. In doing so, converts have brought a new concept of the person into the community, emphasizing soul over blood and the universal spiritual union over town-specific origin. This shift, as I will detail later, has allowed for relatively rapid ladinoization, especially through education.

Catholic Action's problems with its older, more traditional members are microcosmic versions of its difficulties in the wider community. In the last few years, during which the town has witnessed the rapid decline of the brotherhoods to the point that it seems that some will have to close their shrines and return the saints to the bi-ethnic chapel, Catholic Action has turned its attention to the wider community. After many years of quiet feuding and extreme separation from the brotherhood activities, Catholic Action is now sending out peace feelers to the brotherhoods. Orthodox Catholics separate these short-term goals of establishing amicable relations with the brotherhoods from the long-term valued separation from the hierarchy and civil authorities of the town.

Through friendly relations with Indians of the bi-ethnic chapel, the orthodox Catholics are hoping to attract converts from the rapidly declining brotherhoods. Evangelizing in the chapel has been low key. Rather than openly preaching in the chapel, catechists have begun to participate more frequently and positively to reinforce sacramental activities such as baptisms and masses. Converts hope to become a "mirror" in which the brotherhood Catholics can become aware of differences between the doctrine of the Catholic Church and the activities of *costumbre*.

The reaction of the brotherhood Catholics to the activities of Catholic Action has been a very telling one involving a recognition of the changes that the converts have brought to the town. Indians in the broader community now occasionally refer to themselves as the carriers of images in the processions and to the orthodox Catholic Indians as the specialists in religious knowledge. (Thus, when brotherhood members were faced with endless questions about their belief system, they attempted on occasion to direct me to Catholic Action for exegetical information on brotherhood belief and ritual.) This division of labor between Indian religions has its parallel in the wider community where Ladinos are the literate overseers of the plantations on which Indians work as laborers. Thus, in the domain of religion, the brotherhood Indians appear to be recognizing a ladinoized division of labor with orthodox Catholics. Members of Catholic Action, in turn, hope to level this hierarchical division of labor, just as they aspire to the leveling of differences between Indians and Ladinos in politics and economics.

By examining the Indian catechists' self-criticism and cataloging their frustrations, I have attempted to characterize some of the dimensions along which orthodox Catholic and traditional conceptions of the person diverge. Outside Catholic Action, differences between these symbols are embedded in a more inclusive series of contrasts between the religious and traditional communities or, in other words, between orthodox Catholic and Indian identities.

Ethnicity and Universalism in New Catholic Belief

Recalling the discussion of code for conduct and natural identity in Part One, we can realize that the members of the civil-religious hierarchy see both blood and the code for conduct embodied in *costumbre* as highly associated and complementary facets of Indian identity. To be a Trixano is to be born with Trixano blood that is transmitted from the ancestors, just as *costumbre,* which sets out the models for social action, has been "inherited from the ancestors." Those with Trixano blood show commitment to *costumbre* by participating in the civil-religious hierarchy, a town-specific organization. As noted earlier, the paramount code for conduct of *costumbre* refers simultaneously to the domains of ethnicity, kinship, religion, and town citizenship because of the close parallel of these domains of identity in the traditional world view. Both natural identity and code for conduct unify Trixanos.

Members of Catholic Action not only differentiate these domains or aspects of identity but also assert that some of them are not coterminous with the town. They have separated the unified domains of identity in *costumbre* into subsets of cultural identities encompassed by the religious belief system of the Catholic Church. Lower-level cultural identities, such as citizenship and kinship, are given religious counterparts that tie them into the Catholic Church and emphasize spiritual unity. A citizen of the town is also a member of the Catholic Church's territorial unit, the parish. A kinsman is also a "brother in Christ." With this symbolic reorganization, blood loses its central position as a correlate of code for conduct. Whereas to be a Trixano, within the traditional world view, one had to have Trixano blood, to be an orthodox Catholic one does not have to inherit a specific identity but rather a commitment to a spiritual symbol, the soul.

If we are speaking in narrow terms of the pure domain of religion, then Indian blood as a core symbol loses its earlier consequences as the codes for conduct embodied in cultural identities pull apart and are subordinated to the new belief system. Blood, ethnicity, and origin become de-emphasized, secular identities that the Indian "feels inside of himself." Indian converts believe that ethnicity "cannot be denied" as another domain of identity because of the consistency that religion demands between internal thoughts of the person and his external actions. Yet nonspiritual secular identities are clearly secondary to the new religious identity. Universalism unites the Indian with orthodox Catholics throughout the world, not just with the brotherhood Trixanos of the town, who note with some consternation: "We are neither [orthodox] Catholics nor evangelicals. We are like our ancestors. We perform our ritual duties because we have inherited them from our fathers and grandfathers. We respect our fathers and for this reason we must continue the *costumbre,* although there are only a few of us. We cannot permit the *costumbre* to die out." In contrast, the Indian converts do not hold up the ancestors as unequivocal exemplars. They, like all others on earth, are subject to the universal judgment of God and so one must pick and choose one's exemplars: "There were certain ancestors who celebrated these days [Holy Week] in a Christian way and this is what we do. At the same time there also existed ancestors who celebrated these days incorrectly, which is what we do not do. We imitate the Christian ancestors who left us with the inheritance of the Catholic faith. We are eliminating the other, incorrect practices. We cannot analyze if the dead were better people because we cannot see their lives." Since blood is no longer associated with religion, it becomes possible to divide the category of ancestors and follow only those who through their behavior showed commitment to the soul and the teachings of the Catholic Church.

To have such a commitment signifies that the orthodox Catholic looks to a spiritual unity that is universal and to the Catholic Church, centered in Rome, for guidance:

> All Catholics should love each other, we should love each other as if we were one. We share being brothers in Christ. The theme of Catholic Action is our unity and feeling of one spirit with all the Catholics of the world. For this reason, we exchange invitations for celebrations with other groups, participating in rosaries and [orthodox] Catholic processions. Religious obligations educate us to feel one because we have one God and one belief: my belief is the same as that of a Japanese Catholic. We carry on the same doctrine, and the hierarchy of the Catholic Church is our head. The hierarchy of the Catholic Church has studied [the doctrine] and they are exemplars that we follow because they are our pastors.

The unity of converts in the town is expressed by addressing each other by the terms "brother" and "sister" that they emphasize relate to a spiritual unity of brotherhood in Christ and contrast with the relation of common blood that children of the same parents have. Catholic Indians have extended this terminology to the relationship between the parents and godparents of a child, who would address each other as "co-parents" (*compadres*) in the belief system of *costumbre*. In substituting brother in Christ for co-parent, the Catholics reason that while relationships can be terminated, leaving fictive kin with perhaps tense and ambiguous relations with each other, "we are companions in the Church for all time." [36]

Blood is also being replaced by spiritual brotherhood in intertown relations. While the civil-religious hierarchy distinguishes Indians from other towns on the basis of dress and language (which have been handed down from the ancestors just as blood and *costumbre* have), members of Catholic Action distinguish the people of different towns by the strength of their "Catholic faith." Ideally, they take special notice of the towns where orthodox Catholicism flourishes and catechists are knowledgeable in the doctrine, seeking out the help of those considered more sophisticated and assisting those who are less. Naturally, they are not unaware of the material qualities of the people from other towns, although they judge that these emblems of identification are declining in importance as Indians change to Ladino styles of clothing and to Spanish as a universal language.

Within the spiritual community of the Catholic Church, members of Catholic Action may stress an identity defined by the soul and the code for conduct of the catechism. Outside of this domain, however, Indians must cope with the realities of the material world in which the economic and political position of the Indian is defined by the other ethnic group. In the larger society, converts must deal with the social fact that Ladinos still operate in terms of ethnicity. Ladinos invert the stressed and unstressed aspects of orthodox Catholic and Indian identities so that religion is subordinated to ethnic membership.

Within the town, the separatism of the Indian converts parallels some aspects of the separatism of the civil-religious hierarchy in religion and in legal affairs. For instance, Catholic Action has redefined the spiritual and material arenas of life so as to gain control over the adjudication of legal difficulties between converts in much the way the civil-religious hierarchy has used its own brand of customary law for cases between Indians in the municipal court. The consequences of the civil-religious hierarchy's separatism have already been outlined in the discussion of the Trixano contrast of the separatist with the bi-ethnic communities. It was concluded that separatism both masked and perpetuated Ladino domination of local Indians. In dealing with the new religious belief system, the issue I would like to resolve is whether or not the Indian converts to Catholic Action have invented a new version of the Trixanos' adaptive strategy in which Indian separatism is embedded in the larger arena of Ladino domination.

Analysis of Domination and a New Way Out

In San Andrés, members of Catholic Action stress spiritual unity with their brothers in Christ in the community, in neighboring communities, and throughout the world. They have a potential spiritual unity with other Indians in the community who can be converted to orthodox Catholicism, but who are classified until such a conversion with local Ladinos, who exemplify the material aspects of life and the will of the body.

The allegiance of the Indians who are not members of Catholic Action and of Ladinos in the community is to the World. Although Ladinos do not form an official part of the Indian civil-religious hierarchy, they are felt to use its activities in order to make money and to enjoy the dances sponsored by the brotherhoods: "The Ladinos participate more in the brotherhoods and less in Catholic Action because they do not have religion. Catholic Action does not offer them dances, but rather only kneels and says that the person should have humility before God. In contrast, in a *costumbre*, there is only alcohol and marimba. The Ladinos do not do anything spiritually. For instance, at Christmas, they dance to the radios, drink and eat special foods, and give gifts to their children." In this statement, the reference to Christmas is an important one, because for the Indian converts this holiday marks a renewal of the soul, whereas for the brotherhoods and the Ladinos it is a minor celebration.

While both the brotherhoods and Ladinos are classified as materially oriented, Catholic Action distinguishes them on another plane. Local Ladinos are thought to be too proud to humble themselves before God and to be too concerned with material acquisition to engage themselves in spiritual endeavors. In contrast, the brotherhoods are thought to be "ignorant" of religion and Catholic Action sees the possibility of "taking away these beliefs, these ignorances of the people" through the work of the Catholic Church. In short, Catholic Action feels that the brotherhoods can be rehabilitated through evangelizing, whereas the Ladinos, at least on the local level, are incorrigible in their materialism.

Catholic Action does not seem to find this view of the intransigence of local Ladinos at odds with the universalism of the Catholic Church. The universalism of the Catholic Church is predicated on the recognition of the soul. Ladinos do occasionally participate in the sacraments; yet their behavior belies the fact that they see no relation between the state of grace and behavior, and they are talked about in the same terms used for Indian converts who forsake Catholic Action for brotherhood activities. Their intentions are not consonant with the belief system of the Catholic Church. Local Ladinos lack a spiritual concern, whereas Catholic Action is quick to point out that many Ladinos in the capital are practicing orthodox Catholics and have become active in other chapters of Catholic Action.

There is an important difference between local and national Ladinos that sheds some light on Catholic Action's seemingly inconsistent reaction to members of the same ethnic group. Unlike national Ladinos, the local Ladino population has full knowledge of the ethnic origins of all inhabitants of San Andrés. This knowledge, plus their control of local politics and economics, allows Ladinos to limit the negotiability of the new religious identity. On the other hand, outside of the town, Indians who wear Ladino clothing and speak Spanish fluently believe they can stress their religious identity without being first classified as Indians.

At the core of the converts' analysis of interethnic relations is the extension of the spiritual-material contrast used to describe the person, the religious community, and the larger society. Union of the spirit emphasizes equivalence of all individuals for the converts. Just as the spiritual is associated with equivalence, the material is associated with inequality and "distinctions between persons": "For God there are no distinctions between persons. God is good and just, and we were created by Him. He knows our origin and we are his creatures, his work. Distinctions exist only in the World. Otherwise, the rich would not die, nor the kind. The most unfortunate—the beggars, the rich, the ugly, the most friendly—for him there is no distinction. When one dies, the pride, poverty, wealth, evil, honor is finished."

Ladinos are beings who lack spirituality, who make and enforce distinctions between persons. What Catholic Action is arguing is that this should not be the case if one has allegiance to God and not to the World. Catholic Action distinguishes the people of other towns not by the dress and dialect associated with *costumbre* and blood but by competence in orthodox doctrine. For orthodox Indians, then, blood becomes the symbol of inequality rather than a basis for separatism. Those who define society in ethnic terms are the representatives of domination, standing in the way of alternatives for the Indians and perpetuating their inferior self-image.

Although the next chapter details the history of Indian-Ladino relations from the converts' point of view, I would like to introduce some general information on the relation between "distinctions that exist only in the World" and their association with blood and ethnicity. For converts, domination of, and discrimination against, Indians began with the conquest, which perpetuated the categorization of Indians as inferior beings. As one Indian put it, "The Spanish race that conquered us is firm, authoritarian. It has egotistical blood—envious, critical, enslaving—and has and will continue to discriminate against us. [Through] the mixture of Spanish and native [peoples] the Ladino class originated. [This class] affects us now, belittling us, separatiɯg us, discriminating against us, making us seem inferior. They maintain unity by discriminating against us." Indians cite both discrmination on the part of Ladinos and disinterest and separatism on the part of Indians as factors that perpetuate the image of the inferior Indian.

The analysis of Indian converts points to the civil-religious hierarchy's separatism as an ineffectual attempt to evade Ladino domination. The civil-religious hierarchy values the fact that they are allowed to practice customary law in the municipal courts for cases involving Indians. Indian converts directly criticize the discriminatory bases of the dual system that is ultimately controlled by the Ladino mayor. Specifically, they cite a period early in the twentieth century when Ladinos took advantage of the dual system to apply restrictive labor laws only to the Indian population of the town. On the other hand, converts applaud the efforts of later national presidents to extend the law universally.

From the converts' point of view, ethnic discrimination has also been evident in the educational system. Indians were felt to be unable to respond to education because of their presumed inferiority. The universalistic Catholic Church put the basis of such discrimination to a test in response to the negative attitudes of Ladino university students toward Indians. One catechist summarized this test in the following words:

> Most people do not like the idea of progress among Indians. For instance, many years ago the students of San Carlos [the national university] published a bulletin stating that Indians were not suitable for education, but rather only for heavy work in the fields. This [report] was respected because the university was a respected center of high culture. However, the Archbishop [Rossell] felt that there was no distinction between people and saved this bulletin to see if it were true or not. He founded the Indian Institute of Santiago and began with Indian children, teaching them with a group of experts. After some years, the first graduation of teachers from the institute took place. These pure Indians took out the report and responded to it, saying that the Indian was also able and perhaps a little better than the Ladino, but that he did not have

the economic means and opportunities. They demonstrated the truth of their assertion through this graduation of Indian teachers who had studied twelve years.

Through the intervening twenty-five years between this educational experiment of the archbishop and the present, changes have occurred. Some Indians feel that, "Now the people understand that a person who uses his traditional dress has a head and is a human being like all others and is equal." Most, however, feel that this statement is a still-to-be-achieved ideal and one that is threatening to the Ladino. Indians feel that, although some Ladinos are in favor of progress among the Indians, the majority are opposed to such changes because they may lead to the leveling of differences between the two groups and because Indians would no longer be willing to serve as manual laborers on Ladino plantations. Nor, they feel, would the educated Indian be interested in serving in the lowest unpaid positions in the municipal government in any case.

In an ironic way, the orthodox Catholic world view gives Indians the conceptual framework with which both to analyze domination and to conceive of progress as ladinoization. The goal of valued social change for converts is a leveling of differences used by Ladinos to preserve the Indian in an inferior position. Social equivalence in the material aspects of life parallels the universalism of the soul in the spiritual domain. The traditional division of labor, which uses ethnicity to justify the Ladino as the *patrón* and the Indian as laborer, is to be supplanted by equivalent opportunities for both groups. What is looked forward to is an improved socioeconomic standing for the Indians that will bring better levels of hygiene and diet, as well as nonagricultural employment in such positions as drivers, teachers, mechanics, and students. Catholic Indian attitudes toward progress as ladinoization contrast sharply with the civil-religious hierarchy's view that becoming like a Ladino is an alternative outside the conventional set of religious commitments. Converts believe that selective ladinoization is possible as a solution to poverty and discrimination. The civil-religious hierarchy holds that such changes are outside the control of Indian society and the individual and that they will only reinstitute domination in new terms.

For the orthodox Catholics, the locus of progress varies between local and national contexts. In the town where ethnicity is still an issue, progress for orthodox Catholics means the establishment of independent, but equivalent, socioeconomic statuses for Indians and Ladinos.

This model for society has given local Indians the incentive to rally for better education in the local school, for a restructuring of the lowest nonpaid jobs in the municipal government, and for the possibility of better wages for agricultural workers. Within the town, change takes on a collective character because the individual is defined first in terms of his ethnicity by Ladinos. Catholic Action emphasizes that these are areas of life in the wider secular community that are, strictly speaking, outside the domain of religion and in which orthodox Catholics participate but only as private individuals. In institutions in the community, such as the agricultural cooperative and the school, Catholic Action is not formally represented, although a case can be made that Indian converts enact a role parallel to their religious commitments, since they refer to their work in these secular groups as being like that of the Apostles.

Recent collective action among Indians has led to reforms in the local school, but not to confrontations of laborers with the landholders. This situation is due to several factors. First, those Indians who send their children to school and are active in the advisory "Parents of Families" program (an equivalent to the U.S. Parent Teacher Association) already share the new world view that values education and literacy. Indian activism in the school, then, does not have to deal with differences in Indians' evaluation of education in the wider Indian community.

In economics, which affects all Indians not just a special interest group, the different views of traditionalists and converts make collective action difficult. Trixano Indians may be ambivalent about the *patrón*-laborer relationship, but they are most concerned with maintaining ties with "good" *patrones*. Converts tend to see such relationships as repressive and exploitative, blocking the progress of Indians and the leveling of the two ethnic groups. The differences in these two assessments of the Ladino landholder and employer make collective action difficult because it would require the unity of all Indians in the town.

Third, collective action and cooperation are alien strategies within the traditionalist Indian world view in which each individual evaluates and actualizes commitments in a slightly different manner. Fourth, priests in the Catholic Church have intervened in the orthodox Catholic analysis of bi-ethnic towns with short study sessions for Indians that both evaluate the reasons for the unequal distribution of land among townspeople and present alternatives for economic betterment. As I will show in the next section, these courses have directed Indian activism in the community away from confrontation and toward a more conservative view of social change.

In contrast to the town, where ethnic identity is stressed and some institutional changes are contemplated, the national context brings out a more individualistic conception of progress. In the urban centers outside San Andrés, Indian identity is negotiable because others do not know the origins of an individual. Generalized discrimination against Indians in employment encourages Indians to adopt the Ladino lifestyle and to experience ethnicity as an unstressed identity that the individual feels inside of himself but does not necessarily manifest to others. As one young Indian, who was educated outside of the town and has worked in the capital, noted: "If I went to the capital in traditional Indian dress to market the harvest, then I would be discriminated against because Ladinos have always taken the Indians to be inferior to Ladinos in cultural, social, and intellectual matters. If a person wore traditional dress in an office in the capital, he would be discriminated against and given more work or simpler work without responsibility. But if that same person dressed in Ladino clothes, then he would be well treated like the rest." Most Indians who continue their studies or work outside the town find that they must assume the uncomfortable role of the stranger and subordinate Indian or else ladinoize and pass as members of the other ethnic group.

The Indian concept of ethnicity as well as the emblems of Indian identity, such as dress and language, are town-specific. Beyond the limits of the town, the Indian is a stranger to both other Indians and Ladinos. One Indian recounted his travels outside the town in the following way:

> Once I went to Totonicapán for a [Church sponsored] course. We went wearing our native dress, completely clean. After class we took a walk and I noticed that we struck others as being strange and that some people took special note of our traditional ponchos. We were something of a spectacle, like clowns. Everyone looked at us. I felt ashamed. When we went to Quezaltenango we decided to take off the *rodillera* [a wool apron worn by men]. But we were still in white pants and someone commented that we must be Mexican musicians. Another time in the capital, people remarked that we must be going lion-hunting. There are many reasons why people are leaving behind traditional dress.

Not only do Indians feel subject to ridicule, but they also find it difficult to communicate with others unless they adopt the national language: "It is necessary to speak Spanish because in other areas there are different Indian dialects. It is also a problem if we come to a city where there are only Ladinos and we ask for something in a store. They do not understand us, nor would the Indians. Now Spanish has become generalized and it is necessary to speak it." Thus in the wider society both the Ladino image of the inferior Indian and the Indian conception of town-specific ethnicity contribute to the rapid ladinoization of the individual.

In national society, the locus of progress is more clearly the individual who, through advanced education and job experience, may master Ladino codes for conduct to the extent that he is able to pass as a Ladino without having his identity questioned. Although members of Catholic Action assist youths showing promise and seeking education outside the community, they are very ambivalent about the result. They want the educated youth to return to the town and assist the progress of the entire community. At the same time, the Indian converts realize that there is no place for an educated Indian in a community whose division of labor is based on ethnicity. Perhaps the greatest fear of the parental generation is that their sons will cultivate individualistic progress to the extent that they will become dominators of other Indians. This fear echoes those of the civil-religious hierarchy.

Collective concern with the future of San Andrés and individualistic conceptions of progress outside the community are responses to differences in the negotiability of identity in the national and local arenas. They are also reflections of the two aspects of the orthodox Catholic conception of the person. Orthodox Catholic ideology stresses the individual as the locus of choice between good and evil. The individual is responsible for consistency between thought and action in order to be able to regain or maintain the state of grace. Unlike traditional Indians, orthodox Catholics cannot depend on others to speak for them because all are accountable directly to God for their own actions and omissions. Catholic doctrine, however, balances this individualism with the necessity to collaborate in the community of Catholic Action. Grace is both internal and individualistic, but also external and social. Those in the state of grace manifest it through activism in the affairs of Catholic Action and a desire to explain orthodox Catholic teachings to fellow members and potential converts.

Ideally, Catholic Action envisions a balance between the individualistic and collective conceptions of progress. Since education in the broadest sense is felt to be the means through which progress is achieved, the activities of Catholic Action both benefit the spiritual growth of the Catholic and promote possible economic leveling of Indians and Ladinos. Literacy in Spanish and the ability to express oneself and evangelize make the Indian a better Christian because they are directed toward the activities of Catholic Action. They are external manifestations of the internal state of grace. Through preaching and bringing others into the group, the faithful are both practicing these new skills and teaching them to others. Individual achievements should benefit the entire group. These achievements are distinguished from the image of the Ladino who uses education only for economic gain at the expense of others.

Apostles in the Material World

One duty for practicing orthodox Catholics is to carry religious teachings to those outside of the Catholic Church as the Apostles did. One Indian catechist explained his concern for those outside the Catholic Church in the following words:

> If I were a faithful Christian and all alone, I would still have the obligation of being an apostle, of exhibiting good behavior at work and carrying the message of the word of God to others who are not Christians or to fallen Christians. By being a good example and with my explanations, I would be able to assist people so that they would join the congregation, converting to good Christians. I would explain obligations and duties. This can be done not only with individuals but also with groups that work together for a *patrón*. One can speak with workmates, evangelizing them. This is the obligation of the good Christian. Not only the catechists, but all good Christians can carry the message to the fountains and corn mills where many people congregate. If one is a good Christian, one is an apostle because he carries on the word of God.

For the Catholics, one's spiritual state is manifested in daily action within both the orthodox Catholic and the wider communities.

Thus, it is not surprising that Indian converts have carried their spiritual models, the Apostles, over into nonreligious aspects of life. As a community, Catholic Action does not directly participate in other organizations in the town. Active members of the group, however, have been leaders in and promoters of school committees, literacy programs, and an agricultural cooperative. Converts have even stated that they would take on positions in the municipal government if they were appointed to the traditionally Ladino positions that are recognized by the national government and carry no brotherhood obligations.

In consonance with the social ideology of leveling material distinctions, converts have become active in national institutions that impinge on the town. Converts are active in these secular organizations because they deal with skills that are valued within Catholic Action, such as education and literacy, and because the organizations are working to resolve dilemmas in the Christian life, such as the conflict between material obligations to the family and spiritual obligations to the Catholic Church. Orthodox Catholics are eager to send their children to the local six-year elementary school, unlike many brotherhood Indians who feel that education competes with time that would be better spent in learning agriculture and assisting fathers in their fields. In contrast, orthodox Catholics see education as giving the student skills that will benefit both spiritual and material life: "It is very important for our children to study in the school. If they study, they can defend themselves in their lives. Those who are interested in religion can give better explanations and make Catholic Action greater. They will be our successors and will be left more capable than we are through their education in the schools." Materially, education leads to less physically exhausting and higher-paying nonagricultural jobs where fluency in Spanish and literacy are required. Those who are familiar with Ladino ways "can defend themselves" or represent their interests to Ladino authorities within and outside of the town so that they will not be taken advantage of and will be listened to. In religious matters, students will be able to use education to further the work of Catholic Action, increasing the number of members who are literate and can serve as catechists.

In pursuance of these goals, children of Indian converts were, fifteen years ago, the first to secure scholarships and to continue their education on a higher level outside the town. Before this time, scholarships had been made available from time to time; but parents of Indian students had not permitted their children to take advantage of higher education. The orthodox Catholics have been able to reap some of the rewards of education for the wider community through adult literacy programs sponsored by the local school and taught by secondary school students as a requirement for their degrees. The group has encouraged Indians to return to the town to teach these classes and has collaborated with the school in securing adults—who are often hesitant to go to the school and exhausted after a day's work—to attend the classes.

Orthodox Catholics lament the fact that illiteracy is extremely high among adult Indians in the town and that such programs have had only a qualified success for a relatively small number of Indians. Furthermore, they note that a high literacy rate continues to influence the organization of Catholic Action in that leadership positions in the group tend to circulate among a small group of members who are literate.

Through activism in the school, converts have discovered that what they perceive as an egalitarian national policy in education and government is not carried out by local Ladinos who mediate between the town and national government and control the local school. The government's educational policy requires all children in the country to attend elementary school. Local Ladinos have subverted the intent of this policy in the past by requiring a payment for school-sponsored snacks. This payment plus normal school fees is felt to discriminate against Indians by pricing tuition over the heads of poor agriculturalists with large families. Indians have successfully brought complaints against this kind of discrimination to the attention of national officials.

The second institution in which Catholic converts have been active is the wheat growers' cooperative of San Andrés that was established in the early sixties. Even before the cooperative was formed, the Catholic Church had shown interest in cooperativism because "God created the world for all human beings, not just for a few." The bishop recognized that all Catholics have material needs and that "poverty makes one forget God." Through courses offered on religion and cooperativism, the Catholic Church wanted to stimulate the creation of savings and loan cooperatives, so that Indians might avoid the conflict between providing for their families and fulfilling their obligations to the Catholic Church. A catechist from San Andrés attended the course, which pointed out that productive agricultural land belonged to a small minority of the population while the majority was landless.

The proposed solution to uneven land distribution was cooperatives in which Indians could save small amounts of money and take out low-interest loans so that each individual eventually would have his own land and would not have to "sacrifice himself with the *patrones* and live in fatal poverty." The Catholic Church's solution to poverty directs individuals to circumvent the social and economic domination of Ladinos without challenging the foundations of the skewed distribution of economic resources. To this end, the Catholic Church has organized, administered, and financially backed "Indian" cooperatives in other areas of the Guatemalan highlands. The focus of programs within these cooperatives is the individual Indian who, it is hoped, will become a self-sufficient agriculturalist.

The Catholic Church's course in cooperativism sparked interest among the converts; but the cooperative was not founded until the early sixties when a local Ladino brought cooperativism to the attention of the wider community in an attempt to resolve the problem of the large seasonal migration of Indians to coastal plantations. A local, independent agricultural cooperative was organized, and Indian converts as private individuals took an active leadership role from the beginning. Later in the decade, the San Andrés cooperative affiliated itself with Agricultural Cooperatives Development International (ACDI). This move tied the local organization to a national network of cooperatives, educational centers, agricultural extension agencies, and international support through U.S. Agency for International Development. The long-term effect of the national affiliation has been a reduction in the amount of influence local Ladinos can exert within the new organization. The cooperative appears not to have replicated the local ethnic division of labor or the separatist and subordinate models for Indian-Ladino relations on the local level. It is significant that converts conceive of their participation in the cooperative in religious terms.

Converts see their role in the cooperative as one that complements the technicians who staff the bureaucracy as full-time clerks, bookkeepers and managers: "If the cooperative gives seed and fertilizer without advice, one cannot live better. In the course, we learned that we have the obligation to be like apostles. We have to be the propagators of cooperativism and teach the people who are still ignorant." If this comment has a familiar ring, it is because it closely parallels the orthodox Catholics' description of their work in Catholic Action, "just as a cornfield does not grow alone . . . so it is with our soul." The similarities between the two organizations make them counterparts in the material and spiritual arenas of life for orthodox Catholics.

The cooperative is seen as universal by converts in the sense that not only the people of the town, but also those of other places and of both ethnic groups are members. The ideology of the cooperative is "one for all and all for one," a material version of orthodox Catholic beliefs. Furthermore, converts as private individuals are taking on the task of explaining the rights and obligations of cooperative members in Cakchiquel during the general assembly of members. This form of communication is something new for the cooperative, and converts attribute interest in the idea of translating the regulations into Cakchiquel to their own earlier attendance at the cooperativism school where they came to understand how the cooperative worked. The idea that the individual has the obligation to transmit the knowledge that he has gained through study to others in the community seems to have been extended from Catholic Action to the cooperative. Converts also note that their relatively active role in cooperative meetings is not new for those who have participated in Catholic Action and that "we have benefited because we know what a meeting is and what it is to live in society."

On first inspection, it would seem that converts have found a niche in the material world where they can extend the social implications of orthodox Catholic belief. The cooperative reflects a unity of purpose that socially and spatially transcends the "distinctions of the World" used to mark and subordinate Indian ethnic segments of the population. Like the Catholic Church, the cooperative relates the individual to mankind without intervening divisions into ethnic groups. All individuals who choose to join the cooperative are members of equivalent standing who share the same rights and duties. Each contributes wheat to the collective marketing of the harvest and benefits from discounts the cooperative receives on large purchases of seed and fertilizer. Educational programs work to level differences between individuals as they relate to the understanding of cooperative ideology and technical advances in agriculture. Furthermore, increased harvests, which follow from using fertilizer, feed back onto relations in the bi-ethnic community to the extent that self-sufficient Indians do not have to subordinate themselves to Ladino *patrones* as laborers.

Nevertheless, with increasing activism in the cooperative, converts have uncovered a problem with the actualization of the material counterpart of orthodox Catholicism. In brief, some converts have come to believe that the cooperative is unable to deal with an economic situation that is the product of a history of domination based on ethnicity. Converts observe that the economic gap between the Ladino landholder and the Indian peasant has not narrowed significantly from the time of the founding of the cooperative. The two ethnic groups do not benefit equally from the cooperative because most of the land in the municipality is controlled by a handful of Ladino families. These families own much of the flat land adjacent to the town that is especially suitable for wheat and lends itself to the profitable use of modern agricultural machinery. Converts point out that Ladinos reap a decidedly greater benefit from the cooperative than do Indian peasants who occasionally supplement subsistence crops of corn and beans with small plantings of wheat. The Indian remains a marginal agricultural-ist, even with the cooperative, because this form of development does not significantly challenge the disparity in size of landholdings between the ethnic groups.

Ethnicity comes back into the analysis of Indian converts despite the universalism of the orthodox Catholic and cooperative ideologies be-cause it is an historical identity that has molded present-day economics. Orthodox Catholics as apostles in the spiritual or material world are still Indians in the community of San Andrés, and present universalism does not compensate for the history of ethnic subordination. To pre-sent a full account of the way in which Indian converts have begun to see their present position as historically determined, the next chapter will deal with the new Catholic Indian perspective on the social history of the town during the last hundred years.

6. Oral History and the Negotiation of a New Indian Identity

Trixanos in the civil-religious hierarchy have organized their ideas about the creation of society into mythology. In a parallel fashion Indian converts have systematized their explanations of the forces that have shaped Indian subordination through oral history as a belief system. Without a doubt, members of Catholic Action have been taught different versions of the past by elders, the hierarchy of the Catholic Church, and teachers in the bi-ethnic school system. What converts have begun to do is to resynthesize such accounts to develop history as a belief system for representing alternative models of a bi-ethnic society and for presenting different strategies for dealing with ethnic subordination.

Oral history is not a simple narration of the past. Rather, history (like myth) is continually rephrased both to direct and to deal with the changing character of relations within the Indian community and relations between ethnic groups. History as a belief system is filtered through the realities of the present; it has the ideological benefit of hindsight. The question one must ask is, Does this belief system clarify or mystify the Indians' understanding of the mechanisms that subordinate them? In answering this question, this chapter will examine the Indians' movement away from emphasizing mythological models and toward historical models as alternative ways of analyzing their social world and phrasing the relations of ethnic and religious identities.[37]

In describing the history of San Andrés during the last century to show how universalism is compromised, Indian converts single out two periods for special attention. Oral history as a symbol system contrasts the decades of forced labor under President Manuel Estrada Cabrera who governed the country between 1898 and 1920 with the period of educational and labor reforms under Jorge Ubico who was in power from 1931 to 1944.

The ideologies and political actions of both administrations are thought to have had a definitive impact on interethnic relations that has carried over into the present. Cabrera is associated with racism that "enslaved and impoverished" the Trixanos, while Ubico has come to embody a secular universalism that was necessary, though not sufficient, for the leveling of distinctions between ethnic groups. Indians attribute significance to the sequence of these governments because the exploitation and subordination of Indians during the Cabrera administration limited the effectiveness of Ubico's economic and educational reforms. Nevertheless, these reforms are pointed to as the first evidence of a split in social ideology between the government and the local Ladino landholders who had earlier been perceived as politically homogeneous in their desire to control Indians as a subordinate agricultural labor force.

This perceived ideological divergence among Ladinos has allowed converts to localize symbols of domination to the town and to associate secular universalism with such national organizations as the government, which provides scholarships for Indian students, and ACDI, which manages the cooperative. Through the local branches of the school and cooperative, converts have attempted to assert universalism in the material world through separatism from local Ladino-dominated politics and plantation economics. The bi-ethnic membership and administration of the universal organizations, however, has brought constant conflict in San Andrés over definitions of their local activities. Indian strategy for stressing universalistic definitions has been to appeal to higher authorities in the government and ACDI to adjudicate disputes. In these ways earlier dependence on local *patrones* for access to land and work has now been transferred to national organizations that provide financing for advanced schooling and to national banks that advance credits for the cooperative. This chapter will argue that the converts' emerging analysis has left unresolved the new dependence on national institutions.

Racist and Universalist Societies in History

Oral history accounts related by converts begin with descriptions of the late nineteenth century when the social isolation of San Andrés was broken by the settlement of increasing numbers of Ladinos. These outsiders found that governmental legislation and the ignorance of local Indians allowed them to acquire large parcels of land and to subordinate Indians as agricultural laborers. The rapid ascent of Ladinos to local power, loss of Indian lands, decline in productivity on Indian farms, and rapid increase in periodic migration are blamed on new legislation, which required formal deeds to prove land ownership, and on subsequent forced-labor laws. In both cases, Indians are portrayed as being helpless because of the ethnic basis of Ladino domination and the Indians' lack of knowledge of the national political and legal systems.

Although Indians have come to associate this period with increasing contact with Cabrera's forced-labor policy (*el mandamiento*), they point out that the initial penetration of Ladinos into the town occurred during the administration of Justino Rufino Barrios (1873 to 1885), when legislation requiring formal deeds to prove land ownership was enacted. Ladinos are seen as having manipulated the procedure of acquiring deeds and as playing on the Indians' lack of familiarity with the Spanish language and national law. As one Indian noted: "In the times of Barrios, Indians had a great deal of land, large extensions of land near the town. In those times, Indians were very backward; they didn't read or speak Spanish. Ladinos took advantage of this to draw up deeds. They gave a few cents for the land to Indians who did not understand. Their [the Indians'] livelihood was threatened and they became accustomed to working on the coast; they left their lands to be sold. Some Ladinos even gave liquor to the people so that they would sign the deeds." Indians who lost land and gave up subsistence agriculture became a source of labor for plantations both within and outside the town. It is this labor pool drawn on through forced labor that first established the pattern of cyclic migration to the coast.

According to the converts' oral histories, the social reality of the Trixanos was defined in terms of ethnicity by Ladinos during the *mandamiento* of the Cabrera period. Indians as an ethnic group were pressed into service with only token payment as laborers to open up the undeveloped southern coastal region of the country for plantation agriculture. Local Ladinos were not adversely affected by this decree. Instead they took advantage of the precarious economic position in which Indians found themselves by buying up Indian land and setting up large farms on which the remaining Indians could work. This period is credited with regularizing plantation agriculture and the position of Indians as impoverished laborers (*mozos*) for Ladinos on both the local and extra-local levels. Subsequent decades of economic prosperity in San Andrés had little positive influence on the economic position of the Indian population because of the uneven distribution of land resulting from the Barrios and Cabrera periods.

The *mandamiento* (which is not distinguished by Indians from the *repartimiento*) codified plantation owners' rights to draw on the populations of Indian communities as pools of cheap labor for the development of coffee and cotton production on the south coast. Forced labor is described by one Indian in the following terms:

> The *mandamiento* was an order that had to be complied with. The government was on the side of the rich landowners. He who didn't comply was sent to jail because he disobeyed the law. The plantation owners [*finqueros*] did not come here but sent a request to the governor. The governor forwarded the request to the mayor, saying that so many laborers were awaited on a given farm for such a date. The laborer here had to comply. It was not important if he had a harvest, if he was sick, if he didn't have money or could not stand the sadness of his family.

Recruitment of labor under the *mandamiento* was not done directly by the plantation owner, but rather by the administrative chain of command in the government. Local authorities selected laborers to fill the order by leaving money at Indian homes. This payment, which could not be refused, contracted the Indian laborer to work the required period. After the Indian had returned home from two to four weeks, it is said that the Indian was once again liable for service. Those who escaped work as agriculturalists were drafted by the government as laborers for road work or for service in the military.

Oral historians note that because Indians were continually subject to work outside the town, many were unable to cultivate corn and beans on their farms. Agricultural production on Indian lands declined sharply, independent subsistence production was difficult if not impossible, and other sources of income were necessary to finance the purchase of staple foods and clothing. To supplement their incomes and avoid working outside the community, many looked to local Ladino landholders for work so that they might remain with their families. Others avoided the insecurity of forced labor by migrating to large coastal plantations where they became permanent workers in residence (*colonos*). Economic insecurity, migration, and the growing settlement of Ladinos contributed to further sale of Indian landholdings and increased Indian dependence on Ladinos for access to land and work.

For local Ladinos, the *mandamiento* was a period in which workers and land were available and agricultural surpluses found a ready market in the coastal region that was not self-sufficient in the production of staples. Because of the "pull" Ladinos had with local and departmental authorities, they were able to go to the departmental capital with gifts for the governor who then permitted landowners to retain laborers without fear that the workers would be ordered to the coast. From the Indian point of view, Ladinos as an ethnic group had firmly established their position as *patrones* both within and outside the town at this time.

The consistency of Ladino attitudes toward Indians was evident from the collaboration of governmental administrators (who balanced local and regional demands for Indian labor) with local plantation owners. Furthermore, the courts defined the Ladino as the legally backed master of his laborers. Many stories are told by Indians of abuses of the *patrón* position. Beatings and jailings of Indians by Ladinos were not uncommon, especially when a laborer disobeyed or answered back to his *patrón*. The local courts are said to have inevitably backed the claims of the landowner over his laborers.

The close of the Cabrera presidency in 1920 marked the end of forced labor. Indians returned to the town and production on Trixano farms rose, although the loss of land during the *mandamiento* meant that fewer Indians farmed their own soil. Those who managed to hold on to land were often left with peripheral and less-productive lands well outside the town.

Throughout the 1920s and 1930s commerce between the coast and San Andrés increased and the town retained its name as an important commercial center for grains. The most important product was corn, which was sold to the coast during the months of scarcity just before harvest. Because of the loss of lands, however, Indians comment that "this business was for them, not for us." While plantation owners sent wagons to pick up local agricultural surpluses, Indians often transported smaller quantities in hundred-pound bags carried on their backs as they made their way to the coast to work as seasonal laborers.

In contrast to the Barrios and Cabrera period, the presidency of Jorge Ubico is characterized by the Indians as a time of law and order in which Indian rights were protected by legislation that was universally applied to Indians and Ladinos alike. During the tenure of this government, from 1931 to 1944, both Ladinos and Indians were taxed in labor, the rights of agricultural laborers were protected, and schools were opened to Indian attendance. All citizens of the country were required to assist in the construction of new roads linking smaller towns to the capital by contributing six days of work for each half year or by contributing wages for a substitute laborer. During the Ubico period, the rights of laborers were protected by labor reforms restricting corporal punishment and allowing laborers to defend themselves against arbitrary punishment by their *patrones*. In addition, schools were subject to legislation that made universal attendance compulsory. The intent of Ubico's new policies seemed to be centralization of the administration of the country by ending the social isolation of rural population centers. As a result of the implementation of his programs, small towns were tied into a communications network that centered on the capital; plantation owners could not mark their independence of the government by enforcing their own informal labor codes; and Indians were integrated into a nation-wide school system.

The early 1940s are remembered in oral history as "a time of more order" when the presidency of Ubico promoted greater justice for Indians, more understanding between the ethnic groups, and growing communication and transportation facilities. When the subject of Ubico comes up, there is an inevitable contrast between the repressive Cabrera regime and the more universalistic policies of Ubico concerning the rights of the worker with respect to his *patrón*:

> Before the time of Ubico, Ladinos were the dominators of Indians. For making a mistake, *patrones* beat workers and brought them to jail. Cabrera did not care for the indigenous people, only for the Ladinos. He maintained Indians as slaves. When Ubico entered the government, there was a change because he created an article in the constitution which made work sacred. The worker while he is working is in a sacred position. If the *patrón* came to bother him, and the laborer retaliated, it was because the *patrón* deserved it. *Patrones* obeyed this and there was no more offense.

Indians feel that during the Ubico presidency laborers were no longer "slaves" who could be mistreated for mistakes or disagreements with the *patrones*. If the *patrón* offended a laborer, the laborer had the right to defend himself if he was doing his duties. As the rights of the *patrón* came to be legally restricted and agricultural labor "given more respect," Indians talked more of unity and understanding between the ethnic groups.

The second governmental policy that Indians interpret as moving toward more egalitarian treatment was the *vialidad*, or the taxes paid to the government in the form of labor, primarily in road construction. Each adult male was required to work on governmental projects one week every six months or to pay a one-dollar tax instead (cf. Skinner-Klée 1954:107–108). Indians feel that since both groups were liable for the tax, the government did not show favoritism to either group: "In the time of Ubico, there was more unity between Indians and Ladinos. For him there was no distinction [between ethnic groups]. Ladinos also had to do a week of *vialidad*. They paid if they did not want to go. For this reason one sees that this was a government that treated the two [ethnic groups] in the same manner." Indians have chosen to stress the fact that both ethnic groups were subject to the same law, rather than to point out that in practice this policy taxed the ethnic groups in two different ways. Ladinos were economically able to pay the tax directly, whereas Indians contributed in the form of manual labor. Oral history stresses the universalism of this policy rather than noting ethnic differences in fulfilling obligations.

Another of Ubico's innovations, the vagrancy laws, is also not interpreted as having singled out Indians in a discriminatory fashion. Although vagrancy laws tended to regulate Indian labor, Indians in retrospect see them in a positive light as having reinforced the high value placed on work. Agriculturalists with substantial landholdings were exempt from this form of labor regulation. Vagrancy legislation established that laborers (*jornaleros*) who owned at least ten *cuerdas* of land were required to present verification from *patrones* that they had worked at least 100 days a year. Those who owned less than ten *cuerdas* were legally required to show that they worked 150 days a year (cf. Skinner-Klée, 1954:110–114; 118–119). Laborers were dependent on landholders to fill out their booklets indicating that they had worked the requisite number of days. Labor protection laws and freedom to choose whether to work for a *patrón* in or outside the town apparently buffered any feeling that Indians were being singled out for special legislation.

Ubico is also admired by the present-day Indians for making school attendance compulsory and for fining parents who kept their children out of school. At the time, however, it is said that the law was not appreciated by Indian parents who feared the treatment that their children might receive under Ladino school teachers. According to oral histories, Trixanos felt that education was useless for agriculturalists and missed the assistance of the youth in the fields: "Ubico put a school in each municipality. Also there was a law that fined those who did not send their children to school, Q2.50 [$2.50]. As they earned 15 cents [a day], this was a large fine. The government did this because we [Indians] were ignorant and did not want to send our children to school. Because of this law, the Indians can now read, write, and half-speak Spanish." During the Ubico period the local school (which had been a Ladino-oriented institution before this time) was required to educate greater numbers of Indian children than it had before, giving them some exposure to Spanish and literacy. Mandatory school attendance, although often hedged by recalcitrant parents, is now credited with improving interethnic relations and increasing the employment opportunities for Indians. It is felt that as more Indians become fluent and literate in Spanish they could also better explain and defend themselves. As a result, problems between *patrones* and laborers were less common and it was more difficult for Ladinos to take advantage of Indians in the courts. Furthermore, Indians could understand the orders of people outside the town, such as the leaders of the road crews or plantation managers, so that they were no longer punished for misunderstanding instructions.

For Indians, Ubico stands not only for universalism as opposed to racism, but also for a new distinction between local and national Ladinos. Looking back at the Ubico period Indians do not see Ladinos as a monolithic block to the same extent as they were during the Cabrera period. Instead, Indians emphasize the ways in which the national government limited local Ladinos' rights over laborers and restricted their ability to discriminate against Indian children by excluding them from the school system. This view of the government's concerns as distinct from the interests of local Ladinos is also evident in the Indians' interpretation of the subsequent revolutionary period when the Arbenz government set up local agrarian committees to look into the possibility of redistributing lands from large plantations to landless peasants.

The revolutionary governments of Arévalo and Arbenz from 1945 to 1954 came during a period of serious economic decline for San Andrés. A combination of the loss of soil fertility and contracting coastal markets made farming for profit an increasingly marginal enterprise. Chemical fertilizers were unknown in San Andrés and the practice of burning or burying corn stalks after the harvest was not effective enough to replenish the intensively farmed topsoil. In addition, surpluses were no longer grabbed up by corn-hungry markets because the south coast was producing adequate quantities for its own consumption by this time.

As local ecological circumstances and the loss of external markets made local plantations less profitable, Ladinos began to emigrate to urban centers. The closing of small plantations left fewer jobs for landless peasants who in turn were forced to seek employment on coastal plantations. Seasonal migration for plantation work was not a novelty for Trixanos. The Indians note that during the period of forced labor they became accustomed to temporary migration to the coast so that it was natural to continue this pattern in times of local scarcity, especially in the months when local corn reserves had been exhausted and little agricultural work was available in the town.

According to oral histories, the revolutionary governments had little effect on San Andrés (besides giving it a generator for electricity and a school for one of the surrounding hamlets) until 1952 when a local committee was formed to carry out the policies of the agrarian reform. The goals of the reform were to reduce rents on agricultural lands to a token payment and to break up large, underfarmed landholdings to make more land available to landless agriculturalists. Although the program was never effectively implemented in San Andrés, Indians describe the Arbenz period as one of increased antagonism between Indian laborers and Ladino *patrones*. Landholders were afraid that their lands would be chosen for redistribution, while Indians felt that any beneficial changes and their initiators would be wiped out by the next change in government. Both groups avoided open criticism of the reform because they believed this would lead to being denounced as "anticommunists" and result in jailings or other severe punishments.

In San Andrés, the lands owned by local Ladinos were never actually redistributed by the reform, although there were moves to break up a nearby plantation owned by an outsider. Even this move was never carried out since paperwork in the capital was delayed. Local Ladinos successfully put off redistribution of their lands by telling tenants they could cultivate land without paying rent, in addition to their being paid for their work on local plantations. Since the land in these cases would be under cultivation by local peasants, it was felt that no "motive for criticism" would arise and that the lands would remain intact, as they did. Actually, rent-free land was not much of a concession since under the reforms rent had been legally reduced from fifty to five pounds of harvested corn per *cuerda* (cf. Skinner-Klée 1954:134).

With hindsight, oral histories suggest that the counterrevolution of Castillo Armas in 1954 was well received in San Andrés by Ladinos and Indians, both of whom welcomed his Ubico-like attitude toward social reform. Actually, there is some evidence of a gap between oral histories and actual events of the counterrevolution. Evidently, some Indians fled the town and one Ladino family was forced to relocate permanently after the counterrevolution. Nevertheless, Castillo Armas is said to have calmed antagonism between landowners and laborers in the countryside and to have made it clear that agrarian reform committee members who fled during the counterrevolution for fear of reprisals would be safe from governmental attack.

Oral histories as related by converts describe a sequence of models of

Guatemalan society, focusing on the relations between government, local Ladinos, and Indians. The dominant ideologies that guide social relations within each model vary in the extent to which Indians may separate natural identity, or blood, from the code for conduct of subordination. This issue is of first importance to orthodox Catholic Indians who seek universalism in the material world to parallel the spiritual unity of membership in the Catholic Church. Valued universalism provides a national context in which equivalent social and economic opportunities are open to all individuals and orthodox Catholic Indians may negotiate ethnic identity with an encompassing religious commitment.

As a symbol, the Cabrera presidency presents an extreme of Ladino dominance in which Indian identity was defined in inflexible terms both inside and outside the town. Indian blood was the basis for an ascribed inferiority and Trixano separatism only allowed Ladinos to take advantage of the Indian failure to understand national legal and administrative ideologies. In the present, converts point to local parallels to the Cabrera model in the Ladino civil administration of San Andrés, which drafts Indians for the upkeep of the municipality, and in the ties between *patrones* and laborers.

In the present, converts see progress as moving away from the Cabrera model toward the rule system implicit in the Ubico model. Selective ladinoization is looked to as a means for leveling differences used to preserve Indians in inferior social and economic positions. Ubico's secular universalism is seen as relating the individual to society without intervening divisions into ethnic groups by presenting equivalent obligations and opportunities to all individuals. The present-day importance of this ideological transition from Cabrera to Ubico is evident in the following counsel that an Indian convert gave to a laborer: "Why are you suffering in this work? Now is not the time. All your efforts are profiting the *patrón*. With a little [land], enough is harvested. You are killing yourself earning fifty cents [a day]. If I did not have these *cuerdas*, I would be an assistant in the hotel in Sololá and would live happily instead of suffering with these *patrones*." In this advice, the convert is stressing alternatives to subordination to local Ladinos. The cooperative, which is seen as exemplifying Ubico's universalism, allows Indians independence of local *patrones* by offering credits for fertilizer that enable Indians to gain subsistence from even limited amounts of land. Alternatively, Indians can seek employment outside of town that will permit negotiation of identity. Since Ubico, the outside has come to signify both the means for achieving material equivalence and a social order that will accept changes in code for conduct without questioning ethnic origin.

In this context, it is interesting to compare Indian reactions to the Ubico and Arbenz periods because both promulgated social reforms that marked off governmental ideology from the racism of local Ladinos. Both Ubico's universalistic educational and taxation policies and Arbenz' agrarian reforms might be seen as leading to the "leveling of distinctions in the world." Catholic Indians have chosen to make Ubico an exemplar of egalitarian ideology that respected Indians and resulted in more unity and understanding between ethnic groups, while maintaining an ambivalent stance toward Arbenz who is seen as having promoted antagonism between Indians and Ladinos.

Indian converts stress the complementarity of Ubico's policies and orthodox Catholic ideology. Ubico represents the freeing of blood from code for conduct in the secular world through universalistic policy and the opening of educational opportunities to Indians. In contrast, Arbenz' policies are envisioned as negatively competing with Catholicism because they are said to have called for a forceful substitution of an encompassing political commitment for a religious one. Like Cabrera's racism, Arbenz' "communism" is believed to have precluded moral action as defined in orthodox Catholic belief. Converts observe that Catholic Church affairs were not disturbed by the government during this period as long as they did not conflict with revolutionary ideology. Yet Indians strongly disagree with what they interpret as Arbenz' priorities with regard to church and state. In particular they are critical of what they feel children were taught during the revolutionary period: "to worship the president and ask him for things as if he were God." This mixing of religious and secular domains is unforgivable as far as the orthodox Catholics are concerned.

There is little doubt that a very significant source of the Indians' ambivalence toward Arbenz as a symbol of the revolution was Archbishop Rossell's stand on communism through the revolutionary and counterrevolutionary periods. The archbishop's pastoral letters (for instance, 1954a, 1954b, 1955) were strongly anticommunist, arguing that communists manipulated religious symbols to gain rural converts, that they promoted ethnic antagonism to convince the poor that they would benefit from affiliation with the party, and that the state was their only god. He asserted that one could not be a Christian and a communist, or a Guatemalan and a communist because these identities and ideologies are antithetical and mutually exclusive. By implication he closely linked religion, nationality, and patriotism. Certainly there are parallels between Catholic Action's portrayal of the revolution and the archbishop's ideology. There is a good chance that Indians were exposed to similar anticommunist arguments by political groups organizing in rural areas (Adams 1957b).

The archbishop's warning to the faithful not to become involved in politics should also be understood in the context of his commitment to the Catholic Church as an institution. Clearly, the national Church has been continually involved in national and international politics and local congregations have at times aligned themselves with domestic political parties (Calder 1970). In fact during the revolution the archbishop directed faithful Catholics to vote. While he did not publicly endorse particular candidates or parties in pastoral letters, he made it very clear who Catholics should *not* support: communists or their sympathizers, Catholics who had lived notoriously immoral lives or had expressed antichristian beliefs, and anticlerical candidates who had formerly advocated the limitation of the legal rights of the Church in Guatemala (Rossell 1948b).

Generally Catholic converts in San Andrés have been hesitant to involve themselves collectively or as individuals in national party politics because such involvement has been felt to challenge the valued encompassing character of religious identity.[38] By incorporating this position into their oral histories, Catholic Action converts have perpetuated a narrowed set of political options for attaining parity with Ladinos.

Conceptions of Progress in the Material World

Catholic Action converts have avoided participation in local organizations that, they believe, require commitments to encompassing ideologies, such as racism or party politics. Instead they favor organizations, such as the cooperative and the elementary school, where universalistic models are put into action. Converts are able to separate activism in these groups as private individuals from their religious identity so as to maintain the spiritual-material contrast and to avoid bringing Catholic Action into disputes in the secular world. Nevertheless, converts have consistently held leadership positions in the cooperative and worked on committees for the school. They talk of being like apostles in promoting forms of secular universalism as alternatives to ethnic subordination.

Universalistic application of law and opportunity, however, only perpetuates the economic marginality of the Indian population. Converts seek a social order in the material world that will parallel their beliefs about the unity and equivalence of souls in the spiritual order of the Catholic Church. The difficulty in implementing the spiritual model in the world is that in orthodox Catholic belief spiritual equivalence lacks a historical dimension. In the same way, cooperativism and bi-ethnic education introduce universalism without coming to grips with the historic outcome of long-term Indian political and economic subordination. In the cooperative, all members share equivalent standing and access to centralized distribution of credit in the form of seed and fertilizer. Indians have found that economic success is proportionate to the initial size of individual landholdings. Ladinos with large plantations have reaped the greatest profit from centralized distribution and marketing. Indian renters are effectively barred from membership or they benefit on a restricted scale because of limited landholdings. Although cooperative technology has contributed to an increased number of independent peasants with small-scale holdings and to the weakening of overt signs of Ladino domination, it has not narrowed the economic gap between the ethnic groups or come into conflict with the structural position of Ladino landholders.

In defining the cooperative and the school as universalistic institutions, converts stress national affiliations, while in criticizing racism in these organizations, they emphasize local Ladino participation. Universalism signifies that membership is open to all qualified individuals regardless of ethnicity; but the resulting local Ladino participation necessitates constant disagreement and negotiation over racist and universalist definitions of these organizations. Indian strategies for emphasizing a universalistic definition of social relations within the cooperative and the school have involved attempts to separate these organizations from local symbols of racism and an appeal to higher authorities on the national level to mediate disputes. To examine the process of Indians' attempts to negotiate ethnic and universalistic identities, as well as the growing dependence of converts on national institutions, it is necessary to take a closer look at the historical development of the wheat growers' cooperative in San Andrés.

The interlude of radical politics in San Andrés apparently did little to reverse declining production, although it may have temporarily reduced seasonal migration by making more land available to peasant Indians. By the midfifties the agricultural yield is estimated by Indians to have been only one-third of the maximum harvested at the end of the nineteenth century. Also in the 1950s, some 70 percent of the town annually migrated to coastal coffee and cotton plantations for the harvest. The partial solution of these production and migration problems has been credited to one of the most important local landowners and political leaders. In 1956, this Ladino leader experimented for the first time with chemical fertilizers for his wheat crop, drawing the attention of townspeople who noticed the quantity and quality of the harvest. Two years of debate followed these experiments, because some felt that chemical fertilizers would "burn" the soil making it infertile, while others saw fertilizer as a solution to social and economic problems.

The Ladino leader, who administered the town as mayor during these years, discussed the potential of fertilizer with local agricultural extension agents and was successful in soliciting more seed and fertilizer from the ministry of agriculture for demonstration plots. Convincing local agriculturalists that fertilizer would increase the yield was not as major a problem as the facts that few Indians could afford a cash outlay for fertilizer and that lending agencies would not advance money, especially in small amounts, on future harvests. Responding to this predicament, the mayor organized a meeting to found an agricultural cooperative that would allow the purchase of seed and fertilizer on credit. Although many adopted a skeptical attitude, fourteen agriculturalists banded together in 1959 and formed the Wheat Growers' Cooperative of San Andrés. In 1960, the cooperative solicited formal legal status and by the early 1970s, after being chosen for special attention from development agencies, it had expanded to 1,200 members from the departments of Sololá, Quiché, and Guatemala. The cooperative continues to function as an independent private enterprise, receiving loans and technical assistance from national and international development agencies like SCICAS (*Servicio Cooperativo InterAmericano de Crédito Agrícola*), ACDI (Agricultural Cooperative Development International), and AID (Agency for International Development). In 1970, San Andrés was chosen as a regional cooperative center for the administration and instruction of nearby local cooperatives.

Although the cooperative is concerned with better yields for the subsistence crops of corn and beans, it has more directly promoted the planting of wheat as the solution to economic stagnation because that grain is the region's most important cash crop and has a base price guaranteed by the government. The cooperative works on the principle that centralized distribution of agricultural supplies, machinery, transportation, storage, marketing, and education will make agriculturalists more competitive producers by giving access to capital and credit and by cutting out unscrupulous middlemen.

Agricultural production has risen dramatically in the last thirteen years largely because of the introduction of chemical fertilizers, although it is difficult to assess exactly how much the increase has been and who has benefited most. According to one official estimate, between 1959 and 1969 the production of wheat rose eightfold, of corn threefold, and of beans almost eightfold (Aguirre Díaz *et al.* 1970:4). The cooperative claims that this economic upturn has greatly affected the lifestyle of Indian peasants. Seasonal migration to the south coast declined from some 70 percent in the late 1950s to 5 percent in the 1970s. In addition, the creation of thirty nonmanual labor positions in the administrative and technical fields, including transportation, has stemmed Ladino migration to urban centers and taught Indians new skills.

Undoubtedly, the cooperative has benefited the community, although many Indians are uncertain about who has made the most substantial gains. Indians simply do not have time to plant wheat after taking care of their obligations to *patrones*. In addition, Indians may have problems establishing official access to land. One Indian member noted:

> Many cannot be members of the cooperative here. This is the disgrace that we have. If an individual does not have a little land, then he cannot be a member. Yes, he can rent land, but who can take advantage of a planting if it is a few months late? For example, the laborers of this landowner do not plant wheat because they do not have time. Furthermore, in the cooperative, they insist on the tenancy of land amounting to five or six *cuerdas*. The individual has to have tenancy although he does not own the land. The laborer wants to be a member although he does not own land. He wants to be a member because he sees that everyone is making use of the cooperative and making more money. But if he does not own land, but rents land, the *patrón* has to give tenancy. If the harvest does not yield, the *patrón* has to pay the credit or the land is confiscated. Actually, they do not confiscate the land because we have had sessions on this many times. But the *patrones* avoid these issues [by not signing the tenancy papers]. Then the poor cannot be members.

The universalism of the cooperative is caught short because it fails to deal with the historical problem that originated during the Cabrera period: "the land here is in the hands of a few." Ladino *patrones* only aggravate the situation by denying Indian laborers tenancy papers. On the one hand, Indians laud the efforts of such organizations as the co-operative federation based in the capital city and ACDI. On the other hand, Indian critics localize the problem of limited access to the cooperative by blaming large landowners' demands for priority on work and their failures to collaborate with laborers interested in fulfilling the prerequisites for cooperative membership.

Credit for declines in the numbers of migrants to the coast is often taken by the cooperative that claims to have increased production on members' lands so that they no longer have to subsidize agricultural earnings with plantation work (Aguirre Díaz *et al.* 1970). A less official Indian interpretation suggests, however, that the ideas and agricultural techniques that the cooperative has introduced into the community are more important than the institution itself:

> It is said that because of the cooperative Trixanos do not go to the coast. Well, partially it is because of the cooperative, but partially not. Now people are awakening; now people are not like before. For example, earlier, people were more ignorant. They dedicated themselves exclusively to work with their hands. Now, yes, they work with their hands, but they also think a little more. With new ideas from the cooperative they produce better harvests. Many use the ideas of the cooperative but are not members and do not go to the coast. They use what they have learned buying fertilizer and planting a little, with the earth well worked, so that the harvest produces well. They buy fertilizer and wheat seed so that they can plant for themselves. They do not want to govern themselves under the cooperative. They understand that they themselves can solve their problems.

Some Indians who are unable to acquire official tenancy to land or do not want to work under the authority of the cooperative have used modern agricultural methods and fertilizer without affiliating themselves with the new organization. Their resourcefulness and self-reliance are admired. Nevertheless, unaffiliated agriculturalists must seek their own sources of credit and middlemen for marketing.

Despite some misgivings, converts continue to take an active role in cooperative affairs and note that *patrones* are feeling the impact of the small agriculturalists who were earlier laborers. The combination of a larger number of independent small-scale agriculturalists and the growing belief that work on the coast, the roads, or in the capital is preferable to local plantation labor has reduced the labor pool that *patrones* may draw upon. The bind that landowners find themselves in has already led to better treatment of laborers and somewhat higher wages. Modern agricultural techniques and the cooperative itself have had a noticeable, if limited, impact on the extent to which local Ladinos define the social reality of the Indian population. Converts are quick to add that the new "awakening" of Indians and interest in nonagricultural work outside the town have made a substantial contribution to the weakening of Ladino domination. The major vehicle for this awakening has been education, to which I will now turn for an example of the negotiation of racist and universalistic definitions in a local bi-ethnic organization.

In both the cooperative and the elementary school, Indians are tied to national institutions through local bi-ethnic organizations that espouse universalistic social ideologies. While cooperativism and education mutually reinforce each other, the school is thought to present a wider range of alternatives for social progress. On the one hand, the cooperative ideally provides economic growth that makes education a feasible option for Indian youths who in poorer times had to assist their parents in providing for the family. On the other hand, Indians who have become fluent and literate in Spanish are felt to be more inclined to take an active part in cooperative administration. Educated Indians have acted as intermediaries between the cooperative and Indian community, have initiated instruction on cooperativism in Cakchiquel, and have become spokesmen in general assemblies. Unlike the school, however, the cooperative has goals that center on the integration of rural communities into the nation as food producers. The cooperative strategy for development focuses on making Indians better at what they already do. Indian administrators who contribute to these goals remain agriculturalists because the full-time technical staff of the cooperative is drawn from the capital. In contrast, the school, which offers six years of instruction with higher levels on demand, is envisioned as the means to a broader range of occupations that encourage ladinoization and the negotiation of identities on local and national levels. Education with its exposure to Ladino lifestyle and social world view is believed to benefit Indian agriculturalists as well as enable them to seek specialized training for new nonagricultural occupations.

Converts single out education since the Ubico period as the most significant contribution to social change. Such change is exemplified by the ability of Indians to defend their interests with Ladinos in town, to present grievances directly to national authorities, and to promote alternative nonmanual occupations for the youth:

Before, there were no opportunities for the poor to study, and it was thought that only Ladinos were capable of studying or advancing. Now Indians are able to study as we see with our students who are doing the same work as the Ladinos. In the past, we were unaware that we could progress because we lacked the means, the opportunity. No people in my generation could prosper, although they had the intelligence, because they lacked the opportunity and approval. Now, thanks to the involvement of the government in awarding scholarships, we see that Indians are capable of studying widely and the progress of our race is distinguished.

As in the case of the cooperative, consistent national intervention has encouraged the feeling that local organizations can provide alternatives to ethnic-based subordination. For several reasons, the negotiation of racist and universalistic models in the school has been an especially heated and delicate issue. The school has been staffed entirely by Ladinos and administered by a member of one of the most important landowning families in town. Because Indians do not participate in everyday decision making, there have been periodic confrontations over which model for social relations should be promoted in the school. Indian participation in these conflicts must balance demands for change against the fact that successful completion of school is a prerequisite for further occupational training in secondary schools outside the town. In addition, the administration of the school has a say in who receives scholarships for advanced education. Indians have attempted to avoid direct confrontations with the school by enlisting the aid of the ministry of education that has the jurisdiction to decide and enforce new policy. An example will clarify this strategy for putting pressure on local Ladinos to stress universalism and acknowledge the Indian historical position.

In pushing for a more nearly universalistic model for the school, Indians have realized that equivalent access to educational facilities calls for the special recognition of Indian poverty. A dispute early in the 1970s centered on the collection of a fee for the preparation of school snacks. Indians felt that this fee along with the registration costs for the operation of the school discriminated against poor Indians who were unable to raise the necessary money to send their children to school. Not only was the fee an added burden in times when registration costs were rising, but it was spent on snacks including food, such as milk, to which Indians were not accustomed. Some children became sick and most avoided the snack. In 1971, after eight years of complaints, Indians protested by delaying the registration of their children so that the school was not able to open for the beginning of the term. The Ladino reaction was to send municipal authorities to the parents telling them that they were required by law to register their children. Indians belonging to Parents of Families responded to the stalemate by sending a complaint to the state technical supervisor for the ministry of education. State police were called in to investigate the reasons for the school boycott. A meeting of the principal, municipal government, parents, and the representative of the ministry of education was called. Although the state supervisor failed to appear, Indians decided to register their children without paying the fee for the snack. When the representative of the ministry of education finally arrived, he explained that "it was impossible to eliminate the snack because it was a governmental agreement and by [its] being a law, they [the Indians] could not oppose it." As a compromise, the official suggested that poor families would be permitted to pay the fee in installments. An agreement was reached and school opened, although Indians point out that this time was not the last they encountered discrimination in the school system.

Indians have sought to restrict the significance of the concept of ethnicity and its association with the code for conduct of subordination by ladinoizing through the school and by encouraging universalistic alternatives for peasant agriculturalists. They associate themselves with the urban, Ladino world by participating in local branches of national organizations and by bringing in national authorities to decide disputes. Periodic confrontations and compromises concerned with the school have attempted to deal with social ideology and history so that ladinoization is an option for the Indian youth. Some converts believe that by accommodating to local racism through coexistence they will eventually be able to change the system. Like oral history accounts, Indian perception of the social system based on ethnicity is tied to the past through the Cabrera presidency and the *mandamiento* but localized in the present to the town.

Implicit in the strategy of Indian converts is their hesitance to challenge the structural position of Ladinos whom they emulate in occupation and lifestyle. On the local level Ladinos are thought to impose a racist ideology. It is, however, only partially clear to the Indians that on the national level as well the very identity of those whom they emulate is based on the subordination of Indians as food producers and as a source of labor for plantation agriculture. Converts are caught in a bind because they believe that education leading to ladinoization embodies an egalitarian promise of success that may compensate for a history of Indian economic subordination. The way out of poverty and racism is individual education that will permit Indians to work outside the town and negotiate identities so that ethnicity does not imply subordination. The only way to accomplish this task is to pass as Ladino outside the town; yet, in doing so, Indians risk the loss of identification with their own ethnic group.

The following remarks represent the ambivalence of the parental generation toward the forms of success that have been made possible by groups such as Catholic Action:

> I hope that the educated youths understand and are conscious of their race. But I also fear that there might be a youth who will fail to recognize that he is an Indian, who will disregard his race by wanting to present himself as a Ladino. If so, he regresses, because if he is pure Indian, he belittles the race he belongs to. It is possible that such a person might say, "May those Indians stay in their place, I will be more like a Ladino." And this is only because he changed his dress, while his studies, his culture, his education become worthless because they made him different. I hope that our children's egotism does not increase, because what I desire is the salvation of our race and not that they leave us in the backwardness in which we live because they do not return to their race. If they do not collaborate with their own race, then I would criticize them, as would any Indian from the town. I hope that our children carry us from the backwardness of this race and I hope that as they advance all Indians will advance.

The score of Indian students who have continued education outside the town in the last ten years concur in this statement that values the identification of the individual with his "race." None have been able to secure permanent, nonmanual jobs in the town and all agree that agricultural work in the community would cause them to become "frustrated with hard work, suffering, and low salary" because they "are not in agreement with following the same in the future."

Most students and a growing number of locally educated youth are planning permanent migration to urban centers that will contrast with old patterns of seasonal migration tied to agricultural production. The youth think of permanent relocation "for the benefit of the whole life if one finds the means to progress economically" as coming into conflict with community identification: "If there were sources of work here for the educated youth, it would be progress for the town. But as there is no work and the youth must go elsewhere, the town is always the same

as the present. There is no advancement and the people stay the same."
The long-term effects of migration may well be a continual drain of
educated youth away from the town. Since few students have completed their education and settled down to permanent employment, it is
too early to assess the impact of permanent migration on groups like
Catholic Action or on the negotiation of identity for the youth themselves.

While both students and converts seem to be feeling their way along
the path of change, the civil-religious hierarchy has taken a strong, if
situational, stand on ladinoization of the youth that parallels the models of the separatist and bi-ethnic communities.

Ladinoization and the End of the World for
the Civil-Religious Hierarchy

Trixanos committed to the civil-religious hierarchy are ambivalent
about changes that have occurred in San Andrés during the last two
decades. Elders sidestep evaluation of the new religious groups in town
by singling out the youth as the locus of change. Yet in praising or con-
demning activities of the youth, elders are aware of the ties that youths
have with those who introduced new religious groups and social ideologies to the town. Trixano elders take note that virtually all young
innovators are the sons and daughters of Catholic and Protestant converts. Unlike their parents, however, these young adults have begun to
formulate a new and very distinctive lifestyle in accordance with a
commitment to selective ladinoization and education. While the activities of their parents have been largely restricted to the town, the
younger generation has followed out the personal consequences of ideological change outside the town. Most have continued education in
other areas of the country, returning to San Andrés with ladinoized
clothing, speech, aspirations, and attitudes toward religious fervor.
None are willing to continue manual labor in the fields, although all
would like to settle in their natal town even while they realize that
achieving this combination of desires is next to impossible. The educated Indian youth are symbols of both valued and unanticipated effects of alternative conceptions of Indian identity. Though these
youths numbered fewer than fifteen in 1971, they are recognized as
having had a significant impact on the behavior of the rest of the
younger generation in the community.

Change in San Andrés has had both positive and negative aspects from the traditionalist point of view. Indian elders in the civil-religious hierarchy note an increase in freedom and fair treatment accorded Indians in the bi-ethnic community. This modification of Ladino behavior is credited to a great extent to educated Indians, who Indian elders say: "Do not permit Ladinos to bother them, now that they speak out and can give opinions, now that they have ideas and have studied. They know some of the laws and they will not allow Ladinos to do something bad in the municipal government." On the negative side, however, elders describe serious decreases in the amount of respect demonstrated by the youth, a decline in service to the brotherhoods, and a growing self-interested individualism. In pursuing the details of varying assessments of change, I will argue that the elders' ambivalence toward new patterns of social action is a result of the different significance that ladinoization has for the separatist and bi-ethnic conceptions of community.

In the context of agricultural labor, elders discuss change in a positive light, pointing to an increasing ability of Indians to negotiate identity with respect to Ladinos:

> In the old days, Ladinos made it so that they had more privilege, more respect, more honor than our fathers the Indians. Only Ladinos were understood and taken into account in decisions. All this has changed in the present because now there is more freedom. Now it is the free desire of the Indian to work for the Ladino. Before Indians were forced to work because they had to comply with the *mandamiento* [forced labor]. Now, by the grace of God, we do not suffer with this law, but Ladinos still have the feeling of superiority, although it is not as notable. A kind of equality can be observed now because we cultivate their land and they treat us better, not as in the past. If laborers are treated badly, no one will finish the work. For this reason, Ladinos understand us a little more and treat us well.

Whereas in the past, Indians were not given a choice when they were drafted into forced labor, now the elders feel that laborers may register disagreements with Ladinos simply by refusing to work for the landholder. In this commentary, "freedom" signifies that Indians may choose when and for whom they will work, and greater "equality" signals Ladino responsiveness to laborers' demands, that Indians will be taken into account. Additionally, this latter concept calls for an acknowledgement of the interdependence of the two ethnic groups. Both concepts imply that, while Ladinos remain superordinate in terms of ethnicity, they should recognize their dependence on Indians as a source of manual labor in the fields. If Indians decide to withdraw their agricultural services, Ladino *patrones* will be unable to plant and harvest the crops. Neither freedom nor equality, as conceived by the elders, calls for a restructuring of the ethnic division of labor. Labor relations are better from the elders' point of view because there is more give and take in interethnic relations and because Ladinos have come to be less arbitrary in the ways in which they express superiority.

From the point of view of the elders of the civil-religious hierarchy, one of the factors contributing to social change in economics has been the defense of Indian rights in the administrative government of the bi-ethnic community by educated, ladinoized Indians. Ladinoized Indians play a role similar to that of the first Indian councilman who acts as an intermediary and represents Indians in the bi-ethnic court. Unlike the traditionalist councilman, the new intermediaries do not administer *costumbre* as a separatist alternative. The following description indicates the scope of the changes that elders see in the youth and the benefits that accrue to the Indian community because of this change:

> Now Ladinos are not the only ones to give good opinions or advice. Earlier, one had to go to a Ladino to ask the favor of checking to see if a document was filled out correctly. Now members of our race are able to read or fill out documents. Ladino participation is not necessary, and Indians give us a more sincere opinion. For this reason, it is good that youths have changed their dress and language, that they have learned the new language of the Ladinos. I have noticed that the few young people who have succeeded do not forget Cakchiquel or their race. I judge that it is a good thing that they have changed their dress because they have studied and can go to the court without fear. They know how to defend themselves through the legal code. I have noticed that many come to find jobs like those of the Ladinos.

In emphasizing positive aspects of change, Indians of the civil-religious hierarchy talk of the ways in which educated Indians can assist the rest of the Indian community, instead of dominating members of the separatist community (the fear of the mythology about pacted individuals). In appearance and occupation, the young Indians may resemble Ladinos; but they are thought to maintain an identification with their own community and ethnic group in the context of bi-ethnic affairs.

Positively evaluated talents of the Indian youth allow for new kinds of negotiation in the courts and economics. The ability of these Indians to deal effectively with Ladinos is associated with assertiveness and articulateness, as well as with ladinoized dress and occupations. Yet in the separatist community such changes endanger the ideology of blood and *costumbre* as symbols of Indian identity. To suggest that an individual is an Indian through blood without the associated code for conduct of *costumbre* rings of the ideas of the converts. Such a separation of natural identity from code for conduct is a step that traditional elders are not willing to make because it challenges the paramount values of *costumbre*, the respect for social elders, and the interdependence of generations.

Elders express concern for the negative aspects of cultural change in terms of a failure to honor the unity called for in brotherhood discourses. The youth do not express union with their ancestors because they ignore the model of their grandparents and do not seek to adore God through their behavior. They partially deny God's commandment that "we should have love, care, and friendship with our fellows; that we have understanding and mutual sharing to do that which is good." In this way, the ladinoized youth are seen as rejecting the basis of Indian identity as understood by the civil-religious hierarchy. In other words, they question the unity of the individual with family and fellow humans in the separatist community. In place of *costumbre*, the ladinoized youth seem to be following careers of self-interested individualism. One elder complained:

> I believe that not all changes are good. Although our townsmen are moving ahead, they only look out for their own lives and do only that which springs from their own lives, their ideas. They do not respect an elder, like myself, because they want only their lives and this is what they respect. We are not taken into account by them. Everything is being left behind: their modes of being lack order. A person does not say "good day" to you because he does not want to show respect, because the youth do not show respect when they encounter us. In contrast, we are accustomed to greeting another person with respect and reverence suited to his age. But now they scarcely say "good bye" and this is not respect.

Such criticism is often phrased in terms that parallel ritual discourses given in the brotherhoods. The valued and devalued models for behavior toward social elders have come to represent the gap between the ideal and the actual (cf. pp. 67–70).

In a manner that recalls the brotherhood discourses in Chapter Three, Trixanos follow the model of the ancestors by respectfully acknowledging the presence of elders and by acting with reference to them so that the length of life is extended by God and the inhabitants and plantings of the community are fruitful. Elders feel that the community as a whole and the youth specifically are moving away from the values of the *costumbre*, thereby threatening the fertility of the town. "Our ancestors had a good life because they behaved well before God in caring for their fellows. Thus God rewarded them with good plantings, good harvests. But now life has degenerated with bad plantings, bad behavior, because there is much evil on earth." Although the youth do not identify with the separatist community, those who practice *costumbre* suffer because God is punishing the Indian community as a whole. Because of the unity of blood, the elders translate the devalued behavior of the youth into "*our* bad behavior." Lives are shortened, bodies are thought to show signs of decay at an early age, and the celebration of *costumbre* in the brotherhood is threatened.

The decline in community concern for the brotherhoods is a direct challenge to the separatist Indian community. If the civil wing of the hierarchy is unable to recruit new members for the brotherhoods, then the celebration of the paramount values that unify and justify separatism of the Indian community is threatened with extinction. For individuals, *voluntad* (will), or the personal ranking of goals within a larger set of valued commitments, will no longer be forged into the unity of overarching *costumbre*. Decline of the brotherhoods and ritual intermediaries implies a weakening of contrasts between the town and the wilds, between will and luck-destiny, between *costumbre* and envy. The law of Christ, which stands for continuity and unity, is being pushed aside by a law that represents discontinuity and divisiveness.

In the past Trixanos treated the maintenance of society as an issue separate from problems between individuals. Now growing individualism and self-interest, the negative aspects of ladinoization, are coming into direct conflict with the maintenance of Indian society. "People from the hamlets [*aldeas*] are concerned about the continuation of the brotherhoods. They have good intentions [*buena voluntad*]. But all is ending itself, all the ancient *costumbres*. Now there is no one to receive this brotherhood, now that townspeople do not want to continue the *costumbres* of the brotherhoods. It is possible that no one will be found and that this *costumbre* might end. Then the images will be given to the chapel." Both ladinoization of the youth and alternative religious organizations are blamed for the lack of interest in the brotherhoods. To give the images of the saints to the hillside chapel would be to admit the impossibility of continued negotiation between subordination and separatism because the chapel is a part of the bi-ethnic community. To avoid such a final step, minor brotherhoods are consolidating their shrines with brotherhoods that host the celebrations of Holy Week and the titular feast of San Andrés. Also members of brotherhoods are being asked to continue service past the traditional tenure of one year. As one ritual guide explained, "We must continue our *costumbre* although there are only a few of us. We will not permit our *costumbre* to die or be extinguished." For the elders, the death of *costumbre* would be one more example of growing disorder and evil in the world and a sign that a final judgment and destruction of the world is once more at hand.

Conclusions

> Of course this is not to claim that ideology is necessarily the ulti-
> mate reality of social facts and delivers their "explanation," but
> only that it is the condition of their existence. (Dumont 1970:246)

The foregoing chapters have documented, and presented an interpretive framework for analyzing, a radical shift in Indian identity that has
occurred in the Guatemalan community of San Andrés Semetabaj during the last twenty-five years. Unlike the Caste War of the Yucatán
(Reed 1964) or the agrarian revolt in Michoacán, Mexico (Friedrich
1970), the redefinition of Indian identity in San Andrés has not involved sustained civil conflict with the broader society. Like these other
movements, however, the quiet transformation in San Andrés has involved a redefinition of a rural community's relation to the broader
society. Yet Indians of this Guatemalan community are still impoverished peasants who live uncomfortably close to subsistence. Ladinos in
the town still control the large expanses of land that are most productive for cash crops. Their political control of the town has been challenged at times in the recent past by increasing involvement of Indians
in Ladino posts in the civil administration of the town. Furthermore,
some Indians have become national representatives in the cooperative
federation and others are seeking training for nonagricultural occupations. Behind these continuities and changes, Indians of both the civil-
religious hierarchy and Catholic Action feel that there has been a
major transformation in what being an Indian means in San Andrés.[39]

From an anthropological perspective at least two divergent interpretations of the patterns of change in Indian identity can be made on the
bases of the findings of this symbolic analysis of ethnicity. On the one
hand, the analyst can agree with the Indians' perception of a radical
change in their world view and self-images. This interpretation would
argue that there have been fundamental changes in the conceptions
that Indians associate with ethnicity and interethnic relations. Changes
in these conceptions and the way they are interrelated in Indian world
view through religion have influenced Indians' perception of social
reality and their strategies for actions within that reality.[40] In addition,

this position would emphasize important changes in the Indians' consciousness and their analysis of the social ramifications of their subordinate position. Finally, this interpretation would suggest that the vehicle for these changes in identity has been the interplay between the belief system of the civil-religious hierarchy and Catholic Action. Indian converts to Catholic Action have constructed an ideology that deals with the secular implications of their new religious belief system precisely because they were called upon to analyze the differences between *costumbre* and modern orthodox Catholicism. Thus, the social analysis of ethnic subordination that Indian converts have developed is a historical product of both religious systems as evidenced, for example, by the changes in belief that accompanied the forced separation of Catholic Action from the bi-ethnic church and the civil-religious hierarchy.

A second and contrasting line of anthropological interpretation would come to a contrary set of conclusions, noting that there are a series of striking parallels between the world views of the civil-religious hierarchy and Catholic Action. This interpretation would *minimize* the significance of actual changes in Indians' understanding of subordination. The parallels between the two religions' conceptualization of Indian identity would lead these analysts to conclude that Catholic Action has largely replaced the belief system of the civil-religious hierarchy with new symbols for old conceptions. Further, this line of reasoning would argue that innovations in Catholic Action's beliefs have not resulted in insights into the mechanisms of subordination; rather, it would be argued that they have continued to obscure and constrain Indians' perceptions of the mechanisms that maintain them in a subordinate position. At this point, I would like to return to the findings of this study on identity and belief and examine them from the points of view of both interpretations, beginning with the second.

No doubt there are some striking structural parallels between the world views expressed through the two religions. For instance, both world views deal with the relation of religious identity to ethnic identity by contrasting models of egalitarian and hierarchical social orders through religious symbols. In both cases, belief systems show how egalitarian models, which serve as the basis for present religious organization and expression, have been compromised by Ladino domination. Ladino control of the bi-ethnic community has compromised moral action, according to these religious systems, because ethnically subordinated individuals are unable to exercise the ultimate moral choices valued by religion.

Despite ethnic subordination, the civil-religious hierarchy and Catholic Action persist in the belief that Indians can employ strategies to restrict the ways Ladinos control Indian life. Such strategies attempt to limit the contexts in which Ladinos identify Indian blood with codes for conduct entailing subordination. They also seek to extend the situations in which separatist cultural identities are stressed and distinguished from ethnic subordination. Separatism, of course, means very different things in Trixano *costumbre* and Catholic Action social ideologies; yet in both cases separatism calls for the structural avoidance of hierarchical relations in favor of egalitarian relations on the local level. In action, both groups work in their own ways for better treatment of Indians in local bi-ethnic society. The social realities of San Andrés, then, redirect the priorities of Trixano and Catholic Action values toward adjusting to their subordinate position rather than directly challenging it.[41]

Neither world view has effectively challenged the overall structural relation of Ladinos to Indians in San Andrés, although both belief systems deal with the origin and present character of the hierarchical social order. In the case of the civil-religious hierarchy, religion might be interpreted as misportraying the relation of the order of Satanás to the order of Christ as these symbols are vehicles for the conceptions of the bi-ethnic and separatist Indian communities respectively. Separatism based on the blood of ancestors effectively masks the ramifications of subordination based on the blood of ethnicity in the civil administration of the town and in religious institutions. The separatism of the civil-religious hierarchy perpetuates Indian belief systems and a town-specific ethnic identity. It also serves to perpetuate the subordination of Indians to Ladinos.

In the case of Catholic Action, the social ideology of Indian converts might also be interpreted as blocking Indians' understanding of the mechanisms that maintain them in a subordinate position. The analysis of Indian converts localizes the sources of domination to the bi-ethnic town of San Andrés where ethnic identities lend a hierarchical order to Indian-Ladino relations in plantation economics, civil administration, and Trixano religion. In contrast, the broader society that allows orthodox Catholics to stress religious identity and de-emphasize ethnicity is thought to be a source of egalitarian, universalistic options for Ladino-Indian relations. By localizing inequality in terms of ethnicity, Indian converts have failed to understand the mechanisms through which the broader society maintains rural Indians *and* Ladinos in a subordinate position as agricultural producers in an industrializing country. Nor does Catholic Action analysis extend to describing the sources of inequity in the broader society where their children enter the class structure in urban occupations and where universalistic institutions are also stratified in terms of class. Further, by perpetuating Archbishop Rossell's stand on political movements, converts have unnecessarily limited and stereotyped their options for achieving ethnic parity.

In contrast to the foregoing interpretation of Indian belief systems as misportrayers of subordination, an alternative interpretation would find substantial changes in Indian analysis of their subordination. This position notes that Indians have moved through three very different ways of explaining their subordination and the possibility of achieving greater parity with Ladinos.[42] In working through these forms of explanation, Indians have gained insights into the mechanisms that have maintained the relative social position of the two ethnic groups.

First, the civil-religious hierarchy takes what I will call a "separate spheres" approach to the problem of subordination. Through core symbols that contrast the law of Christ with the law of Satanás, Trixanos have distinguished a separate sphere of control in the Indian community as it contrasts with the bi-ethnic community. Within this separate sphere of control, Trixanos celebrate an identity that they believe is distinct from their economic and political subordination to Ladinos in the bi-ethnic social system of San Andrés.

Blood, land, and *costumbre* inherited from the ancestors are the core symbols of this separatist identity. Among Indians, interpersonal relations are governed by values that stress the unity and equivalence of all Trixano individuals, cooperation between generations, and respect for social elders. Ideally, this separatist identity should be manifested in economics, political and jural affairs, and religious celebrations.

What I have termed the negotiation of Trixano identity involves Indian attempts to regulate the extent to which Ladinos control Indian lives by maintaining their own control of a separate sphere in which Trixano belief serves as the model for behavior. Indians prefer separatism as mythologically portrayed in the contrast between the order of Christ and the order of Satanás. Religion describes these orders as independent ones while noting that the order of Satanás (or of the natural wilds) may endanger the town and the fields. To minimize such threats Trixanos are enjoined by the guardian saint not to "bother" the Devil but rather to turn their attention toward gaining fertility through activism in the order of Christ, which is located in the separatist Indian community. In fact, Trixanos follow this advice not by challenging the bi-ethnic government but by working to limit Ladino encroachment into the separate sphere of Indian civil government and judicial affairs.

Trixano participation in the bi-ethnic community, where Ladinos control the land and the civil administration of the town, limits the extent to which separatism can be expressed. Indians acknowledge that much of their life in the bi-ethnic community involves them in the sphere of Ladino control. Within this sphere, separatism becomes ethnic subordination justified in terms of an ethnic division of labor that associates the natural positions of Indians with manual labor and those of Ladinos with supervisory roles and nonmanual occupations. Mythology presents the origin of this division of labor as the conquest of Guatemala, which established a hierarchical social order based on ethnic identities.

The moral order portrayed in the belief of the civil-religious hierarchy compensates Indians for their subordinate position in the sphere of Ladino control. Mythology pictures the conquest as an extension of Christ's moral order to San Andrés through the conversion of Indians to colonial Catholicism. Yet the Spaniards denied the moral choices offered to individuals in this new religion by subordinating the individual to her or his ethnic identity. Religious belief resolves the tension between a paradoxical offer of moral choices and a simultaneous denial of these choices within the belief system itself. The Indians' suffering under subordination will be rewarded and the domination of Ladinos will be punished after death. The moral order does not direct Trixanos to challenge hierarchical social relations in the Ladino sphere of control. Furthermore, social change is pictured as being outside the control of both individuals and the separatist Indian community through the contrast between the activities of the ritual guides and the sorcerers.

Second, Trixanos who have converted to orthodox Catholicism and joined Catholic Action have criticized the separate spheres adaptation to subordination in favor of an "ethnic division-of-labor" explanation. Converts believe that Indians will gain greater parity with Ladinos as they move out of low-status work as laborers by gaining access to universal institutions (such as cooperatives and schools) that will permit economic and occupational mobility.

In developing the ethnic division-of-labor explanation, converts have taken analytic categories and values from Catholic orthodoxy and extended their scope in order to analyze interethnic relations. Converts contrast allegiance to the World and allegiance to God. Unlike the civil-religious hierarchy, Catholic Action believes that the order of the World should be subordinated to the competing order of God. The order of the World entails hatred, envy, vice, and distinctions between persons, such as wealth and ethnicity. In contrast, the order of God stresses the unity and equivalence of all individuals in the spiritual dimension of life. This unity transcends the social divisions of the material world and calls on all individuals to phrase their identities in terms of a universalistic soul rather than in terms of divisive blood. Catholic Action stresses the universalism of the soul and a parallel goal of social equivalence of individuals in the material world. Discrimination from Ladinos and lack of interest and separatism on the part of Trixanos are factors that Indian converts think have perpetuated inequities in the social order. By freeing codes for conduct from their formerly strong association with Trixano blood, Indian converts have been able to analyze the ethnic basis of Ladino domination *and* to conceive of greater social and economic parity through ladinoization.

Initially Indian converts believed that the ethnic division of labor, which was used to justify Ladinos as *patrones* and Indians as laborers, was the stumbling block to greater material parity. To level distinctions between ethnic groups, converts sought new institutions that would offer equivalent opportunities for individuals of both ethnic groups. They proposed new activism in universalistic, national institutions, such as the school and cooperative, that would allow Indians wider participation in the economy and training for nonmanual occupations.

Third, in implementing their social ideology Indian converts have found that the present ethnic division of labor is not the only obstacle to be surmounted in the quest for greater parity. History as a symbol system distinct from atemporal religion has been used by Indian converts to develop a more comprehensive analysis of subordination. I will call this the "historical-racism" explanation of subordination. History shows that Indians have not been rewarded in this life for separatism and that the more egalitarian policies of some governments in the past have not compensated for earlier periods of institutionalized ethnic discrimination. Through this historical-racism explanation, converts argue that Ladinos have maintained power over Indians by historically linking access to society's critical institutions and bases of wealth to the ethnic division of labor and ethnic stereotyping.

During the last century Ladinos gained a dominant position as an ethnic group in San Andrés by acquiring major landholdings and roles as *patrones* for Indian laborers. Ladinos rose to power in the community by taking advantage of their access to the state government and the courts. Periods of forced labor involving only the Indian population allowed local *patrones* to consolidate their economic positions in the community and to dominate economically dependent Indians. As a result, Ladinos have been able to restrict local access of Indians, as a group, to nonmanual occupations and to education. Indians have been unable to secure access to such institutions because of their poverty and because Ladino world view has limited Indians to subordinate roles, through arguments that Indians would not respond to education and were naturally endowed specifically to engage in heavy manual labor. This history of interethnic relations has meant that Ladinos in the present will reap disproportionate rewards from participation in such new economic institutions as the agricultural cooperative.

In Stavenhagen's terminology (1970), Indian converts have used history as a symbol system to analyze the way in which colonial relations and class relations have defined Indian subordination. Through their division-of-labor explanation, converts have come to an understanding of the class relations dimension of ethnic subordination. By extending their analysis through the historical-racism explanation, they have come to an interpretation of the interplay between colonial and class relations. Thus converts have come to an understanding of the mechanisms that subordinate them as an ethnic group and as a class of peasant agriculturalists. By localizing the sources of oppression, however, they have limited the scope of their analysis and blocked awareness of their new dependence on national institutions.

The paradoxical situation in which converts find themselves at present is the result of social change in the broader society where class relations are diverging from and replacing colonial relations with increasing industrialization, regional economic integration, and a consumer-oriented market. For Stavenhagen these changes are part of a broad transformation of class structures caused by the historical expansion of capitalism in Latin America. The growth of capitalism has been accompanied by the introduction of private property, the expansion of commercial agriculture, the establishment of seasonal and permanent labor migrations, the growth of urban centers, and the development of policies to direct national integration. Together, these processes undermine ethnic-based subordination and promote cultural assimilation (Stavenhagen 1975:53–63). Both the school and cooperative are examples of the social forms through which this transition is taking place in San Andrés. In the future, I would expect that Indian youths caught between passing into an economically marginal urban lower class and continuing loyalty to fellow Indians in their home communities will begin a new examination of the ties between class relations in urban and rural areas.

At this point, Indian converts are compromised in daily life where they feel that they are unable fully to act on the historical-racism explanation of subordination. For them, activism in the cooperative aims at an amelioration of local economic subordination. They recognize, however, that the cooperative will not solve the problem of larger disparities in wealth between ethnic groups. Education and the ethnic passing of Indian youths is also felt to be only a partially successful strategy because these are individualistic solutions to the problem of subordination. At present, converts see a compromising hope in education through which Indians may train for nonmanual occupations and gain skills to defend themselves, to present themselves so that they will be taken into account, and to pass as Ladinos in the broader society.

Notes

1. For international examples of this growing literature, see Comaroff (1985), Lan (1985), Scott (1976; 1985), and Ong (1987). Latin Americanists writing on these issues would include J. Nash (1979), Taussig (1980), Bricker (1981), and Stern (1982; 1987).

2. See, for example, Warren and Bourque 1985, as well as Bourque and Warren 1979, 1980, 1981, 1989.

3. I am not implying that Indian religion and world view have been neglected issues in Mesoamerican ethnography. In fact, religion has been a major concern for several generations of ethnographers (see, for example, La Farge and Byers 1931; La Farge 1947; Wagley 1949; Oakes 1951; Bunzel 1952; Guiteras-Holmes 1961; Moore 1966; Vogt 1969; Blaffer 1972; Bricker 1973, 1981; Smith 1977; Falla 1978; Brintnall 1979; Tedlock 1982; Annis 1987). Many analyses of Indian world view before the 1960s failed to find ethnicity problematic because of an early and continuing interest in disentangling Mayan belief from syncretistic Mayan-Catholic religious systems. In addition, it was often assumed in early studies that Indian communities were like Redfield's "folk societies" and could be treated as cultural wholes (Redfield 1947, 1953, 1960).

4. Of course, notions of what is "traditional" and "indigenous" may be central ways that communities justify current cultural practices, as will be shown later in this study when the Trixano conception of *costumbre* is examined at length.

5. Differences in the theoretical perspectives of the investigators may account for these contrasting findings. It is also likely that historical and contemporary economic differences, as well as different national policies toward Indians, explain differences between the neighboring countries. Colby and van den Berghe (1961) have written about differences in the rigidity of ethnic stratification in southern Mexico and Guatemala. Pitt-Rivers (1969) has discussed variations in the historical definition of ethnic categories. These analyses, plus the following presentation of Stavenhagen's framework, might be used to specify the reasons for variations in the significance of ethnicity and class between southern Mexico and Guatemala. De la Fuente (1965) reviews the anthropological literature on Mesoamerican ethnicity and documents the notable variation in specific forms of Ladino-Indian and Indian-Indian relations in Guatemala and Mexico. Wasserstrom (1983) makes an effective historical case for variations in the elaboration and centrality of the civil-religious hierarchy.

6. Pitt-Rivers (1967) notes that the characterization of a cultural practice as "Indian" in Chiapas is enough to cause Ladinos either to drop the practice or to deny knowledge of it. This reaction may be an example of non-Indian responses to economically competitive relations with Indians, as examined by Colby (1966).

7. Passive resistance through the formation of closed corporate communities was not the only Indian reaction to colonial and republican exploitation. For instance, in the sixteenth century Indians revolted against Spanish control, excessive demands for tribute, and the use of Indian children for gold washing. In the seventeenth century, when Indians were pressed into service to assist in the transfer of the colonial capital to its present site, they moved to outlying towns, fled to the mountains, and refused to pay tribute. In the eighteenth and nineteenth centuries, revolts were sparked by taxation, land losses to Ladinos, and challenges to the authority of the *principales*. In the nineteenth century, when Ladinos were encouraged to resettle in Indian regions and communal lands were abolished, Indians of one town rose up and slaughtered Ladino settlers. Finally, in the twentieth century labor revolts have been a common reaction to forced labor. Also, Indians have attemped to avoid vagrancy laws, which required them to work on plantations, by claiming to be traveling merchants instead of agriculturalists (Jones 1940:9–10, 146, 161, 165; Adams 1967:480; Handy 1984:47–55; Wasserstrom 1983).

8. For a good summary of the debates concerning the civil-religious hierarchy as a mechanism that acts to level economic differences in contrast to the hierarchy as a way of justifying economic stratification, see Cancian (1965, 1967) and Smith (1977).

9. Jean-Loup Herbert (1967) notes that by focusing on ladinoization we may fail to notice growing levels of Indian class stratification, Indian-Ladino competition, and discrimination against economically mobile Indians. In addition we may miss new forms of Indian ethnic diversity (cf. Brintnall 1979). The creation of prosperous, nonpeasant alternatives by Indians has been documented by Colby and van den Berghe (1969), Smith (1977), and Hawkins (1984).

10. Many anthropologists argue that Indian communities have responded to change with conservative strategies. Attempts to channel change and buffer the community from the full impact of contact include the grafting of new economic functions onto old institutions, such as interethnic ritual kinship (Tumin 1950, 1952) and the selective incorporation of new commercial values (Colby and van den Berghe 1969). Some communities appear to segregate communal values and world views from new commercial enterprises (see Tax 1941; M. Nash 1958; Reina 1966; Cancian 1965, 1972). June Nash's study of a Chiapas community shows how Indians incorporate Ladino strategies to preserve Indian control over the local judicial system, religious ceremonies, and land. She concludes that Indians are conscious of the advantages of their ethnic identity as opposed to the marginal class identity of landless laborers

who live at the margins of Ladino society and have no political representation (1970). Wasserstrom (1983) argues strongly against these positions.

11. The interpretive approach used in this study was initially informed by the writings of Geertz (1965, 1973), Turner (1967, 1969), Douglas (1966, 1970), Dumont (1970), Ortner (1973, 1975), Schneider (1968, 1969), Barnett (1973), and Silverman (1969, 1971). In rewriting this introduction it is clear that, early or recent, the more interactive approaches to the creation of meaning capture more fully the process of ethnic living and change (cf. note 1 and the following discussion of meaning and cultural process).

12. Mendelson (1957, 1958, 1959, 1965) has done an exemplary analysis of these "pre-Columbian" themes for Santiago Atitlán. What is most fascinating is his conclusion that Judas (Maximón), as a guardian of sexual fertility, embodies the paradoxes of Mayan-Catholic belief. He notes the difficulty of ethical syncretism given the differences in Mayan and Spanish concepts of sexuality (1967).

13. Here I am concerned with the political consequences of belief and, thus, share Geertz's preoccupation with "the role that ideologies play in defining (or obscuring) social categories, stabilizing (or upsetting) social expectations, maintaining (or undermining) social norms, strengthening (or weakening) social consensus, relieving (or exacerbating) social tensions" (1973:203).

14. Clearly, a complementary study might be written to examine Ladino world views and negotiations of identity. Pitt-Rivers (1967) describes an inconsistency in Ladino identification with local community and metropolis and, in passing, mentions history as a meaning system used by rural Ladinos to interrelate different concepts of identity. Both Méndez Domínguez (1967) and Adams (1957a) have done important work on Ladino world views, social forms, and systems of stratification. Hawkins (1984) has formulated a model of derived, contrastive identities. My initial goal of investigating both groups proved impossible in the field.

15. Tax (1937) was the first anthropologist to point out that the *municipio* (rather than the "tribe" or language group) is the appropriate minimal unit of study for the highlands. Ethnic identity, religion, social and political organization, marriage patterns, and economic specializations are all specific to municipal units and relevant to regional political economies.

16. Nancy Munn, in a personal communication, pointed out a fundamental ambiguity between the principles of hierarchy and equality basic to the Trixano definition of the civil-religious hierarchy. Certainly, the issue of the ranking of equivalent options (in myth, in the Trixano concept of individual moral choice, in Trixano and Catholic Action social organizations, and in relations with external groups) deserves more attention. Another line of analysis might pursue the relation between the significance of the ranking of individuals in Indian social organization and the meaning of the ranking of ethnic groups in the wider community.

17. This analysis argues against the overgeneralization of Taussig's interpre-

tation (1980) of the devil contract as an indigenous Marxist critique of capitalism. In Guatemala contracts symbolically mediate ethnicities, not so-called precapitalist and capitalist modes of production and the cost of worker alienation on commercial plantations (cf. Warren 1986).

18. What I refer to as Trixano mythology is actually a loosely bound collection of short stories and commentaries describing a complex series of changes producing the bi-ethnic town of San Andrés. Virtually all Trixanos can narrate some of the stories, although only a handful of elders, who are especially active in civil-religious hierarchy celebrations, are familiar with the widest range of stories and commentaries. Myths are directly recounted by the elders on some occasions, such as wakes. In addition, mythical sequences are brought together and alluded to in the brotherhood-shrine rituals through discourses given by elders, processions of the saints, and ceremonies of the sorcerers.

19. There is a broad consensus among Mesoamericanists that differences between Ladinos and Indians are phrased more commonly in "cultural" rather than in "racial" terms, as evidenced by the possibility of Indians passing as Ladinos outside the natal community (Tax 1941, 1942; Roberts 1945; Colby and van den Berghe 1961; Pitt-Rivers 1969). Trixanos use the word *raza* (which has been translated as "race" or "stock") to contrast the origins of Indians and Ladinos. Whether the analyst uses the labels races or ethnic groups for Ladinos and Indians is probably of secondary importance. In either case, blood, descent, origin, and other putative differences (such as skin color, height, hair texture, and posture) are part of a culturally created set of concepts used to differentiate ranked categories of people believed to be naturally different. In addition, wide-ranging differences in behavior and belief are ranked and associated with the ideology of inequivalence. Throughout this analysis, we are dealing with a culturally specific ideological reality that is often felt to have physical manifestations, despite observed individual variations and despite passing. Dumont (1970), Barnett (1973), and Dolgin (1977) provide insightful analyses of the relation of ideology to systems of ranking and stratification.

20. Throughout this analysis, I have used Schneider's distinctions between natural identity and code for conduct (1968, 1969).

21. This presentation of the significance of unity for Trixanos has benefited from Schneider's discussion of diffuse enduring solidarity (1968).

22. Rosaldo (1968) suggests that through religious brotherhood rituals, the contradiction between ideal ranking by ascribed status (social age) and alternative secular rankings by achieved status (wealth) is expressed.

23. Negotiation, in a more clearly diplomatic rather than bargaining sense, is the metaphor I use for the actualization of models of identity in daily social interaction. This phenomenological process is one of exploring and responding to the expectations of others in a particular set of social contexts and historical moments. Indians' negotiation from a subordinate position involves patterned attempts to assert valued definitions of reality and identity. Strate-

gies for regulating others' control over Indians are dependent on accurate knowledge of others, but not on a common world view or definition of the situation. Some situations are inflexibly defined by Ladinos; others are subject to varying strategies (including violence) on the part of Indians who wish to limit the exercise of Ladino power. Ultimately, attempts to negotiate identity reorient priorities for the expression of different aspects of identity. Various dimensions of this process are discussed throughout this study and the conceptualization of this process deserves additional theoretical attention. Cicourel's analysis of the social construction of reality (1970) has informed my understanding of the interpretive dimensions of negotiation. In the present study, ethnic subordination presents a dynamic series of constraints that influence Indians' ongoing interactions through which they interpret, create, modify, and justify identities, roles, and statuses.

24. Other Indian officials in the civil government are unable to press for separatism because they are invariably defined, in terms of bi-ethnic social ideology, as subordinates in charge of the upkeep of the municipal buildings or as message carriers. These positions have no counterparts among Ladino civil officials.

25. The liminality of these rituals would seem to reside in the concurrence of both sets of interpretations of Indian identity, as well as in the role reversals typical of the *communitas* of the brotherhood dances. Yet even this preliminary examination of variations points to a historical dimension of Turner's antistructure (1969).

26. Silverman's model (1969) of the ways in which cultural systems deal with priorities, through which actors express commitments to codes for conduct, has been very helpful in analyzing this material. To his model, I have added the notion of the actor as a cultural construct. In addition, I am interested in emphasizing the historical circumstances in which the enactment of commitments produces feedback to influence the cultural rule system for structuring priorities.

27. It would be a mistake to see this belief system as associating all goodness with God, the saints, and ritual guides and all evil with Satanás, the animals of the wilds, and the sorcerers. As with other divinities in the town and wilds, the forces of nature are sources of both fertility and punishment.

28. In Trixano world view, an ideological principle resembling Foster's image of limited good (1967) is restricted to the domain of interpersonal relations as structured by the sorcerers in the wilds. Through pact mythology, this principle is tied to contrasting images of the Indian and Ladino and to tension between identification with the Indian community and individualized self-interest. As will be shown in subsequent chapters, once the moral actor is no longer thought to be necessarily subordinated to race, the locus of limited good is redefined as a historical problem resulting from long-term Ladino domination.

29. Pacted humans are anomalous, incorporating both human and animal

characteristics. They are often portrayed in the mythology as rapidly changing back and forth between animal and human forms. A more detailed analysis of these symbols might be made along the lines of Blaffer's analysis (1972) of the winged black demon (*h?ik'al*) in highland Chiapas.

30. Bricker (1973) analyzes ritual humor in Chiapas as another symbolic form through which deviant behavior is criticized and the moral order upheld. She finds that behavior that departs from Indian cultural norms in terms of ethnic identities, sex roles, and performance of public duties is satirized in parallel ways through liminal rituals. Although I have not analyzed ritual humor in San Andrés, the festival of Corpus Christi appears to dramatize similar themes. In San Andrés, the ritual enacts a humorous Ladino-Indian marriage and represents hacienda life in a dance where participants masquerade as wild animals.

31. The pastoral letters, published addresses, and prayers that I cite in this analysis can be found as part of the Taracena Flores Collection at the Benson Latin American Collection, University of Texas at Austin. I would like especially to thank Ann Hartness Graham, public service librarian at the Benson Collection for assistance in locating these materials and for sharing my interest in their contents. Ann Hartness Graham is now compiling an annotated bibliography of primary source materials found in the Benson Collection that deal with Guatemalan politics from 1944 to 1960.

32. The presentation of a fuller analysis of the controversial Guatemalan revolutionary period from 1944 to 1954 is beyond the scope of this study. Adams (1970), Jonas (1974), Jones (1940), Melville and Melville (1971), and Monteforte Toledo (1965), and Whetten (1961) provide macro-analyses of the national political systems during the revolutionary period. Adams (1957b), Falla (1970), and Wasserstrom (1975) examine variations in the impact of national politics on highland communities.

33. The long history of largely unsuccessful mission attempts in the town calls for an explanation of the acceptance of the Tecpán catechist's offer to come to San Andrés and the apparently easy time that the Indian catechists had in converting a core group of Trixanos. Orthodox Catholic Indians explain that in this circumstance "God gives special insight and openness" to particular people. I would like to add that there was a constellation of political and economic factors that probably made a certain segment of the population of San Andrés especially receptive to the new religion. As will be shown in Chapter Six, the early fifties was a time of exposure to radical political ideologies calling for peasant activism in local agrarian reform committees. The subsequent counterrevolution coincides with increasing international interest in evangelization. These historical circumstances, as well as local ecological factors, undoubtedly influenced the initial reception of Catholic Action in the town.

34. The Indian converts were sharply criticizing the liminal aspects of civil-religious hierarchy celebrations. These ritual contexts invert the secular pat-

terns of authority that elders have over youths, husbands over wives, and Ladinos over Indians. Adultery, for instance, is negatively sanctioned in secular contexts. Mythology tells of Indian women who are sent to the underworld and transformed into animals because they "desired" Ladino men. As in the case of Indians who make pacts, these women threaten the separatist order of the Indian community that stresses endogamy. In addition, their potential offspring are ambiguous in terms of national identity, just as the pacted are ambiguous in terms of code for conduct. In both cases the strong association of blood with behavior in *costumbre* is violated. Although orthodox Catholic belief separates blood from codes for conduct, Indians of Catholic Action maintain endogamy within the Indian segment of the town for other reasons as will become clear in subsequent discussions of orthodox Catholic separatism.

35. Unfortunately there is little exegetical information from either group on the significance of these processions.

36. A further implication, though not made explicit by the converts, is that the use of "brother" de-emphasizes what is often a hierarchical relationship between the parents of a child and the child's godparents. Godparents are often selected on the basis of their economic or political position, and a significant number of Indians have chosen Ladino godparents for at least some of their children. The converts seem to be forgoing the advantages of such relations that in the past have tied the laborer to his *patrón* through ritual kinship. Converts prefer to turn to members of their congregation for godparents, apparently preferring the flexibility of not tying themselves to the *patrones*.

37. In a recent publication, Dolgin (1977) analyzes the complex relation between history, mythology, and ideology in a class-stratified society where the individual is the ultimate locus of value and inequality is tied to natural identity. Pursuing the parallel between the present study and Dolgin's work would undoubtedly be a productive line of inquiry.

38. In the early seventies, this stand was reinforced by great confusion and violence in national politics. To combat urban guerrillas, President Carlos Arana Osorio (1970–1974) called a prolonged state of siege shortly after his inauguration. During the state of siege, civil rights were suspended, curfews enacted, and the capital city was searched for guerrillas. Although the state of siege did not greatly affect rural areas, peasants were reminded of urban violence through newspaper reports of murders on the right and left of the political spectrum and through searches of rural buses, as they approached urban areas, by the military.

39. Schneider's "pure domain" contrast of Judaism and Christianity is very useful in describing this transition: "If Judaism is the clearest and simplest case where kinship, religion and nationality are all a single domain, then the transformation of Christianity centers on the separation of a natural and supernatural element, so that kinship becomes differentiated as being based on relationship as material substance, religion as relationship as supernatural

(spiritual) substance. In other words, kinship and religion are more highly differentiated in Christianity than in Judaism, and this differentiation depends on a different form of the distinction between supernatural and natural" (1969:123). For Trixanos, blood and *costumbre* are the defining elements of religion, kinship, ethnicity, and town citizenship. In contrast, orthodox Catholics have differentiated religion from kinship, ethnicity, and citizenship by emphasizing the element of volition for a religious identity that necessitates conversion. Orthodox Catholicism stresses relationship as spiritual substance (the soul) and relationship as code for conduct (Christian love that unifies all Catholics and is expressed through the models for behavior in the Bible and catechism).

The pure domain approach does not spell out the full story of cultural change in San Andrés. Nevertheless, Schneider's model does clarify the most problematic issue for the study of cultural identity: the interrelationship of different domains of identity that contrast at varying symbolic levels. In pursuing the ideological dimension of belief, this analysis moves into the area of conglomerate domains (cf. Silverman 1971 and Dolgin 1977 for companion approaches to these issues).

40. Religion discusses the highest-level models for identity by structurally relating scared, esoteric symbol systems to secular orderings of everyday experience and by indicating the role of the person in each. On the one hand, in *costumbre* mythology unfolds the problem of evil in ecological surroundings familiar to the Indian peasant. In turn, the agriculturalists reaffirm mythological models through their labors in the fields. Both mythology and ecological space as symbol systems present separatist and bi-ethnic models for Indian identity as well as an explanation for the asymmetry between these models. On the other hand, in Catholic Action belief, the problem of evil is articulated in parallel terms through universally applicable sacred scripture and the particulars of history as a belief system. Once again different models of identity and the logic of their interrelations are presented. Part of the strengths of both *costumbre* and Catholic Action belief comes from the association of esoteric knowledge (which, though not monopolized by, is most familiar to the hierarchy elders or the orthodox Catholic catechists) with symbolic forms that are part of everyday life.

41. On a theoretical level, this analysis suggests that in complex societies symbol systems present multiple models for cultural identity. These models are translated into social action through systems of rules for the negotiation of domains of identity. The very enactment of social ideology, however, produces feedback that restructures the priorities, or values, attached to domains of identity, potentially influencing the way in which subordination is perceived.

42. The analytic distinctions between these forms of explanation are further elaborated by Bourque and Warren (1976, 1981). These models were first developed to examine various explanations of female subordination and to analyze differences in perception of subordination in the Peruvian Andes. The

usefulness of similar models for analysis of interethnic subordination points toward some strong parallels between subordination in terms of sexual and ethnic identities. Further research might analyze the impact that changes in ethnic-based belief systems have had on women's cultural identities in Guatemala. In addition, future analysis of ethnic and sexual identities might question the ways in which these identities cut across class distinctions.

Bibliography

ADAMS, RICHARD NEWBOLD

1957a   *Cultural Surveys of Panama—Nicaragua—Guatemala—El Salvador —Honduras.* Scientific Publications No. 33. Washington, D.C.: Pan American Sanitary Bureau.

1959   "La ladinización en Guatemala." In *Integración social en Guatemala.* Guatemala City: Seminario de Integración Social Guatemalteca No. 9, Vol. II:123–137.

1967   "Nationalization." In *Handbook of Middle American Indians* 6:469–489. Austin: University of Texas Press.

1970   *Crucifixion by Power: Essays on Guatemalan National Social Structure, 1944–1966.* Austin: University of Texas Press.

ADAMS, RICHARD NEWBOLD, ed.

1957b   *Political Changes in Guatemalan Indian Communities.* Publication No. 21. New Orleans: Tulane University Middle American Research Institute.

ADAMS, RICHARD NEWBOLD, and ARTHUR J. RUBEL

1967   "Sickness and Social Relations." In *Handbook of Middle American Indians* 6:333–355. Austin: University of Texas Press.

AGUIRRE DÍAZ, ENRIQUE; ANTONIO COROXÓN TOBÍAS; et al.

1970   *Cooperativa de agricultores trigueros de San Andrés Semetabaj.* Quezaltenango: Imprenta Atlántida.

ANNIS, SHELDON

1987   *God and Production in a Guatemalan Town.* Austin: University of Texas Press.

BARNETT, STEPHEN

1973   "Urban Is as Urban Does: Two Incidents on One Street in Madras City, South India." *Urban Anthropology* 2:129–160.

BEALS, RALPH L.

1969   "Indian-Mestizo-White Relations in Spanish America." In *Comparative Perspectives on Race Relations,* ed. Melvin Tumin, pp. 239–257. Boston: Little, Brown.

BLAFFER, SARAH D.

1972   *The Black-man of Zinacantan.* Austin: University of Texas Press.

BOURDIEU, PIERRE

1977   *Outline of a Series of Practice.* Trans. Richard Nice. Cambridge: Cambridge University Press.

BOURQUE, SUSAN C., and KAY B. WARREN

1976 "Campesinas and Comuneras: Subordination in the Sierra." *Journal of Marriage and the Family* 38:781–788.

1978 "Denial and Reaffirmation of Ethnic Identities: A Comparative Examination of Guatemalan and Peruvian Communities." Program in Latin American Studies Occasional Papers Series. Amherst: International Area Studies Programs, University of Massachusetts.

1979 "Female Participation, Perception and Power: An Examination of Two Andean Communities." In *Political Participation and the Poor in Latin America*, ed. John Booth and Mitchell Seligson, pp. 116–133. New York: Holmes and Meier.

1979 "Political Participation and the Revolution: Lessons from Rural Peru." Latin American Program, Working Papers Series, No. 25. Washington: Wilson Center.

1980 "Multiple Arenas for State Expansion: Class, Ethnicity, and Sex in Rural Peru." *Ethnic and Racial Studies* 3:264–280.

1981 *Women of the Andes: Patriarchy and Social Change in Two Peruvian Towns.* Ann Arbor: University of Michigan Press.

1989 "Democracy without Peace: The Cultural Politics of Terror in Peru." *Latin American Research Review* 24 (no. 1).

BRICKER, VICTORIA REIFLER

1973 *Ritual Humor in Highland Chiapas.* Austin: University of Texas Press.

1981 *The Indian Christ, the Indian King: The Historical Substrate of Maya Myth and Ritual.* Austin: University of Texas Press.

BRINTNALL, DOUGLAS E.

1979 *Revolt against the Dead: The Modernization of a Mayan Community in the Highlands of Guatemala.* New York: Gordon and Breach.

BUNZEL, RUTH

1952 *Chichicastenango, a Guatemalan Village.* Publications of the American Ethnological Society No. 22. Locust Valley, N.Y.: J. S. Augustin.

BURGOS-DEBRAY, ELISABETH, ed.

1984 *I . . . Rigoberta Menchú: An Indian Woman in Guatemala.* London: Verso Editions.

CALDER, BRUCE JOHNSON

1970 *Crecimiento y cambio de la iglesia Católica guatemalteca 1944–1966.* Estudios Centroamericanos No. 6. Guatemala City: Seminario de Integración Social Guatemalteca.

CANCIAN, FRANK

1965 *Economics and Prestige in a Mayan Community.* Stanford: Stanford University Press.

1967 "Political and Religious Organizations." In *Handbook of Middle American Indians* 6:283–298. Austin: University of Texas Press.

1972 *Change and Uncertainty in a Peasant Economy.* Stanford: Stanford University Press.

CARMACK, ROBERT M.

1981 *The Quiché Mayas of Utatlán: The Evolution of a Highland Guatemala Kingdom.* Norman: University of Oklahoma Press.

CARMACK, ROBERT M., ed.

1988 *Harvest of Violence: The Maya Indians and the Guatemalan Crisis.* Norman: University of Oklahoma Press.

CHRISTIAN, WILLIAM A.

1981 *Local Religion in Sixteenth-Century Spain.* Princeton: Princeton University Press.

CICOUREL, AARON V.

1970 "Basic and Normative Rules in the Negotiation of Status and Role." In *Recent Sociology No. 2: Patterns of Communicating Behavior,* ed. Hans Peter Dreitzel, pp. 4–45. New York: Macmillan.

COLBY, BENJAMIN

1961 "Indian Attitudes Towards Education and Interethnic Contact in Mexico." *Practical Anthropology* 8:77–85.

1966 *Ethnic Relations in the Chiapas Highlands of Mexico.* Santa Fe: Museum of New Mexico Press.

COLBY, BENJAMIN N., and PIERRE L. VAN DEN BERGHE

1961 "Ethnic Relations in Southeastern Mexico." *American Anthropologist* 63:772–792.

1969 *Ixil Country: A Plural Society in Highland Guatemala.* Berkeley: University of California Press.

COMAROFF, JEAN

1985 *Body of Power and Spirit of Resistance: The Culture and History of a South African People.* Chicago: University of Chicago Press.

DE DIOS ROSALES, JUAN

1968 "San Andrés Semetabaj." In *Los pueblos del Lago de Atitlán.* Guatemala City: Seminario de Integración Social No. 23:159–200.

DE LA FUENTE, JULIO

1965 *Relaciones interétnicas.* Mexico City: Instituto Nacional Indigenista.

DOLGIN, JANET L.

1977 *Jewish Identity and the JDL.* Princeton: Princeton University Press.

DOUGLAS, MARY

1966 *Purity and Danger: An Analysis of Concepts of Pollution and Taboo.* London: Routledge and Kegan Paul.

1970 *Natural Symbols: Explorations in Cosmology.* New York: Pantheon Books.

DUMONT, LOUIS

1970   *Homo Hierarchicus.* Chicago: University of Chicago Press.

FALLA, RICARDO, S.J.

1970   "Evolución político-religiosa del indígena rural en Guatemala (1945–1965)." San José, Costa Rica: *Estudios Sociales Centroamericanos* 1:27–43.

1971   "Juan el Gordo: Visión Indígena de su Explotación." *Estudios Centro-Americanos* 268:98–107.

1978   *Quiché Rebelde: Estudio de un movimiento de conversión religiosa, rebelde a las creencias tradicionales, en San Antonio Ilotenango, Quiché (1948–70).* Guatemala: Editorial Universitaria de Guatemala.

FOSTER, GEORGE

1967   *Tzintzuntzan: Mexican Peasants in a Changing World.* Boston: Little, Brown.

FRANK, ANDRE GUNDER

1967   "On the 'Indian Problem' in Latin America." In *Capitalism and Underdevelopment in Latin America,* pp. 121–142. New York: Monthly Review Press.

FRIEDLANDER, JUDITH

1975   *Being Indian in Hueyapan: A Study of Forced Identity in Contemporary Mexico.* New York: St. Martin's Press.

FRIEDRICH, PAUL

1970   *Agrarian Revolt in a Mexican Village.* Englewood Cliffs, N.J.: Prentice-Hall.

GEERTZ, CLIFFORD

1965   *The Social History of an Indonesian Town.* Cambridge, Mass.: MIT Press.

1973   *Interpretation of Cultures.* New York: Basic Books.

1983   *Local Knowledge: Further Essays in Interpretive Anthropology.* New York: Basic Books.

GILLIN, JOHN PHILIP

1945   "Parallel Cultures and the Inhibitions to Acculturation in a Guatemalan Community." *Social Forces* 24:1–14.

1947   " 'Race' Relations without Conflict: A Guatemalan Town." *American Journal of Sociology* 53:337–343.

1951   *The Culture of Security in San Carlos: A Study of a Guatemalan Community of Indians and Ladinos.* Publication No. 16. New Orleans: Tulane University Middle American Research Institute.

GUITERAS-HOLMES, CALIXTA

1961   *Perils of the Soul: The World View of a Tzotzil Indian.* New York: Free Press of Glencoe.

GUZMÁN BÖCKLER, CARLOS, and JEAN-LOUP HERBERT

1970   *Guatemala: Una interpretación histórico-social.* Mexico City: Siglo Veintiuno Editores.

HANDY, JIM
1984   *Gift of the Devil: A History of Guatemala.* Boston: South End Press.

HARRIS, MARVIN
1964   *Patterns of Race in the Americas.* New York: W. W. Norton and Co.

HAWKINS, JOHN
1984   *Inverse Images: The Meaning of Culture, Ethnicity, and Family in Postcolonial Guatemala.* Albuquerque: University of New Mexico Press.

HELMS, MARY W.
1975   *Middle America: A Cultural History of Heartland and Frontiers.* Englewood Cliffs, N.J.: Prentice-Hall.

HERBERT, JEAN-LOUP
1967   "Apuntes sobre la estructura nacional de Guatemala y el movimiento de ladinización." *Revista Mexicana de Sociología* 29:761–773.

HINSHAW, ROBERT E.
1975   *Panajachel: A Guatemalan Town in Thirty-Year Perspective.* Pittsburgh: University of Pittsburgh Press.

HOBSBAWM, ERIC, and TERENCE RANGER, eds.
1983   *The Invention of Tradition.* Cambridge: Cambridge University Press.

HOLLERAN, MARY P.
1949   *Church and State in Guatemala.* New York: Columbia University Press.

JONAS, SUSANNE, and DAVID TOBIS, eds.
1974   *Guatemala.* Berkeley: North American Congress on Latin America.

JONES, CHESTER LLOYD
1940   *Guatemala, Past and Present.* Minneapolis: University of Minnesota Press.

KUHN, THOMAS
1962   *The Structure of Scientific Revolution.* Chicago: University of Chicago Press.

LA FARGE, OLIVER
1947   *Santa Eulalia: Religion of a Cuchumatán Indian Town.* Chicago: University of Chicago Press.

LA FARGE, OLIVER, and DOUGLAS BYERS
1931   *The Year Bearer's People.* Publication No. 3. New Orleans: Tulane University Middle American Research Institute.

LAN, DAVID
1985   *Guns and Rain: Guerrillas and Spirit Mediums in Zimbabwe.* Berkeley: University of California Press.

MANZ, BEATRIZ
1988   *Refugees of a Hidden War: The Aftermath of Counterinsurgency in Guatemala.* Albany: SUNY Press.
MARCUS, GEORGE E., and MICHAEL M. J. FISCHER
1986   *Anthropology as Cultural Critique: An Experimental Moment in the Human Sciences.* Chicago: University of Chicago Press.
MELVILLE, THOMAS, and MARJORIE MELVILLE
1971   *Guatemala: The Politics of Land Ownership.* New York: The Free Press.
MENDELSON, E. MICHAEL
1957   *Religion and World-view in Santiago Atitlan.* No. 52. Chicago: University of Chicago, Microfilm Collection of Manuscripts on Middle American Cultural Anthropology.
1958   "The King, the Traitor, and the Cross: An Interpretation of a Highland Maya Religious Conflict." *Diogenes* 21:1–10.
1959   "Maximón: An Iconographical Introduction." *Man* 59:57–60.
1965   *Los escándalos de Maximón.* Guatemala City: Seminario de Integración Social Guatemalteca No. 19.
1967   "Ritual and Mythology." In *Handbook of Middle American Indians* 6:392–415. Austin: University of Texas Press.
MÉNDEZ DOMÍNGUEZ, ALFREDO
1967   *Zaragoza: La estratificación social de una comunidad ladina guatemalteca.* Guatemala City: Seminario de Integración Social Guatemalteca.
MIGDAL, JOEL
1974   *Peasants, Politics, and Revolution.* Princeton: Princeton University Press.
MONTEFORTE TOLEDO, MARIO
1965   *Guatemala: Monografía sociológica.* 2nd ed. Mexico City: Universidad Nacional Autónoma de México.
MONTEJO, VICTOR
1987   *Testimony: Death of a Guatemalan Village.* Willimantic, Conn.: Curbstone Press.
MOORE, GRANVILLE ALEXANDER
1966   "Social and Ritual Change in a Guatemala Town." Ph.D. dissertation, Columbia University, New York.
NASH, JUNE
1966   "Social Resources of a Latin American Peasantry: The Case of a Mexican Peasantry." *Social and Economic Studies* 15:353–367.
1967/68   "The Passion Play in Maya Indian Communities." *Comparative Studies in Society and History* 10:318–327.
1970   *In the Eyes of the Ancestors: Belief and Behavior in a Maya Community.* New Haven: Yale University Press.
1979   *We Eat the Mines and the Mines Eat Us: Dependency and Ex-*

ploitation in Bolivian Tin Mines. New York: Columbia University Press.

NASH, MANNING

1955 "The Reaction of a Civil-Religious Hierarchy to a Factory in Guatemala." *Human Organization* 13:26–28.

1957 "The Multiple Society in Economic Development." *American Anthropologist* 59:825–833.

1958 *Machine Age Maya: Industrialization of a Guatemalan Community.* Memoir No. 87. Menasha, Wis.: American Anthropological Association.

1970 "The Impact of Mid-nineteenth Century Economic Change Upon the Indians of Middle America." In *Race and Class in Latin America,* ed. Magnus Mörner, pp. 170–183. New York: Columbia University Press.

NASH, MANNING, ed.

1967 "Social Anthropology." *Handbook of Middle American Indians,* 6. Austin: University of Texas Press.

NOVAL, JOAQUÍN

1967 *Resumen etnográfico de Guatemala.* Guatemala: Universidad de San Carlos.

OAKES, MAUDE

1951 *The Two Crosses of Todos Santos.* Princeton: Princeton University Press.

ONG, AIHWA

1987 *Spirits of Resistance and Capitalist Discipline: Factory Women in Malaysia.* Albany: State University of New York Press.

ORTNER, SHERRY B.

1973 "On Key Symbols." *American Anthropologist* 75:1138–1346.

1975 "God's Bodies, God's Food: A Symbolic Analysis of a Sherpa Ritual." In *The Interpretation of Symbolism,* ed. Roy Willis, pp. 133–169. New York: John Wiley.

PITT-RIVERS, JULIAN

1967 "Words and Deeds: The Ladinos of Chiapas." *Man* (new series) 2:71–87.

1969 "Mestizo or Ladino?" *Race* 10:463–477.

1971 "Race, Color and Class in Central America and the Andes." In *Majority and Minority,* eds. Norman R. Yetman and C. Hay Steele, pp. 90–97. Boston: Allyn and Bacon.

REDFIELD, ROBERT

1947 "The Folk Society." *American Journal of Sociology* 51:393–408.

1953 *The Primitive World and Its Transformations.* Ithaca, N.Y.: Cornell University Press.

1956 "The Relations between Indians and Ladinos in Agua Escondida, Guatemala." *América Indígena* 16:253–276.

1960   *The Little Community and Peasant Society and Culture.* Chicago: University of Chicago Press.

REED, NELSON

1964   *The Caste War of Yucatán.* Stanford: Stanford University Press.

REINA, RUBÉN

1966   *The Law of the Saints: A Pokomam Pueblo and Its Community Culture.* Indianapolis: Bobbs-Merrill.

REYNOLDS, FRANK

1985   "Multiple Cosmogonies and Ethics: The Case of Theravada Buddhism." In *Cosmogony and Ethical Order: New Studies in Comparative Ethics,* ed. Robin Lovin and Frank Reynolds, pp. 203–224. Chicago: University of Chicago Press.

ROBERTS, BRYAN R.

1973   *Organizing Strangers: Poor Families in Guatemala City.* Austin: University of Texas Press.

ROBERTS, ROBERT E. T.

1945   "A Comparison of Ethnic Relations in Two Guatemalan Communities." *Acta Americana* 6:135–151.

ROJAS LIMA, FLAVIO

1968   "Consideraciones generales." In *Los pueblos del Lago de Atitlán.* Guatemala City: Seminario de Integración Social Guatemalteca No. 23:41–67.

ROSALDO, RENATO

1968   "Metaphors of Hierarchy in a Mayan Ritual." *American Anthropologist* 70:524–536.

ROSSELL Y ARELLANA, MARIANO

1943   Carta Pastoral con ocasión del segundo centenario de la sede arzobispal de Guatemala. Guatemala City: Muñoz Plaza.

1945   Carta pastoral con ocasión de la cuaresma de 1945 acerca de la obra de la iglesia Católica. Guatemala City: Sánchez y de Guise.

1946*a*   A las Clases laborante y patronal. Guatemala City: Castañeda, Avila.

1946*b*   Carta pastoral sobre la Acción Católica. Guatemala City: Sánchez y de Guise.

1948*a*   Carta pastoral sobre la justicia social, fundamento del bienstar social. Guatemala City: Castañeda, Avila.

1948*b*   Instrucción pastoral sobre el deber del sufragio. Guatemala City: Sansur.

1949   "Discurso del arzobispo con motivo de la bendición de nuevo local del instituto indígena de Nuestra Señora de Socorro." *Verbum* (Guatemala City), January 30, p. 1.

1954*a*   Carta pastoral sobre los avances del comunismo en Guatemala. Guatemala City: Sánchez y de Guise.

1954*b*   Oración funebre en los funerales celebrados en la Catedral Metropolitana por el eterno descanso de las almas de todas víctimas asesinadas en Guatemala durante el terror comunista y de los muertos en los campos de batalla. Guatemala City.

1955   Conferencia en el tercer congreso Católico de la vida rural el 21 de abril de 1955, en la Ciudad de Panamá. Guatemala City: Sánchez y de Guise.

1958   "Monseñor Rossell y Arellano convoca la nueva cruzada nacional contra el comunismo ateo." *El Imparcial* (Guatemala City) July 8, p. 8.

1962   "2da carta pastoral sobre el peligro del comunismo." *Diario de Centroamérica* (Guatemala City), February 15, p. 2.

SCHNEIDER, DAVID

1968   *American Kinship: A Cultural Account.* Englewood Cliffs, N.J.: Prentice-Hall.

1969   "Kinship, Nationality and Religion in American Culture: Toward a Definition of Kinship." *Forms of Symbolic Action,* ed. Robert F. Spencer, pp. 116–125. Seattle: University of Washington Press.

SCOTT, JAMES C.

1976   *The Moral Economy of the Peasant: Subsistence and Rebellion in Southeast Asia.* New Haven: Yale University Press.

1985   *Weapons of the Weak: Everyday Forms of Peasant Resistance.* New Haven: Yale University Press.

SERVICE, ELMAN

1955   "Indian-European Relations in Colonial Latin America." *American Anthropologist* 57:411–425.

SEXTON, JAMES D., ed.

1985   *Son of Tecún Umán: A Maya Indian Tells His Life Story.* Tucson: University of Arizona Press.

SHERMAN, WILLIAM L.

1979   *Forced Native Labor in Sixteenth-Century Central America.* Lincoln: University of Nebraska Press.

SIEGEL, MORRIS

1941   "Religion in Western Guatemala: A Product of Acculturation." *American Anthropologist* 43:62–76.

1942   " 'Horns, Tails, and Easter Sport': A Study of a Stereotype." *Social Forces* 20:382–386.

1943   "The Creation Myth and Acculturation in Acatán, Guatemala." *Journal of American Folklore* 56:120–126.

SILVERMAN, MARTIN G.

1969   "Maximize Your Options: A Study in Values, Symbols, and Social Structure." In *Forms of Symbolic Action,* ed. Robert F. Spencer, pp. 97–115. Seattle: University of Washington Press.

1971   *Disconcerting Issue: Meaning and Struggle in a Resettled Pacific Community.* Chicago: University of Chicago Press.

SILVERT, K. H.
1954   *A Study in Government: Guatemala.* Publication No. 21. New Orleans: Tulane University Middle American Research Institute.

SKINNER-KLÉE, JORGE, compiler
1954   *Legislación indigenista de Guatemala.* Mexico City: Instituto Indigenista Interamericano.

SMITH, WALDEMAR R.
1977   *The Fiesta System and Economic Change.* New York: Columbia University Press.

SPERBER, DAN
1975   *Rethinking Symbolism.* Cambridge: Cambridge University Press.

STAVENHAGEN, RODOLFO
1968   "Seven Fallacies about Latin America." In *Latin America: Reform or Revolution,* ed. James Petras and Maurice Zeitlin, pp. 13–31. Greenwich, Conn.: Fawcett.

1970   "Classes, Colonialism and Acculturation." In *Masses in Latin America,* ed. Irving Louis Horowitz, pp. 235–288. New York: Oxford University Press.

1975   *Social Classes in Agrarian Societies.* Garden City, N.Y.: Anchor Books.

STERN, STEVE
1982   *Peru's Indian Peoples and the Challenge of the Spanish Conquest: Huamanga to 1640.* Madison: University of Wisconsin Press.

STERN, STEVE, ed.
1987   *Resistance, Rebellion, and Consciousness in the Andean Peasant World: 18th to 20th Centuries.* Madison: University of Wisconsin Press.

TAUSSIG, MICHAEL
1980   *The Devil and Commodity Fetishism in South America.* Chapel Hill: University of North Carolina Press.

TAX, SOL
1937   "The Municipios of the Midwestern Highland of Guatemala." *American Anthropologist* 39:423–444.

1941   "World View and Social Relations in Guatemala." *American Anthropologist* 43:27–42.

1942   "Ethnic Relations in Guatemala." *América Indígena* 2:43–48.

1949   "Folk Tales in Chichicastenango: An Unsolved Puzzle." *Journal of American Folklore* 52:125–135.

1953   *Penny Capitalism: A Guatemalan Indian Economy.* Publication No. 16. Washington, D.C.: Smithsonian Institution Institute of Social Anthropology.

1957   "Changing Consumption in Indian Guatemala." *Journal of Economic Development and Cultural Change* 5:147–158.

TAX, SOL, ed.
1952   *Heritage of Conquest*. Glencoe, Ill.: Free Press.

TEDLOCK, BARBARA
1982   *Time and the Highland Maya*. Albuquerque: University of New Mexico Press.

TUMIN, MELVIN
1945   "Culture, Genuine and Spurious: A Re-evaluation." *American Sociological Review* 10:199–207.
1949   "Reciprocity and Stability of Caste in Guatemala." *American Sociological Review* 14:17–25.
1950   "The Dynamics of Cultural Discontinuity in a Peasant Society." *Social Forces* 29:135–141.
1952   *Caste in a Peasant Society*. Princeton: Princeton University Press.

TURNER, FREDERICK
1971   *Catholicism and Political Development in Latin America*. Chapel Hill: University of North Carolina Press.

TURNER, VICTOR W.
1967   *The Forest of Symbols*. Ithaca, N.Y.: Cornell University Press.
1969   *The Ritual Process*. Chicago: Aldine.

TURNER, VICTOR W., and EDWARD M. BRUNER, eds.
1986   *The Anthropology of Experience*. Urbana: University of Illinois Press.

VALLIER, IVAN
1970   "Extraction, Insulation and Re-entry: Toward a Theory of Religious Change." In *The Church and Social Change in Latin America*, ed. Henry A. Landsberger, pp. 9–35. Notre Dame, Ind.: University of Notre Dame Press.

VAN DEN BERGHE, PIERRE L., and BENJAMIN N. COLBY
1961   "Ladino-Indian Relations in the Highlands of Chiapas, Mexico." *Social Forces* 40:63–71.
1966   "Compadrazgo and Class in Southeastern Mexico." *American Anthropologist* 68:1236–1244.

VOGT, EVON Z.
1969   *Zinacantan: A Mayan Community in the Highlands of Chiapas*. Cambridge, Mass.: Belknap Press of Harvard University Press.

WAGLEY, CHARLES
1949   *The Social and Religious Life of a Guatemalan Village*. Memoir No. 71. Menasha, Wis.: American Anthropological Association.

WAGLEY, CHARLES, and MARVIN HARRIS
1955   "A Typology of Latin American Subcultures." *American Anthropologist* 57:428–451.

WALLACE, ANTHONY F. C.
1972   *The Death and Rebirth of the Seneca*. New York: Vintage Press.

WARREN, KAY B.
1974   "When the Devil Tempts: Cultural Identity in a Highland Gua-

temalan Indian Community." Ph.D. dissertation, Princeton University, Princeton, N.J.

1985   "Creation Narratives and the Moral Order: Implications of Multiple Models in Highland Guatemala." In *Cosmogony and Ethical Order: New Studies in Comparative Ethics,* ed. Frank Reynolds and Robin Lovin, pp. 251–276. Chicago: University of Chicago Press.

1986   "Capitalist Expansion and the Moral Order: Anthropological Perspectives." In *Christianity and Capitalism: Perspectives on Religion, Liberalism, and the Economy,* ed. David Krueger and Bruce Gruelle, pp. 161–176. Chicago: Center for the Scientific Study of Religion.

WARREN, KAY B., and SUSAN C. BOURQUE [see also Bourque and Warren]

1985   "Gender, Power, and Communication: Women's Responses to Political Muting in the Andes." In *Women Living Change: Cross-Cultural Perspectives,* ed. Susan C. Bourque and Donna R. Divine, pp. 255–286. Philadelphia: Temple University Press.

WASSERSTROM, ROBERT

1975   "Revolution in Guatemala: Peasants and Politics under the Arbenz Government." *Comparative Studies in Society and History* 17:473–478.

1983   *Class and Society in Central Chiapas.* Berkeley: University of California Press.

WHETTEN, NATHAN N.

1961   *Guatemala: The Land and the People.* New Haven: Yale University Press.

WOLF, ERIC R.

1957   "Closed Corporate Communities in Mesoamerica and Central Java." *Southwestern Journal of Anthropology* 13:1–18.

1959   *Sons of the Shaking Earth.* Chicago: University of Chicago Press.

Index